The Taiwan Issue in Sino-American Strategic Relations

Westview Replica Editions

The concept of Westview Replica Editions is a response to the continuing crisis in academic and informational publishing. Library budgets for books have been severely curtailed. Ever larger portions of general library budgets are being diverted from the purchase of books and used for data banks, computers, micromedia, and other methods of information retrieval. Interlibrary loan structures further reduce the edition sizes required to satisfy the needs of the scholarly community. Economic pressures on the university presses and the few private scholarly publishing companies have severely limited the capacity of the industry to properly serve the academic and research communities. As a result, many manuscripts dealing with important subjects, often representing the highest level of scholarship, are no longer economically viable publishing projects--or, if accepted for publication, are typically subject to lead times ranging from one to three years.

Westview Replica Editions are our practical solution to the problem. We accept a manuscript in camera-ready form, typed according to our specifications, and move it immediately into the production process. As always, the selection criteria include the importance of the subject, the work's contribution to scholarship, and its insight, originality of thought, and excellence of exposition. The responsibility for editing and proofreading lies with the author or sponsoring institution. We prepare chapter headings and display pages, file for copyright, and obtain Library of Congress Cataloging in Publication Data. A detailed manual contains simple instructions for preparing the final typescript, and our editorial staff is always available to answer questions.

The end result is a book printed on acid-free paper and bound in sturdy library-quality soft covers. We manufacture these books ourselves using equipment that does not require a lengthy make-ready process and that allows us to publish first editions of 300 to 600 copies and to reprint even smaller quantities as needed. Thus we can produce Replica Editions quickly and can keep even very specialized books in print as long as there is a demand for them.

About the Book and Author

The Taiwan Issue in Sino-American Strategic Relations
Martin L. Lasater

The first two years of the Reagan administration saw a close correlation between improved unofficial relations between Washington and Taipei and a deterioration of strategic cooperation between Washington and Beijing. These developments led many U.S. officials and scholars to conclude that U.S. security interests may require periodic concessions over Taiwan to ensure China's cooperation in countering the Soviet threat.

Rejecting this view, Mr. Lasater argues that Washington's and Beijing's bilateral relations with Moscow and not the Taiwan issue are the key international determinants of Sino-American strategic cooperation. Examining the parameters of that cooperation and the role of Taiwan in Sino-American relations, Mr. Lasater suggests that Beijing is deliberately using U.S. security concerns to seek concessions on Taiwan and other issues. He advises a policy that stands firm in negotiations with the Chinese and that resists the temptation to make politically expedient concessions--a more balanced course of action whereby improved relations with Beijing are sought concurrently with the maintenance of friendly, unofficial ties with Taipei.

Martin L. Lasater is president of Martin L. Lasater and Associates, a consulting firm specializing in foreign policy and security affairs.

For Celeste, Zara, Keyne, Kieran,
Chryseis, and Kendrik

The Taiwan Issue in Sino-American Strategic Relations

Martin L. Lasater

Westview Press / Boulder and London

The paper used in this publication meets the requirements of the American National Standard for Permanence of Paper for Printed Library Materials Z39.48-1984.

A Westview Replica Edition

All rights reserved. No part of this publication may be reproduced or transmitted in any form or by any means, electronic or mechanical, including photocopy, recording, or any information storage and retrieval system, without permission in writing from the publisher.

Copyright © 1984 by Westview Press, Inc.

Published in 1984 in the United States of America by
  Westview Press, Inc.
  5500 Central Avenue
  Boulder, Colorado 80301
  Frederick A. Praeger, Publisher

Library of Congress Cataloging in Publication Data
Lasater, Martin L.
  The Taiwan issue in Sino-American strategic relations.
  (A Westview replica edition)
  Bibliography: p.
  1. United States--Foreign relations--China. 2. China--Foreign relations --United States. 3. United States--Foreign relations--Taiwan. 4. Taiwan --Foreign relations--United States. 5. United States--Foreign relations-- Soviet Union. 6. Soviet Union--Foriegn relations--United States. 7. China --Foreign relations--Soviet Union. 8. Soviet Union--Foreign relations-- China. I. Title.
  E183.8.C5L27 1984   327.73051   84-7407
  ISBN 0-86531-842-5

Printed and bound in the United States of America
10 9 8 7 6 5 4

Contents

LIST OF TABLES. x
ACKNOWLEDGMENTS xi

    PART I -- Sino-American Strategic Relations

1. INTRODUCTION 2
2. THE NATIONAL POWER OF THE PRC 12

    Geography 12
    Military Capabilities 13
    Economy 14
    Sociopsychology 18
    Leadership 18

3. SINO-SOVIET RELATIONS 22

    The Sino-Soviet Split 23
    U.S.-Soviet Balance of Power in East Asia . . 40
    Soviet Strategic Perceptions 43
    Korea and Japan 49
    Soviet Statements on U.S.-PRC Relations . . . 53

4. CHINA'S INDEPENDENT FOREIGN POLICY 58

    Normalization of Sino-Soviet Relations . . . 63
    Future Sino-Soviet Relations 75

5. PARAMETERS OF SINO-AMERICAN STRATEGIC
    COOPERATION 77

    The Soviet Card 77

	Sino-American Military Cooperation	80
	PRC Rejection of Close Military Ties	85
	Future Sino-American Strategic Cooperation	87

PART II -- The Role of Taiwan

6. TAIWAN TODAY: AN OVERVIEW 91

    Background 91
    Economic Conditions 96
    Political System 102
    Recent Political Developments 105
    Foreign Policy 110
    The Importance of Taiwan 116

7. THE SECURITY OF TAIWAN 122

    PRC Military Threat 123
    PRC Intentions 130
    Taiwan's Reunification Policy 148

8. THE TAIWAN ISSUE 153

    The Shanghai Communique 153
    Normalization of Sino-American Relations . 156
    The Taiwan Relations Act 160
    The Mid-1980 Turning Point 164
    China Becomes Inflexible 173

9. PERIOD OF CONTENTION: 1981-1982 178

    The FX Decision 182
    The Arms Sales Controversy 191

10. THE AUGUST 17, 1982 JOINT COMMUNIQUE 202

    Provisions 205
    U.S. Interpretations 208
    PRC Interpretations 213
    Relations in the Post-Communique Period . . 215

11. EPILOGUE 219

    A More Realistic China Policy 219
    Relations Sour Once Again 223
    Sale of High Technology to the PRC 228
    Exchange Visits of Premier Zhao Ziyang and
        President Reagan 230

PART III -- Conclusion

12. SUMMARY AND POLICY RECOMMENDATIONS 238

    Limits of Sino-American Strategic
        Cooperation 238
    The Taiwan Question 242
    Taiwan as a Variable in Sino-American
        Strategic Relations 246
    Policy Implications 248

APPENDIXES 251

SELECTED BIBLIOGRAPHY 278

Tables

1. USSR and PRC Armed Forces in East Asia 30
2. PRC Trade with Centrally Planned and Market Economies 38
3. PRC National Interests and Elements of Policy . 39
4. US and USSR Pacific-Based Forces 40
5. Major Trading Partners of Taiwan, 1983 98
6. Central Government Budget, FY 1983 100
7. PRC-ROC Military Forces 124
8. Main Ground Forces 125
9. Large Naval Vessels 126
10. Air Forces 127

Acknowledgments

I am indebted to many individuals in official and unofficial capacities for their time and assistance in helping me to gather the information required to write this analysis. The research began in the fall of 1979. Special thanks goes to Colonel Angus M. Fraser (USMC, Ret.) for wading through the initial draft and making many helpful suggestions. I am also grateful to the Pacific Cultural Foundation for providing research and writing support during the early stages of the endeavor.

Martin L. Lasater
Washington, D.C.
August 30, 1984

Part I
Sino-American Strategic Relations

1
Introduction

The initial decision on the part of the United States to normalize Sino-American relations was based upon perceptions of the Soviet Union as a mutual threat to both countries. The two chief American architects of improved relations with the PRC, President Richard Nixon and his national security affairs advisor Henry Kissinger, have both referred to this strategic imperative as the motive behind their efforts to establish a cooperative relationship with China during 1969-1972. President Nixon wrote in the New York Times on October 11, 1982:

> The key factor that brought us together ten years ago was our common concern with the Soviet threat, and our recognition that we had a better chance of containing that threat if we replaced hostility with cooperation between Peking and Washington. This overriding strategic concern dominated our dialogue, and our relationship, during the first decade.[1]

Henry Kissinger, in a guest editorial appearing in the January 30, 1983, issue of the Washington Post, described the strategic perspective of the Nixon Administration in this way:

> What brought the two nations together was not sentiment but awareness of a common threat....There were powerful incentives for a rapprochement with China: to balance the Soviet Union, either to restrain it or to induce it to negotiate seriously; to isolate

---

[1] Richard M. Nixon, "America and China: The Next Ten Years," New York Times, October 11, 1982, p. A19.

> Hanoi to give it an incentive to end the Vietnam War; to maintain American self-assurance amid our messy withdrawal from Indochina by demonstrating our continuing capacity for major positive initiatives.[2]

Kissinger was even more explicit in his memoirs regarding the strategic origins of Sino-American relations. In White House Years he wrote: "It had been the Soviet Union whose menace had brought China and us together; our cooperation reflected a geopolitical reality produced by concern at the growth of Soviet military power."[3]

The Carter Administration carried the Nixon initiative to a logical conclusion by extending diplomatic recognition to the People's Republic of China on January 1, 1979. Zbigniew Brzezinski, President Carter's national security advisor, outlined the strategic perceptions held by the Democratic administration:

> It is essential that we treat the Chinese as a serious global and strategic partner.
>
> Nor need we pretend that the American-Chinese connection isn't heavily influenced by the Soviet threat. Alliances are usually the product of a third-party threat. We should not be shy in saying to the world and to the Chinese that there is a mutual American-Chinese interest in stemming Soviet hegemonism....We have an interest in a strong and secure China.[4]

During the early normalization period, Deng Xiaoping openly advocated close strategic relations between the United States, Japan, Western Europe, and China to counter Soviet expansionism. In a February 1979 interview with Time magazine, Deng stressed the need to unite against the Soviet Union, saying:

---

[2] Henry A. Kissinger, "Mr. Shultz Goes to China," Washington Post, January 30, 1983, p. C8.

[3] Henry A. Kissinger, White House Years, (Boston, MA: Little, Brown and Co., 1979), p. 1053.

[4] Zbigniew Brzezinski, "If the Russians and the Chinese Make Up," Washington Post, November 22, 1982, p. A15.

After setting up this relationship between China, Japan and the U.S., we must further develop the relationship in a deepening way. If we really want to be able to place curbs on the polar bear, the only realistic thing for us is to unite. If we only depend on the strength of the U.S., it is not enough. If we only depend on the strength of Europe, it is not enough. We are an insignificant, poor country, but if we unite, well, it will then carry weight.[5]

The visit of Secretary of Defense Harold Brown to the PRC in January 1980 laid the initial foundation for a defense relationship between the United States and China. As envisioned by American planners, the relationship was to be composed of three elements: (1) "a strategic dialogue between senior defense leaders to promote understanding of each other's policies and interests so that parallel actions could be taken when interests were seen to coincide"; (2) "reciprocal visits between...defense establishments in various mutually agreed functional areas, such as military education and training, logistics, and military medicine...to identify areas where limited cooperation might be mutually beneficial"; and (3) "the willingness of the United States to cooperate with China in selected areas of defense technological development."[6]

The Reagan Administration continued to place high value on the strategic aspects of Sino-American relations. The Administration described the PRC as "a friendly, non-allied country with which we share important strategic interests, including a common perception of threatening Soviet ambitions worldwide."[7]

A fundamental question, therefore, is what are the interests of the United States and how does strategic cooperation with the PRC further those interests?

---

[5] "An Interview with Teng Hsiao-ping: Calling for Stronger U.S.-China Ties and a United Front Against Moscow," *Time*, February 5, 1979, p. 34.

[6] Prepared statement of James A. Kelly, "Defense Relations with the People's Republic of China," given before U.S. House of Representatives, Committee on Foreign Affairs, Subcommittee on Asian and Pacific Affairs, June 5, 1984, p. 1, ms.

[7] Prepared statement of Walter J. Stoessel, Jr., given before U.S. Senate, Committee on Foreign Relations, *East-West Relations: Focus on the Pacific*, 97th Cong., 2d sess., June 10, 1982, p. 9.

According to the FY 1984 Posture Statement of the Secretary of Defense, the fundamental vital interests of the United States and the foreign policy needed to protect them are:

> --To preserve our freedom, our political identify, and the institutions that are their foundation--the Constitution and the rule of law.
>
> --To protect the territory of the United States, its citizens, and its vital interests abroad from armed attack.
>
> --To foster an international order supportive of the interests of the United States through alliances and cooperative relationships with friendly nations; and by encouraging democratic institutions, economic development, and self-determination throughout the world.
>
> --To protect access to foreign markets and overseas resources in order to maintain the strength of the United States' industrial, agricultural, and technological base and the nation's economic well-being.[8]

The Posture Statement defines the Soviet Union as the major, and only serious, threat to these interests: "The Soviet Union poses, and for the foreseeable future will continue to pose, the most formidable military threat to the United States and its interests. Threats to our interests may arise from other sources or circumstances, but only the Soviet Union has the military power directly to inflict mortal damage to the United States."[9]

To counter the Soviet threat to U.S. vital interests, the Reagan Administration established the following as the highest priority national security objectives of the United States:

---

[8] U.S. Department of Defense, _Annual Report to the Congress, Fiscal Year 1984_ (Washington, D.C.: Government Printing Office, 1983), p. 15.

[9] Ibid.

--To deter military attack by the USSR and its allies against the United States, its allies, and other friendly countries; and to deter, or to counter, use of Soviet military power to coerce or intimidate our friends and allies.

--In the event of an attack, to deny the enemy his objectives and bring a rapid end to the conflict on terms favorable to our interests; and to maintain the political and territorial integrity of the United States and its allies.

--To promote meaningful and verifiable mutual reductions in nuclear and conventional forces through negotiations with the Soviet Union and the Warsaw Pact, respectively; and to discourage further proliferation of nuclear weapons throughout the world.

--To inhibit further expansion of Soviet control and military presence, and to induce the Soviet Union to withdraw from those countries, such as Afghanistan, where it has imposed and maintains its presence and control by force of arms.

--To foster a reduction in the Soviet Union's overall capability to sustain a military buildup by preventing, in concert with our allies, the flow of military significant technologies and material to the Soviet Union, and by refraining from actions that serve to subsidize the Soviet economy.[10]

China's role in overall U.S. strategy becomes apparent in the discussion of regional objectives in the Posture Statement. Regarding U.S. security objectives in East Asia and the Pacific, the Statement says:

> The importance to the United States of the security of East Asia and the Pacific is demonstrated by the bilateral treaties with Japan, Korea, and the Philippines; the Manila Pact, which adds Thailand to our treaty partners; and our treaty with Australia and New Zealand--the ANZUS Treaty. It is further enhanced by the deployment of land and air

---

[10] Ibid., p. 16.

forces in Korea and Japan, and the forward deployment of the Seventh Fleet in the Western Pacific. Our foremost regional objectives, in conjunction with our regional friends and allies, are:

--To maintain the security of our essential sea lanes and of the United States' interests in the region; to maintain the capability to fulfill our treaty commitments to the Pacific and East Asia; to prevent the Soviet Union, North Korea, and Vietnam from interfering in the affairs of others; to build toward a durable strategic relationship with the People's Republic of China; and to support the stability and independence of friendly countries.[11]

"To build toward a durable strategic relationship with the People's Republic of China" is, therefore, an objective of U.S. national security policy defined as being in the vital interests of the United States. President Ronald Reagan affirmed the strategic value of China to the United States in his official statement accompanying the August 17, 1982 Joint Communique between Washington and Beijing. The President said:

Building a strong and lasting friendship with China has been an important foreign policy goal of four consecutive American administrations. Such a relationship is vital to our long-term national security interests and contributes to stability in East Asia. It is in the national interest of the United States that this important strategic relationship be advanced.

In June 1982 testimony before the Senate Committee on Foreign Relations, Under Secretary of Defense Fred Ikle discussed U.S. security interests and strategic objectives in terms of China:

Although not an ally, the People's Republic of China seems to share our view of the dangers from Moscow's expansionist drive into Asia. Indeed, the growing convergence of Chinese and American strategic interests has been the primary reason for the steady

---

[11] Ibid., p. 17. (emphasis added)

improvement in our bilateral relations over the past decade. Increasingly, we have found that where our common interests are threatened, it is useful to take parallel actions.

The People's Republic of China appears to have decided that containment of Soviet expansionism and the maintenance of a global balance of power depends for the foreseeable future on the viability of U.S. military power and America's alliances throughout the world. As a result, the Chinese actively support our security partnership with Japan; they are enthusiastic supporters of NATO; they support a continued U.S. military presence in the Philippines and the Western Pacific. Like us and our allies, China firmly opposes the continued Soviet occupation of Afghanistan and the Soviet-backed Vietnamese occupation of Kampuchea.[12]

Following Secretary of State George Shultz's visit to the PRC in February 1983, Paul Wolfowitz, Assistant Secretary of State for Asian and Pacific Affairs, told the House Committee on Foreign Affairs: "Developing a strong, stable, and enduring U.S.-China relationship is an important element of President Reagan's foreign policy." He then went on to list some of the principal benefits the relationship had for the United States:

> We no longer have to plan and spend to confront a Chinese threat; our parallel interests in containing the Soviet Union have been repeatedly reaffirmed and we are in fundamental agreement that the Soviets remain the principal threat to peace in the world; we have common interests in containing not only Vietnamese aggression in Southeast Asia and encouraging a peaceful settlement of the Kampuchean problem based on Khmer self-determination, but also in resisting Soviet aggression in Afghanistan; we are able to maintain a useful dialogue with China on a wide range of important international problems of common concern; China has developed

---

[12] Prepared statement of Fred Ikle, "Soviet Challenge in the Pacific and U.S. and Allied Responses," given before U.S. Senate, Committee on Foreign Relations, June 10, 1982, p. 11, ms.

constructive regional policies and cooperative relations with our Asian allies; China has developed increasingly strong ties to the western-oriented international economic system; trade and investment opportunities for American business have grown tremendously; despite problems, East Asia has emerged as one of the more stable and prosperous regions of the world, with China playing an increasingly responsible regional role.[13]

In mid-1983 the Reagan Administration decided to broaden the base of Sino-American relations. As noted by Wolfowitz in testimony before Congress in June 1984: "The particular goal of this Administration has been to put U.S.-China relations on a more stable and increasingly comprehensive basis--one that avoids the extreme of hostility and suspicion without succumbing to the opposite extreme of euphoria and sentimentality."[14]

Deputy Assistant Secretary of State William Brown elaborated on this comprehensive approach to U.S. China policy:

> Our still developing relationship with China is an event of momentous importance to both countries and to the stability of East Asia. We are, of course, aware of certain perspectives we share with the Chinese concerning Soviet activities in the region. We also recognize that a certain degree of cooperation in security matters could be natural and mutually beneficial as the relationship with China evolves. But the U.S. will neither press this possibility nor make it the centerpiece of our bilateral contacts with Beijing simply because we wish that relationship to rest on a far broader, firmer foundation than a common reaction to Soviet policy. Instead we will work for a balanced development of economic, political and people-to-people contacts with China and

---

[13] Prepared statement of Paul Wolfowitz, "Sino-American Relations Eleven Years After the Shanghai Communique," given before U.S. House of Representatives, Committee on Foreign Affairs, Subcommittee on Asian and Pacific Affairs, February 28, 1983, pp. 1, 3, ms.

[14] Prepared statement of Paul Wolfowitz, given before U.S. House of Representatives, Committee on Foreign Affairs, June 5, 1984, p. 1, ms.

encourage China's greater participation in the regional and international arrangements which we support. We are convinced that only such a far-sighted approach will sustain U.S.-Chinese ties over the long term. And such an approach should also provide an even better basis for security cooperation if that should seem desirable to both sides in the future.[15]

The Reagan Administration has attempted to use its broad approach to Sino-American relations not only to enhance the value of strategic cooperation to the Chinese, but also to help moderate PRC domestic and foreign policies. As summarized by James Kelly, Deputy Assistant Secretary of Defense, on June 5, 1984:

> The United States' aim is to build an enduring, friendly but not allied relationship with China that recognizes both our common interests and our differences and which will enable us to take complimentary actions with the Chinese when our common interests are challenged. A strong, secure, successfully modernizing China can be a force for peace and stability. China's stake in having a stable and secure international environment for its modernization efforts make it unlikely to become a threat. Over the past several years, China has moderated its foreign policies and demonstrated a real desire to improve state-to-state relations with its Asian neighbors. One of our aims in strengthening the defense component of our relations with China is to reinforce these positive trends in Beijing's foreign policies.[16]

At the close of writing in July 1984, Sino-American strategic relations had begun to improve after more than two years of limited cooperation. These were years characterized by continuous controversy over the Taiwan issue and by gradual improvement in Sino-Soviet

---

[15] Prepared statement of William A. Brown, "The Soviet Role in Asia," given before U.S. House of Representatives, Committee on Foreign Affairs, Subcommittees on Asian and Pacific Affairs and on Europe and the Middle East, The Soviet Role in Asia, (Washington, D.C.: GPO, 1983), pp. 536-537.

[16] James A. Kelly, "Defense Relations with the People's Republic of China," p. 8, ms.

relations. In mid-1984, the Taiwan issue remained unresolved, but the Sino-Soviet normalization process had slowed because of bitter disagreement over Vietnam.

The remaining chapters of Part One examine the close relationship between the Soviet threat and Sino-American strategic cooperation. Among the factors examined will be the national power of the PRC, the nature of the Sino-Soviet split and the probability of its continuation, and the military and political parameters of the U.S.-PRC strategic relationship. The objective of the analysis is to determine the extent to which Sino-American strategic cooperation is possible and of benefit to the United States.

2
The National Power of the PRC

China's national power may be considered in terms of its geography, military capabilities, economic strength, and various sociopsychological factors. Equally important is how China's leaders will likely use the nation's resources. Each of these elements will be introduced briefly in this chapter in terms of U.S. security interests. References to the various elements of PRC national power will appear throughout the remainder of the text.

2.1   GEOGRAPHY

From the point of view of American security interests--that is, the extent to which the PRC diverts the Soviet threat away from the United States and the free world as a whole--the geographic elements of China's national power are paramount. The PRC is the third largest nation in the world, having about 3.7 million square miles and roughly one-quarter of the world's population. The PRC has the world's longest land boundary, roughly 13,000 miles, of which some 4,500 miles lay adjacent to the Soviet Union. The sheer mass of China, both physically and demographically, effectively restricts Soviet expansion into Asia. From the geographic perspective, it matters little to the United States who controls China, as long as that government is sufficiently strong to maintain social cohesion and sufficiently nationalistic to resist USSR encroachment on China's territory. China forms a natural barrier to Soviet domination of Asia, and the preservation of that barrier is strategically important to the United States.

2.2 MILITARY CAPABILITIES

As important as geography and population are to a nation's power, its government must command sufficient military forces to defend national interests. In the case of the PRC, analysts have noted the paradoxical nature of China's military capabilities. Although the nation possesses four million men in uniform, their ability to defend China against a determined Soviet attack is questionable. As Harlan Jencks summarized: "The gross numbers are staggering. The People's Liberation Army constitutes the world's largest land army, the second largest navy, and the third largest air force. Yet there is considerable doubt as to how effectively this huge force can defend China."[17] John J. Sloan of the U.S. Defense Intelligence Agency described China's military capabilities in this way:

> Discussion of China's current and future military capabilities is filled with paradoxes. On the one hand, its overall military capabilities can be viewed as impressive. This is particularly true when the nation's level of economic development and the problems associated with adequately providing for the livelihood of about one billion people are considered. China is the only developing nation possessing a strategic missile system capable of reaching both superpowers. It possesses the world's largest standing army, an army equipped with large numbers of standard weapons, albeit not sufficiently modern. China's air force is the third largest in the world, and its navy includes more submarines and aircraft than any other, save the United States and the USSR. These large numbers of forces and unsophisticated weapons have often been creatively adapted and deployed to maximize other assets available, such as geography, a large population, and political communication skills. Chinese military defense capabilities are better than at any point in modern history.
>
> On the other hand, China's armed forces possess many serious weaknesses which belie the strengths suggested by force numbers

---

[17] Harlan W. Jencks, "Defending China in 1982," *Current History*, 81, 476 (September 1982), p. 250.

alone. Many of these weaknesses have become convincingly apparent or have been openly acknowledged only in relatively recent times.[18]

Most analysts agree that the most serious weaknesses within the PLA in its ground, air, and naval branches are: lack of mobility and mechanization, poor logistics systems for sustained offensive operations, marginal command and control for combined arms or joint service operations, obsolescent weaponry, limited power projection capability, obsolescent aircraft and avionics, poor pilot training, inadequate communications, limited capability of its defense industry, obsolescent ships and onboard equipment, and limited amphibious lift capability.

Although it is in the U.S. interest that China be strong enough to protect its borders and to prevent Soviet encroachment, it is not in the U.S. interest that the PRC become a threat either to the United States or to friendly governments in the region. This leads to one of the most difficult problems facing U.S. policymakers: to what extent should the United States help build up the PLA? At the heart of U.S. strategic cooperation with China is the assumption that, through military and economic assistance, Washington will be better able to leverage future PRC policy along lines in keeping with U.S. interests. This is a dangerous assumption; but one which American leaders risk, given the growing military strength of the Soviet Union and the hostility evident in U.S.-USSR relations.

2.3   ECONOMY

China has enormous potential economic power; but, like its military, the PRC economy has great weaknesses to overcome. China's gross national product (GNP) in 1983 was $264.5 billion, but its per capita income averaged only $258. Total trade was $43.66 billion, of which $22.33 billion were exports and $21.33 billion were imports. Reserves at the close of 1983 totalled $19.3 billion, of which $14.5 billion were foreign exchange reserves. China's agricultural output exceeded $270 billion yuan ($1.98 yuan = US$1) and industrial output totalled $614.7 billion yuan. State revenues in 1983

---

[18] U.S. Senate, Committee on Foreign Relations, and Library of Congress, Congressional Research Service, *The Implications of U.S.-China Military Cooperation: A Workshop* (Washington, D.C.: GPO, 1981), p. 31.

were $124.9 billion yuan and expenditures totalled $129.2 billion yuan.[19]

China's current leadership has set socialist economic modernization as the essential national goal of this decade and the remainder of the century. Deng Xiaoping in his opening speech to the important Twelfth National Congress of the Communist Party of China (CPC) on September 1, 1982, said:

> The 1980s will be an important decade in the historical development of our Party and state. To step up socialist modernization, to strive for China's reunification and particularly for the return of Taiwan to the motherland, and to oppose hegemonism and safeguard world peace--these are the three major tasks of our people in the 1980s. Economic construction is at the core of these tasks, as it is the basis for the solution of China's external and domestic problems.[20]

Echoing the senior statesman's remarks, Hu Yaobang in his report to the CPC Congress said:

> The general task of the Communist Party of China in this new historical period is to unite the people of all our nationalities in working hard and self-reliantly to achieve, step by step, the modernization of our industry, agriculture, national defense, and science and technology and to make China a culturally advanced and highly democratic socialist country....
>
> Of the various tasks for bringing about an all-round new situation, the most important one is to push foward the socialist modernization of China's economy.[21]

---

[19] Data on China's economy in 1983 may be found in Zhang Zhongji, "China's Economy: Achievements in 1983," Beijing Review, 27, 8 (February 20, 1984), pp. 14-17; "Report on the State Financial Situation," ibid., 27, 22 (May 28, 1984), p. 21; and "China Data," China Business Review, 11, 1 (January-February 1984), pp. 52-53.

[20] The text of Deng's speech can be found in The Twelfth National Congress of the CPC (Beijing: Foreign Languages Press, 1982), pp. 1-6.

Donald Zagoria addressed the problem of socialist modernization in an important <u>Foreign Affairs</u> article.[22] Zagoria pointed out that the present leadership is in the midst of dismantling the China created by Mao Zedong. This process is essential because of the loss of popular confidence in the Chinese Communist Party caused by the Cultural Revolution and other policy failures. Zagoria noted several important features of the "quiet revolution" now underway in the PRC: the decollectivization of agriculture through the "household responsibility" system; the shift from heavy to light industry; the placing of emphasis upon labor productivity and efficiency instead of ideological "purity"; the decentralization of economic decision-making; the expansion of private enterprise; the creation of special economic zones; and the increased emphasis on science and technology and the resulting improved status of Chinese intellectuals. Each of these initiatives are resisted by many individuals in the party, bureaucracy, and military who, for personal or ideological reasons, find fault with the reformists' program. Moreover, the current leadership is itself undecided about the ultimate propriety of many of its reforms. As Zagoria observed, "China's economic system is just beginning to experiment with market forces." He warned:

> The true tests lie ahead. Will the Chinese move further in the direction of trying to create a market socialist society of the Hungarian or Yugoslav variety, or will they tightly restrict the market forces they are beginning to unleash? There is still no coherent strategy for combining Plan and market and the problems of running a mixed system are bound to be enormous. Indeed, the present situation is unstable....At some point a decision will have to be made whether to go forward or backward.[23]

Industrialization is one of the keys to China's modernization. According to Joyce Kallgren, China's major industrial goals are (1) to increase the growth of light industry and slow the growth of heavy industry; (2) to break the bottleneck caused by limited energy

---

[21] <u>Ibid.</u>, pp. 18-19.

[22] Donald S. Zagoria, "China's Quiet Revolution," <u>Foreign Affairs</u>, 62, 4 (Spring 1984), pp. 879-904.

[23] <u>Ibid.</u>, p. 895.

resources; (3) to facilitate foreign investment, especially the transfer of science and technology; (4) to increase factory productivity; and (5) to establish a fiscal system which will give the central government appropriate revenues and yet retain local initiative and self-reliance.[24]

Problems abound. Western businessmen have been particularly concerned about the uncertainties surrounding investments in China. The February 1983 cancellation of the Daqing ethylene glycol plant is an example of setbacks which can occur without warning. The cancellation of the plant, scheduled to be built at a cost of $26 million with Japanese assistance, caught Tokyo by surprise because the project had been viewed as the first of a series of new construction projects. Previous Japanese and Western expectations of investment opportunities were dashed in 1979, when ongoing negotiations valued at $40 billion were suddenly cut off in the wake of China's economic retrenchment.[25]

U.S. security interests are served by a China sufficiently strong economically to prevent a return to the social chaos which plagued the mainland in earlier decades. But care needs to be exercised here as well. It would not be in the U.S. interest for the PRC to develop into a superpower rival like the Soviet Union, or even for China to emerge as a economic competitor on the scale of Japan.

---

[24] Joyce Kallgren, "China in 1983: The Turmoil of Modernization," Asian Survey, 24, 1 (January 1984), pp. 71-72.

[25] Kyodo, February 16, 1983, in U.S. Government, Foreign Broadcast Information Service, Daily Report: Asia & Pacific, February 16, 1983, p. C1. (Hereafter FBIS-Asia & Pacific). Also see U.S. Congress, Joint Economic Committee, East-West Trade: The Prospects to 1985, 97th Cong., 2d sess., August 18, 1982, p. 56.

2.4 SOCIOPSYCHOLOGY

Sociopsychological factors also contribute to China's national power. China is an ancient civilization which has withstood upheavals far better than its western counterparts. Despite its resilience, China has suffered tremendous social shocks since 1949. Indeed, Mao's objective was the forced transformation of Chinese society down to its very roots. The collectivization of agriculture in 1953-1957, the Great Leap Forward of 1958-1960, the Great Proletarian Cultural Revolution of 1966-1968, and ten years of CPC factional fighting during 1968-1978 are only the peaks of the social cataclysm wrought by the communist revolution.

To these ideologically inspired disruptions must be added the challenges of modernization and westernization now confronting mainland China. In their efforts to assist China to modernize, the United States and other western powers may well introduce the ideas which will eventually transform the PRC into something far different than what it is today. If change can be brought about peacefully in a direction reflecting a positive integration of western and Chinese values, then China in the future may greatly complement the security interests of the United States. If, however, the transformation moves into an ultra-nationalistic or radical communist direction, then U.S. interests will not be served.

2.5 LEADERSHIP

The policies designed to harnass China's national power are formulated and implemented by those who sit in Beijing. Since 1949 the communist government of China has practiced a wide range of domestic and international policies. These have reflected not only the international situation at the time, but also the CPC's experience in the past and the results of political infighting among the various elite factions. A comparison of the policies followed by Mao Zedong in 1972 and Deng Xiaoping ten years later illustrates the profound differences that can occur in the space of a decade in the PRC.

Michel Oksenberg and Richard Bush noted that in 1972 Mao believed that revolution was the preferred method of political change, whereas in 1982 Deng advocated change by reform. Instead of implementing policy through class struggle, as Mao did a decade earlier, Deng sought to instill a sense of regularity and rule through the bureaucracy. Under Mao, the state intruded into all aspects of the life of the individual;

under Deng, the rights of private interests and non-involvement in political affairs were at least partially recognized. Mao dominated China's leadership, while Deng led more by consensus. These differences in personal style, ideological interpretation, domestic and foreign policy, and other aspects of political behavior illustrate the key importance in the Chinese totalitarian system of the personalities of the major power holders and the circumstances which they face. The current Chinese communist system, like its predecessors, is subject to rapid and unpredictable change.[26]

Some scholars have pointed out that there are at least four groups which influence PRC domestic and foreign policy: the reformists, the Maoists, the military, and the disenchanted.[27] The reformists, led by Deng Xiaoping, argue that only through pragmatic economic/social/political reform can China modernize, play an important role in the world community, and avoid domination by the superpowers. Currently the strongest in Beijing, Deng's faction faces external opposition and internal dissent. Zhao Ziyang and Hu Yaobang, for instance, are known to have strong disagreements over several areas of policy.

The Maoist faction includes many of the old, traditional cadre who carried out the communist revolution, plus those who rose to power during the Cultural Revolution. The reformists identify these individuals as leftists and are seeking to purge the more radical from the party's ranks.[28]

The military is also more conservative than the reformists, although less so than the Maoists. Many PLA leaders are known to be dissatisfied with the low priority given to defense modernization and other aspects of Deng's domestic and foreign policies. The

---

[26] Michel Oksenberg and Richard Bush, "China's Political Evolution: 1972-1982," Problems of Communism, 31 (September-October 1982), p. 15.

[27] For a discussion of various political factions within the CPC, including the disenchanted, see "The Political Spectrum: Three Views," China News Analysis, No. 1220 (November 20, 1981).

[28] Yu Yaobang told a delegation from the Socialist Party of Japan in September 1983 that the PRC's Central Committee would start a campaign to remove "leftists" who have resisted change. The campaign is aimed at the approximately ten million members of the CPC who joined the party during the Cultural Revolution. See New York Times, September 30, 1983, p. A3.

military is the biggest institutional threat to the reformists, because the PLA is the only organization other than the party and bureaucracy capable of running the country. The PLA was in de facto control of China during the latter stages of the Cultural Revolution, as the party and bureaucracy struggled to recover from the ravages of the Red Guards.

The last group which influences policy has been called the "disenchanted." These are individuals within and without the party who have become contemptuous of party efforts at reform and doubt if the CPC will ever be able to function justly and efficiently. Their pessimism and cynicism pervade much of society.

Since the death of Mao in 1976, no one has been able to persuade or coerce members of the various factions--or the society at large--to unite under a single leadership. Much of Deng's recent efforts have been directed toward this problem; his program of modernization requires a continuity far beyond his lifespan into the twenty-first century. The publication of Deng's selected works, renewed emphasis on carefully chosen aspects of Mao Zedong thought, and institutional and personnel changes within the party and state bureaucracies are designed to ensure that Deng's pragmatic approach to China's socialist modernization continues after his retirement. The success of this endeavor may be fundamental to the future stability of the PRC. As Oksenberg and Bush concluded: "Until a censensus on ideology exists, it is impossible that China's political system will be fully stable."[29]

The reformists, by emphasizing the economic modernization of China and by opening the door to Western investment and trade, contribute to stability in East Asia and provide immediate benefits to U.S. citizens. Therefore, it is in the U.S. interest to support the reformists when appropriate. But this support should be conditioned by the understanding that Washington can do little to alter Beijing's policies and that Deng's reforms may not long outlive his career. The emergence of another leadership faction, particularly one radical or pro-Soviet in orientation, would be damaging to American interests.

In terms of China's national power, therefore, U.S. interests are best served by a moderately strong, stable society, open to the West and evolving in a direction compatible with American democratic and commercial values. A greatly weakened China is not in U.S. interests, nor is a strong China pursuing anti-Western goals. Above all, it would not be in American interests

---

[29] Oksenberg and Bush, "China's Political Evolution: 1972-1982," p. 19.

for China and the Soviet Union to ally against the United States. The challenge to U.S. policymakers is to evolve a policy which will influence China's development along lines serving American interests. This is difficult for a number of reasons. First, a consensus on U.S. interests vis-a-vis China is lacking. Second, long-range policy planning is difficult to implement in the United States given the nature of the American policy system. Third, the course of China's Four Modernizations is uncertain and may not last beyond the current leadership. And fourth, the influence the United States can bring to bear upon Chinese policy is limited. The above difficulties, plus the uncertainties surrounding the extent of China's national power and the uses to which Beijing may apply that power in the future, dictate a strong dose of caution in U.S. policy toward China.

3
Sino-Soviet Relations

Sino-American strategic cooperation is deeply affected by the state of relations between the People's Republic of China and the Soviet Union. A Sino-Soviet alliance would pose a serious threat to U.S. interests. At the other end of the spectrum, a war between Moscow and Beijing--especially one involving nuclear weapons--would also threaten U.S. interests because of the possibility of escalation. In reality, Sino-Soviet relations have shifted between these poles rather spectacularly.

China and the Soviet Union formed an alliance in 1949, although the official treaty of friendship, alliance, and mutual assistance did not become effective until April of the following year. The two countries cooperated in the Korean War against the United States. Throughout much of the 1950s the Soviets gave considerable amounts of economic and military assistance to the Chinese. By the middle of the decade, however, relations began to cool as a series of disagreements arose between the two sides. By 1960 the dispute had emerged into the open, with Moscow cutting off all aid and withdrawing its technicians from the PRC. The dispute continued to fester throughout the 1960s, reaching a critical point in 1969 when the two countries clashed at several points along the Sino-Soviet border. In the wake of the clashes, Moscow signalled its intention to attack China if Beijing continued to refuse to negotiate border differences. Under the pressure of a deadline, China agreed to Soviet demands for talks.

Despite periodic discussions held by the two sides during the 1970s, relations remained strained. China's decisions to move toward normalized relations with the United States in 1969-1972 and to consummate the relationship in 1978-1979 were heavily influenced by the hostility of the Soviet Union and the immediacy of its threat. Moscow's invasion of Afghanistan in December 1979 as part of its southern strategy to outflank both the United States and the PRC served to push the two countries into close strategic cooperation against their common enemy.

In 1980 China allowed the 30-year treaty of friendship to elapse, although it also indicated that Sino-Soviet relations might be improved under certain conditions. By 1982 both the Soviet Union and China were expressing their desire to normalize state-to-state relations. In mid-1984, however, Sino-Soviet relations again became strained as a result of disagreement over Vietnam and other issues. Thus, over a 35-year period, there has been a rather complete range of Sino-Soviet relations: from close alliance in the early 1950s, to intense antagonism throughout most of the 1960s and 1970s, to limited rapprochement in the 1980s. The vacillation in PRC-USSR relations becomes more understandable in light of the elements of the Sino-Soviet dispute, one of the most important political developments of our time.

3.1   THE SINO-SOVIET SPLIT

In an historical sense, the Sino-Soviet dispute can be seen as a continuation of the China-Russia confrontation which had its origins in the distant past. As early as 138 B.C. the Chinese occupied territory in Soviet Uzbek and Kirgiz. From the twelfth to the fifteenth centuries A.D., the Mongols controlled large segments of Russia, resulting in today's deep-seated Soviet fear and hatred of the "yellow hordes" from Asia. In the seventeenth century the Russians and Chinese came into contact and confrontation in the Manchurian region. By the Treaty of Nerchinsk (1689), Russian settlement was restricted to north of the Amur River. During the eighteenth century, nomads crossing the border led to more conflict. In the Treaty of Burinsk (1727), Russia promised to seal its border to the nomads, but China lost some 40,000 square miles as a concession.

During the nineteenth century, while imperial China was in the process of disintegration, czarist Russia was expanding rapidly into Asia. In numerous treaties--Aigun, Peking, Chuguchak, Livadia, and St. Petersburg to name the more important--China again ceded large portions of its border regions to Russia. It was also during this period that construction began on the Trans-Siberian Railway. Russian encroachment on Chinese territory continued into the early twentieth century, but was arrested by the defeat of Russia by Japan in 1905 and by the outbreak of the Russian Revolution in 1917.

Early relations between the new governments of the Soviet Union and the Republic of China were generally smooth. The Soviets helped to reorganize the Kuomintang (Nationalist Party) and urged members of the Communist

Party of China (which Moscow's agents also organized and attempted to direct) to cooperate with Dr. Sun Yat-sen and Chiang Kai-shek. In 1927, when it became apparent that General Chiang was intent on destroying the communist movement, Moscow directed its Chinese contacts to pursue a disastrous policy of urban revolt. The remnants of the communist party fled to Yan'an in the "Long March" in 1934-1935, during which time Mao Zedong assumed control of the CPC. The USSR had little confidence in Mao's ability to defeat the Nationalists and maintained contact with the ROC until the last moment of the civil war.

At the close of World War Two the Soviets again encroached upon Chinese territory. In 1945 the USSR forced the Nationalists to renounce all claims to Mongolia, which Moscow had earlier declared a Soviet republic, in exchange for a Soviet pledge not to intervene in Xinjiang. Also during 1945, Soviet forces invaded Manchuria, defeated the occupying Japanese army, carried off many industrial plants, and turned over vast quantities of captured Japanese weapons to Mao's communist forces. Since 1949 the Soviet Union has not permanently occupied portions of Chinese territory, but neither has it demonstrated a willingness to withdraw from areas seized in the past.

Geographically, both nations have reason to fear the other. The Central Asian frontier, which extends roughly 1,900 miles from Afghanistan to Mongolia, provides access to the heartlands of both the Soviet Union and China. The border provinces of the two countries are backward and sparsely populated. The border populations are generally of non-Han and non-Great Russian stock.

The Chinese feel especially vulnerable through Mongolia, which borders China for some 2,500 miles. Mao called Mongolia a "fist in China's back." Important invasion corridors lead east, south, and west into the most strategic regions of northern China. The fact that the Soviets dominate Mongolia and station large numbers of troops along the Sino-Mongolian border adds immeasurably to Beijing's perception of the USSR threat.

The eastern frontier, largely defined by the Amur and Ussuri Rivers, extends about 2,300 miles. Manchuria and the bordering provinces of the Soviet Union are areas of high population, rich agriculture, heavy industry, and valuable mineral deposits. The region is of great strategic importance to both nations. China's administrative and industrial heartland is vulnerable to a Soviet attack through Manchuria, and the vital Soviet naval base at Vladivostok and other military facilities are within the range of a Chinese attack from Manchuria.

The geographical proximity of and historical tensions between China and Russia intensify other elements of their disagreement. Both the Chinese and Russians are racially antagonistic and believe the other aims to displace them in Asia. The Chinese fear Russian territorial and political expansion, while the Soviets are concerned over long-term Chinese demographic and cultural expansion into areas now under USSR control.

3.1.1 The Breakdown of the Alliance

Following the victory of the Chinese communists, there was a decade of cooperation between the Soviet Union and the PRC. Starting around 1955, however, serious disputes over ideology, intra-block relations, global strategy, and personal roles in the international communist movement began to emerge.[30]

In terms of ideology, the Sino-Soviet alliance seemed to break down because China adopted a much more ideological solution to economic problems than did the Soviet Union. In essence, the PRC attempted with the Great Leap Forward in 1958 to leap into the final stages of communism without going through the various stages of industrialization and socialism which Soviet ideologists felt necessary before true communism could be realized. The PRC presented itself as being more communist than the Soviet Union, and thus the true model for other communist countries.

Under Nikita Khrushchev, the Soviet Union adopted a more pragmatic course to communism. Khrushchev maintained that material incentives must be used to build the economy, not just ideological fervor as preached by Mao. This fundamental debate between two approaches to communism, which centered over the issue of China's communes, not only antagonized the Soviet and Chinese communist parties, but also led to splits in communist parties throughout the world.

There was also serious disagreement over the question of centralization vs. decentralization within the communist bloc. On this issue, Moscow and Beijing reversed themselves several times, but nearly always on opposite ends of the argument. Initially, the PRC wanted the Soviet Union to exert its leadership and to put down dissident communist movements such as that in Yugoslavia. The USSR preferred to resolve these differences peacefully. Later, when the Soviet Union adopted a much harder line on wayward communist nations like Albania, it was China which argued that each

---

[30] See Donald S. Zagoria, *The Sino-Soviet Conflict, 1956-1961* (Princeton, NJ: Princeton University Press, 1962).

country must define its own path to communism.

China and the Soviet Union also disagreed on global strategy. After the launching of Sputnik and the successful test of an ICBM in 1957, Mao argued that the strategic correlation of forces so heavily favored the Soviet Union that Moscow should press forward and militarily oppose the United States whenever the interests of East and West collided. Mao felt the strength of the USSR would deter the United States and that local conflicts could be contained at levels below the nuclear threshold. Mao further argued that, with the help of the Soviet Union, the outcome of these local conflicts could be manipulated to the advantage of the local communist parties or governments. Thus, Mao wanted Soviet backing during the 1958 Taiwan Strait crisis and urged that Moscow take a harder line on issues such as Cuba, Algeria, and other areas of East-West conflict.[31]

Khrushchev, while no doubt accepting the spirit of Mao's "East wind prevailing over the West wind" analogy, nonetheless viewed the threat of nuclear confrontation much more seriously than did the PRC leader. Convinced that communism would eventually prevail over the West because of socialism's superior economic strength, Khrushchev felt the wisest policy was to contain the threat of nuclear war through diplomatic efforts. Local conflicts were seen as the most likely point of escalation to a major nuclear holocaust and thus were to be avoided whenever possible. Should hostilities break out, they should be contained quickly through political means. Moscow could not justify a possible confrontation with the United States over issues such as Taiwan, which had little impact on Soviet interests. Moreover, the Soviet Union was wary about China's possible intention to push Moscow into a war with the United States. After all, Mao had said that his country would survive a nuclear exchange between the superpowers.

The conflicting personalities of Khrushchev and Mao also played an important role in the breakdown of the Sino-Soviet alliance. Neither leader liked nor trusted the other. Both felt the other to be a danger to the world communist movement. The intense personal dislike between the two leaders centered on Khrushchev's decision to criticize Stalin during the 20th Congress in 1956 without first consulting Mao. The Chinese leader realized that much of what Khrushchev said of Stalin

---

[31] Mao's reasoning during the 1958 Quemoy crisis and other Taiwan-related incidents can be found in Harold C. Hinton, *Communist China in World Politics* (Boston: Houghton Mifflin Co., 1966), pp. 258-272.

could be applied to himself.

Contributing to the personality conflict was Mao's view of himself as Stalin's legitimate successor as leading communist theoretician and statesman. Khrushchev took strong exception to Mao's presumptions, particularly in view of the USSR's superior strength, the leading Soviet role in communist affairs, and the questionable validity of some of Mao's interpretations of Marxism-Leninism. As substantive disagreements between the two countries grew in intensity, both leaders publicly traded insults and tried to discredit the other. By the end of 1960, it was apparent that, if for no other reason, the personal antagonism of Mao and Khrushchev would prevent Sino-Soviet rapprochement.

3.1.2   The 1969 Military Confrontation

With the breakdown of the Sino-Soviet alliance, some sort of military confrontation along their common border was inevitable. The border issue was injected into the dispute in 1963, when Beijing claimed areas it said czarist Russia had seized through illegal treaties dating back to the eighteenth century. China demanded that the Soviet Union acknowledge these treaties as being "unequal" and the territory unfairly ceded. Beijing also demanded as a precondition for any final settlement of the issue the pullout of Soviet troops from at least two of the areas so seized: some 3,900 square miles in Soviet Central Asia and several hundred islands in the Ussuri and Amur rivers near Vladivostok. Moscow, for its part, pledged to defend the existing boundaries and refused to surrender one inch of its sacred territory.

During the Vietnam War, China and the Soviet Union could not agree on measures to aid North Vietnam. In 1967 both countries withdrew their ambassadors from the other's capital. All during this period, the Soviet Union was slowly increasing the size of its forces along the Sino-Soviet border. China, in the midst of the Cultural Revolution, was more concerned with the PLA's reestablishing domestic order than guarding against a Soviet attack.

The Soviet invasion of Czechoslovakia in 1968 had a profound effect upon the Chinese leadership. Beijing realized that the Brezhnev Doctrine, which justified Soviet intervention in socialist countries in which socialism was seen to be at risk, could also be applied to China in the throes of the Cultural Revolution. As early as 1967 Moscow had begun to patrol in earnest the Sino-Soviet border (as defined by the USSR) and several minor skirmishes had occurred between those patrols and

Red Guard or PLA units intent on defending what they perceived to be China's borders. Moreover, Moscow had on more than one occasion hinted that it might intervene on behalf of non-radical Chinese forces to put an end to excesses occuring in the PRC.

Moscow was tempted to intervene for several reasons. First, China appeared to be in a severely weakened and demoralized state. Since a strong China on the border of the USSR would always pose a security threat, Soviet leaders probably reasoned that intervention could be used either to install a pro-Soviet leadership in Beijing or to reduce China's military capabilities to an insignificant level for the foreseeable future. Second, the Sino-Soviet dispute had become very bitter by this point and many in Moscow probably wanted to see the matter settled once and for all in the USSR's favor. And third, the Kremlin may have seen the opportunity as being ripe to end the Chinese challenge to Soviet leadership in the communist movement.

The most critical period of Sino-Soviet military confrontation occurred in March 1969, when the Chinese ambushed a Soviet patrol on Zhenbao Island in the Ussuri (Wusuli) River. The reasons China wanted to precipitate such an incident are related to the complex political maneuvering then going on in Beijing between Mao, Lin Biao, and Zhou Enlai.[32] Various interpretations have Lin or Zhou actually initiating the border clash to discredit the other and gain additional power.

Whoever bears the responsibility, the impact of the Zhenbao incident was immediate and far-reaching. The Soviets responded with a well-planned ambush of their own on the island a short time later. This, as well as several other sharp attacks along the border, resulted in complete defeat for the Chinese. It was at this point that the Soviet Union began a massive military buildup along the Sino-Soviet border. Moscow threatened to attack China unless Beijing quickly resumed discussions on the border issue.

---

[32] The close relationship between the Sino-Soviet dispute, Sino-American rapprochement, and political infighting between Mao Zedong, the military, moderates, and radicals is well documented in John W. Garver, China's Decision for Rapprochement with the United States, 1968-1971 (Boulder, CO: Westview Press, 1982). Another useful discussion of the interrelationship between competing consensus groups and China's foreign policy can be found in Carol Lee Hamrin, "Competing 'Policy-Packages' in Post-Mao China," Asian Survey, 24, 5 (May 1984), pp. 487-518.

Feelers were put out to the United States to test its response to a Soviet attack on the PRC. Henry Kissinger reported that in April 1969, Soviet Ambassador Anatoly Dobrynin suggested that "there was still time for the two superpowers to order events (in China), but they might not have this power much longer."[33] Rather than accepting the veiled invitation to eliminate the Chinese problem, the Nixon Administration signalled instead that the United States would view a Soviet attack on China as being against U.S. interests. This was one of the most important gestures to the PRC of Washington's interest in normalizing Sino-American relations.

Whether the Soviet objective was to attack China, to force it to the negotiating table, or to precipitate a change in Chinese policy is difficult to determine. Without question, Soviet preparations were for war, going so far as the creation of a new Central Asian Military District opposite Xinjiang. But the USSR also gave Beijing several ultimatums to resume negotiations. The most forceful of these was delivered in June 1969 and accepted by the PRC at the very last moment in a Beijing airport meeting in September between Premiers Aleksey Kosygin and Zhou Enlai. Indirectly, the Soviet military response also resulted in a change in PRC policy, although not along lines preferred by Moscow. Within a few months of the border clashes, Lin Biao and his faction were purged from the top Chinese leadership and the moderates emerged as the most important policy-making faction.[34] Two of the most important policy initiatives of the moderates were the normalization of relations with the United States and the opening of China to the West in order to modernize the PRC economy.

3.1.3 The Soviet Military Threat to China

Since 1969 the Sino-Soviet border has become the most militarized in the world. Table 1 indicates the relative strength of the USSR and China in East Asia.[35]

---

[33] Henry A. Kissinger, White House Years (Boston: Little, Brown and Co., 1979), p. 173.

[34] See Thomas M. Gottlieb, Chinese Foreign Policy Factionalism and the Origins of the Strategic Triangle (Santa Monica, CA: Rand, November 1977).

[35] From The Military Balance: 1982-1983 (London: International Institute of Strategic Studies, 1982).

It should be noted that Soviet deployments in East Asia represent roughly one-quarter of their total forces, whereas China's figures are for the entire country. Beijing deploys over 50% of its regular forces to the north to meet the Soviet threat.

TABLE 1

USSR and PRC Armed Forces in East Asia

Category	USSR	PRC
Ground Forces		
Personnel	400,000	3,150,000
Infantry Div.	54	131
(Mechanized)	(54)	(12)
Tanks	12,500	5,000
Air Forces		
Bombers	400+	850
Fighters	1,300+	5,100
(Ground Attack)	(800)	(500)
Naval Forces		
Submarines	120	106
Aircraft Carriers	2	0
Cruisers	12	0
Destroyers	20	10
Frigates	50	30

In testimony before the Committee on Foreign Affairs of the U.S. House of Representatives in June 1984, Assistant Secretary of Defense James Kelly summarized the force structure along the Sino-Soviet border:

> Ground forces poised against each other equate to approximately one million Chinese troops and .5 million much better equipped Soviet military personnel. Chinese forces in the border region include 58 infantry and 8 armored divisions and about 2,000 combat aircraft. China has about 114-155 nuclear armed ballistic missiles. In comparison, the

Soviet military forces in the Far East total 52 divisions, 47 of which are along the Sino-Soviet border. These 41 mechanized and 6 tank divisions have almost five times as many tanks and armored vehicles as the Chinese divisions in the frontier regions. Soviet forces also include 1,800 advanced combat aircraft, and over 750 intermediate and short-range surface-to-surface missiles ranging from the SS-20 to battlefield tactical systems.[36]

Included in the Soviet arsenal are approximately 135 of the highly accurate and mobile SS-20s. One U.S. expert has said of the SS-20: "Perhaps the single most important reason for the erosion of the U.S. nuclear umbrella in Asia has been the Soviet development and deployment of the 'SS-20' intermediate-range ballistic missile system."[37] Although qualitatively and quantitatively inferior to the Soviet missiles, Chinese missiles are well concealed, providing some deterrence against a Soviet first strike.[38]

Improving deterrence against the Soviet Union has high priority for the Chinese military. In March 1983 Defense Minister Zhang Aiping reaffirmed the importance of missile and nuclear programs. He noted that as early as 1956 the "CPC Central Committee decided that developing guided missiles and atomic energy were the two key projects in our national defense modernization."[39] The Chinese leadership realizes it cannot match Soviet missile deployments; yet PRC planners believe continued research and development in these fields will lead to an adequate deterrence under

---

[36] Prepared statement of James A. Kelly, "Defense Relations with the People's Republic of China," given before U.S. House of Representatives, Committee on Foreign Affairs, Subcommittee on Asian and Pacific Affairs, June 5, 1984, p. 3, ms.

[37] K. Dunlop Scott, "The 'SS-20' and the Erosion of U.S. Credibility in Asia," Proceedings, 108, 2, 948 (February 1982), p. 88.

[38] Valuable insight into the Chinese missile program can be found in Mark Wade, "The Chinese Ballistic Missile Program," International Defense Review, 13, 8 (1980), pp. 1190-1192.

[39] Hongqi, March 1, 1983, in U.S. Government, Foreign Broadcast Information Service, Daily Report: China, March 17, 1983, p. K4. (Hereafter, FBIS-China.)

most conditions.

Conventionally, the two armies have quite different missions. The USSR Red Army, emphasizing armored mobility and heavy offensive capabilities, is opposed by the PLA, which continues to adhere to an essentially defensive doctrine of "people's war," or popular resistance against any invading force. What the Chinese lack in sophisticated weaponry, they hope to remedy by numbers and strategy. Beijing plans, in the event of a large-scale conventional attack by the Soviet Union, to channel penetrating Russian forces to choke points within China where they would be annihilated. Small mobile strike units would cross into the Soviet Union to cut lines of communication and to seize or destroy targets of high value to Moscow.[40]

As a result of this mismatch of forces, there is continuing debate over whether the PLA could effectively stop invading Soviet forces by fighting a "people's war under modern conditions." The basic assumption that the Soviet Union would allow itself to be drawn deeply into China may be false. Other options available to Moscow include: (1) the destabilization of Tibet, Xinjiang, and Inner Mongolia and the creation therein of "independent" countries like Mongolia; (2) a preemptive strike against China's nuclear weapons and missile production facilities; (3) the seizure of Manchuria; and (4) nuclear, chemical, or bacteriological assaults against selected administrative and/or industrial centers. These and other Soviet options would severely set back China's development, yet avoid the pitfalls of being drawn into a prolonged guerrilla war in China's interior.[41]

The questionable ability of the Chinese to counter these types of attack has led some analysts to conclude that China would be helpless--even if it were inclined--to assist the West in a two-front war against the USSR. William Green and David Yost argued:

---

[40] Useful insight into PLA strategy can be found in U.S. Defense Intelligence Agency, Handbook on the Chinese Armed Forces, DDI-2680-32-76, July 1976. See also Ray Bonds, ed., The Chinese War Machine (London: Salamander Books Ltd., 1979).

[41] A discussion of Soviet military options can be found in William C. Green and David S. Yost, "Soviet Strategic Options Regarding Mainland China: Notes on a Range of Alternatives," Issues and Studies, 17 (April 1981), pp. 10-31.

>Even in the event of a two-front war--Europe and mainland China--the Soviets may be presumed capable of dealing with Communist China and avoiding entrapment in a "people's war" situation. Indeed, the wisest course for the Soviet Union could be--in the event of a war against the West--to stand on the defensive as regards mainland China. If the panoply of Soviet options deterred the Communist Chinese from taking any action against the Soviet Union, so much the better. The Soviet Union would have avoided a two-front war and part of the Soviet Far Eastern forces would have been released for use against the West. If the Chinese Communists were so rash as to attack the Soviet Union in a two-front war, the meagernes of their logistical capability, the 1950s-quality of their arms and equipment, and the thoroughness of Soviet frontier defenses could readily combine to frustrate the Chinese Communist offensive, which would have to travel far to achieve much of substance. The Soviet Union would still be free to focus the vast bulk of its military power against the West, while the Chinese Communist armed forces would be irrelevant in terms of inhibiting a Soviet blitzkrieg against the West. In short, the range of Soviet strategic options regarding mainland China is sufficiently robust to demonstrate that Western nations would be ill-advised to put too many hopes in the deterrent capacity of the Chinese Communists in the years ahead.[42]

The Chinese are aware of their limitations in defending the PRC against a Soviet attack. Top political commissar General Wu Quili said in July 1983: "The People's Liberation Army would not be able to match a better equipped aggressor even if it modernized its weaponry over the next ten to twenty years."[43]

PLA modernization is fourth priority in the Four Modernizations, a status not pleasing to all military officers, but nonetheless reasonable given the heavy dependence of modern armed forces on a sound economy and healthy industrial base. Defense Minister Zhang Aiping has emphasized that China's "guideline for stepping up modernization of national defense is still primarily

---

[42] Ibid., p. 31.

[43] Washington Post, July 27, 1983, p. A24.

self-reliance. But at the same time, we should import advanced technology."⁴⁴ The Defense Minister cautioned, however, against over-reliance on imported weapons or technology. In <u>Hongqi</u>, he said:

> In order to achieve modernization of our national defense, our first task is to develop and produce sophisticated military equipment.
>
> Our country is a big country and it is not realistic or possible for us to buy national defense modernization from abroad....At the outset it is necessary to obtain some technology that can be imported and model some weaponry on that of others. However, if we are content with copying, we will only be crawling behind others and still be unable to attain our anticipated goal. The fundamental way is to rely on ourselves.⁴⁵

Despite its large size, the PLA has many fundamental obstacles to overcome in its modernization. The major weaknesses of the PLA are:

Ground Forces

-- lack of mobility and mobilization
-- poor logistics and sustained offensive operations
-- limited power projection capability
-- obsolescent equipment
-- weak command and control abilities
-- limited experience in combined forces operations

Air Forces

-- obsolescent aircraft, avionics, and weaponry
-- insufficient pilot training and low proficiency
-- inadequate communications
-- inadequate engine and aircraft production capabilities

---

⁴⁴ <u>Xinhua</u>, February 28, 1983, in <u>FBIS-China</u>, March 2, 1983, pp. K6-K7.

⁴⁵ <u>Hongqi</u>, March 1, 1983, in <u>FBIS-China</u>, March 17, 1983, pp. K3-K4.

Naval Forces
-- obsolescent ships, sensors, and weapons
-- extremely limited shipboard surface-to-air (SAM) capabilities
-- limited amphibious capabilities
-- limited anti-submarine warfare (ASW) capabilities

CIA analysts Sydney Jammes and G. Lawrence Lamborn have studied the PLA's liabilities and assets in some detail. The liabilities faced by the Chinese in their defense modernization program include: the low supply of trained researchers and engineers; the extent of China's nonmilitary needs that compete with the military for limited resources; serious technological weaknesses affecting China's ability to produce high quality weapons; severe problems in China's defense industry from basic research to maintenance of finished products; and organizational deficiencies within the PLA itself. Among the assets noted by Jammes and Lamborn are a dedicated leadership committed to modernization; excellent international credit ratings; availability of advanced technology from abroad; and determination to avoid future costly military engagements such as the conflict with Vietnam in 1979. Weighing these assets and liabilities, the CIA analysts concluded that over the next fifteen years "China will not develop an offensive capability against the USSR," but that "China's defensive capabilities will be significantly improved by 1995 if political stability, economic growth, and scientific and industrial modernization continue unobstructed."[46]

China's deterrent calculations include not only its present and future nuclear and conventional capabilities, but also the notion that the United States would not stand idly by while the Soviet Union destroyed China. The concept of a U.S. unofficial nuclear umbrella over China was indirectly articulated by President Nixon and Henry Kissinger in 1969, when the danger of a Soviet attack against China was high. As Kissinger related in his memoirs:

> From the beginning Nixon and I were convinced--alone among senior policymakers--that the United States could not

---

[46] Sydney H. Jammes and G. Lawrence Lamborn, "China's Military Strategic Requirements," in U.S. Congress, Joint Economic Committee, *China Under the Four Modernizations*, Part 1 (Washington, D.C.: GPO, 1982), pp. 599-602, 604.

accept a Soviet military assault on China....We imposed contingency planning on a reluctant bureaucracy as early as the summer of 1969.[47]

The merits of this strategic concept will be examined in greater detail in Chapter Five. Psychologically, it is appealing and may introduce an element of caution into Soviet planning. Practically speaking, however, the concept may be invalid because of the reluctance of Congress and the American people to support U.S. intervention on the side of China on a scale sufficient to make any difference in a major Sino-Soviet conflict. Such intervention would carry a high risk of escalation into a war between the superpowers.

3.1.4 Other Elements of the Dispute

Three other elements of the Sino-Soviet split should be briefly noted: the border dispute, economic incompatibility, and competition to influence events in Asia and the world.

History provides both countries with enough boundary issues to last for decades. From a long-term perspective, Beijing views with suspicion Moscow's traditional strategic objective of advancing the Russian border to the Kuropatkin Line--running from Vladivostok to Khan Tengri mountain in the Tian Shan range between the Soviet Kirgiz Republic and China's Xinjiang Province. The USSR, on the other hand, is fearful of Chinese cultural absorption of border territories, particularly in view of the fact that Moscow has difficulty convincing white Russians to live in territories along the Sino-Soviet border.

For the short-term, both countries use the border issue as a convenient point of dispute in their larger confict. As Robert Sutter observed:

> The Sino-Soviet border negotiations over the last decade have reflected a variety of incompatible interests of the two sides. The Soviets have not seriously considered the Chinese demands in these negotiations because they are thought to involve the surrender of important Soviet territorial interests that could seriously complicate Moscow's position

---

[47] Kissinger, White House Years, p. 764.

on other disputed borders, notably with Japan;
and because major concessions would be
considered appeasement of an enemy and
acceptance of defeat in a much broader
political struggle. Similarly, the Chinese
for their part have adhered to the border
claims not so much because of the importance
they assign to the territory in question, or
because they expect the Soviets ever to yield,
but rather because these claims represent a
major instrument of political warfare against
an antagonist.[48]

In mid-July 1984 there were signs that China might be attempting to resolve its border dispute with the Soviet Union in a more serious fashion. During that month, representatives from Beijing and Ulan Bator met to sign a final agreement marking the 2,500-mile border between China and Mongolia. Diplomats felt the accord signalled Beijing's interest in resuming border talks with Moscow, suspended since the Soviet invasion of Afghanistan in 1979.[49]

Economic incompatibility is yet another element of the Sino-Soviet dispute. Economic cooperation between Siberia and the industrial base in northern China would seem to be in the interests of both countries. In reality, however, Sino-Soviet trade is quite small. In 1982, PRC-USSR trade totalled only $316 million, compared to $5.2 billion in Sino-American trade and $8.9 billion in Sino-Japanese trade during the same period. In 1983 trade between the PRC and the USSR approached $1 billion, still far below China's trade with the West.

As Table 2 illustrates, the direction of China's trade has shifted significantly since the founding of the People's Republic. In 1979 only 12% of PRC trade was with countries possessing centrally planned economies, while 88% was with market economy nations. By way of contrast, in 1979 only 32% of the Soviet Union's total trade volume of $122.8 billion went to the industrialized West and Japan.[50]

---

[48] Robert G. Sutter, Future Sino-Soviet Relations and Their Implications for the United States (Washington, D.C.: Library of Congress, Congressional Research Service, December 30, 1982), pp. 32-33.

[49] Washington Post, July 13, 1984, p. A20.

[50] U.S. Government, National Foreign Assessment Center, The World Factbook, 1981 (Washington, D.C.: GPO, April 1981), p. 183.

TABLE 2

PRC Trade with Centrally Planned and Market Economies

Year	Total Trade	Centrally Planned	Market Economies
	(Figures in U.S. million dollars)		
1950	1,135	368	767
1953	2,368	1,662	706
1957	3,103	2,065	1,038
1962	2,663	1,180	1,483
1966	4,614	1,014	3,600
1970	4,586	739	3,847
1975	14,750	2,269	12,481
1976	13,433	2,140	11,293
1977	14,804	2,276	12,528
1978	20,638	2,836	17,802
1979	29,332	3,566	25,766

Source: PRC Ministry of Foreign Trade

Unless a profound political change should occur within the PRC, it is unlikely that the direction of China's trade will once again shift toward the centrally planned economies. Although Beijing has expressed an interest in gradually increasing trade with the Soviet Union and in receiving help to modernize factories built with USSR assistance in the 1950s, the Four Modernizations require massive infusions of trade, technology, and assistance from the western democracies. Therefore, the trends noted in Table 2 will probably continue.

Sino-Soviet competition to influence events in Asia is perhaps second only to military deployments along the border in its destabilizing effect on relations between the PRC and the USSR. Because of their strong sense of nationalism and ideological mission, both communist states seek to improve their geostrategic position and to expand their political influence. In Asia, particularly, there is an unavoidable conflict of interest between the two countries.

China, traditionally a major power in East Asia, is attempting to reestablish its role as an arbiter of regional affairs. Patiently but inexorably, Beijing is acquiring the elements of national power necessary to achieve this goal. It may be within reach sometime during the twenty-first century, a century many Chinese--whether from the mainland, Taiwan, or Overseas Chinese communities--view as "China's century."

Table 3 lists the most important categories of PRC national interests and elements of policy.

TABLE 3

PRC National Interests and Elements of Policy

Categories of National Interest	Elements of Policy
Survival	-- Deterrence of nuclear war involving China -- Counterbalance Soviet threat -- Modernize as quickly as possible
Territorial Integrity	-- Regain lost territories, including Taiwan -- Prevent Soviet hegemony in region -- Establish friendly border states as buffers
Economic Well-Being	-- Achieve self-sufficiency -- Maintain and expand trade with West -- Succeed in Four Modernizations -- Develop oil reserves
World Order	-- Assume leadership of Third World -- Oppose superpower dominance -- Expand influence in world communist movement -- Prevent outbreak of regional hostilities threatening PRC interests

China clearly aims to challenge the superpowers in Asia. Although the United States presents a long-term threat to PRC interests, the more immediate and dangerous threat is the Soviet Union. This threat is amplified because the Soviet Union sees an expansionist policy in Asia as essential to its own security. The basic conflict of security interests becomes apparent in the three conditions the PRC has set for the normalization of Sino-Soviet relations: (1) the withdrawal of Soviet troops from Afghanistan, (2) a major reduction of Soviet forces along the Sino-Soviet and Sino-Mongolian borders, and (3) the withdrawal of Soviet-backed Vietnamese troops from Kampuchea. The PRC views the Soviet involvement in these areas as direct threats to its security. The Kremlin, on the other hand, considers its position in Afghanistan, Mongolia, Vietnam, and along the Sino-Soviet border as essential not only to its strategic posture vis-a-vis the People's Republic of China but also as necessary to counter the U.S. presence in Asia. The U.S.-Soviet balance of power in the Far East, therefore, must be factored into the Sino-Soviet equation.

3.2 U.S.-SOVIET BALANCE OF POWER IN EAST ASIA

Table 4 shows the forces of the United States and the Soviet Union in the Far East.[51]

TABLE 4

US and USSR Pacific-Based Forces

Category	US West Pac	US East Pac	US Total	USSR
Ground Forces				
Divisions	1 2/3	2 1/3	4	54
Tanks	190	135	325	12,500
Air Forces				
Bombers	14	0	14	435
Fighters	425	300	725	1,300
(Attack)	(425)	(300)	(725)	800
Naval Forces				
Submarines	--	--	46	122
Carriers				
Attack	3	3	6	0
Helicopter	1	6	7	2
Cruisers	4	10	14	12
Frigates	11	27	38	50

---

[51] From John M. Collins, U.S./Soviet Military Balance, Statistical Trends, 1970-1981 (Washington, D.C.: Library of Congress, September 15, 1982).

Also taken into consideration by Soviet planners are South Korea's 23 divisions, 19 surface combatants, and 400 fighter/bombers. Japanese Self-Defense Forces contribute some 13 divisions, 54 surface combatants, 14 submarines, and 380 fighter/bombers to the allied cause.[52]

The Reagan Administration is seriously concerned about the Soviet military buildup in the Far East. Fred Ikle, Under Secretary of Defense for Policy, told Congress in June 1982: "During the past decade and a half, the Soviets have taken disturbing steps to improve their military capabilities and expand their influence throughout the region. These efforts continue unabated, and five years from now the threat will be even more dangerous." Among the specific concerns cited by Ikle:

> 1. The more than 50 Soviet divisions along the Sino-Soviet border, plus an additional 120,000 Soviet troops facing Southwest Asia, and more than 105,000 conducting combat operations in Afghanistan.
>
> 2. The more than 3,000 combat aircraft stationed in the four easternmost military districts of the USSR. These include the most modern Soviet aircraft, such as the Foxbat interceptor, Flogger fighter, Fencer fighter-bomber, and the Backfire bomber. The Backfire is especially threatening because it can deliver conventional or nuclear bombs and cruise missiles throughout the region.
>
> 3. The deployment to Asia of one-third of the total Soviet force of SS-20s.
>
> 4. The rapid growth and modernization of the Soviet Pacific Fleet, now the largest of the Soviet fleets and home to some of the most sophisticated Russian ships, including the V/STOL aircraft carriers Minsk and Novorossiysk. At least three Kara-class guided missile cruisers are also deployed with the Soviet Pacific Fleet.[53]

---

[52] U.S. Department of Defense, Soviet Military Power, 1983 (Washington, D.C.: GPO, March 1983), p. 56.

[53] Prepared statement of Fred Ikle, "Soviet Challenge in the Pacific and U.S. and Allied Responses," given before U.S. Senate, Committee on Foreign Relations, June 10, 1982, p. 2, ms.

Also of worry to the United States is the acquisition by the Soviet Union since 1979 of increased basing rights in Indochina. In early 1983 the USSR deployed a task force of ten ships in the South China Sea, operating out of Cam Ranh Bay. Cam Ranh is being equipped with the spare parts, fuel, and other material necessary to sustain large deployments of Backfire bombers and naval combatants. Some 50% of the free world's oil transits are now within easy striking distance of Soviet forces based in Vietnam. Presently in Vietnam are 5,000 to 8,000 Soviet military advisors and technicians who repair and service weapons, train pilots and missile crews, guard key Soviet facilities, and operate radar installations at Tan Son Nhut airfield at Ho Chi Minh City (Saigon), Da Nang, Bien Hoa, and Cam Ran Bay. China claims that in addition to these major facilities the Soviets are building another naval base on Con Son Island, about 80 miles southeast of Vinh Loi.[54]

The United States views with apprehension Soviet deployments and bases in the Indian Ocean. At the present time, the USSR normally deploys about 15 major ships in the Indian Ocean, including at least one submarine. Ports of call for Soviet vessels include Aden, the Seychelles, Colombo, Port Louis, Basra, Umm Qasr, Bombay, Madras, and Singapore.

The political challenge presented by the Soviet Union in Asia is also noted with deeping concern by the United States. Moscow uses its highly visible military presence to challenge American political influence in the region. ASEAN and other regional countries carefully monitor the balance of power between Washington and Moscow in the Far East. Given the American defeat in Vietnam and the subsequent reduction of U.S. forces in the Pacific, local governments are susceptible to the argument that the Soviet Union is there to stay whereas the future role of the United States is questionable.

As a result of the increased challenge it faces from the Soviet Union in the Far East, the Reagan Administration discarded the "swing strategy" of previous administrations and began to build up U.S. forces in the region. As Secretary of the Navy John Lehman explained in a December 1982 interview with the Washington Post, the United States can no longer swing the Pacific Fleet to the Atlantic Ocean in case of conflict:

---

[54] New York Times, December 30, 1982, p. A4.

> We have to provide force simultaneously in Asia....Otherwise, Japan must acccommodate immediately with the Soviets, because they depend entirely on imports of oil and everything else. You've got to worry about Alaska, which now provides more oil to the United States than does the Persian Gulf. These are all new developments, so obviously we can't swing the Pacific Fleet, and that fleet is not big enough now to do both the Persian Gulf, Indian Ocean and the minimum defense of the Pacific.[55]

Moscow, seemingly unmindful that its buildup led to the U.S. response, sees the Reagan Administration's renewed emphasis on military preparedness in the Far East as threatening USSR interests.

3.3 SOVIET STRATEGIC PERCEPTIONS

The Soviet Union views Asia, the Pacific, and the Indian Ocean as part of its global strategic competition with the United States. Moscow believes the United States has three objectives in these regions: (1) to overcome the image of the post-Vietnam withdrawal; (2) to solidify military relations with Japan and Korea; and (3) to draw ANZUS and ASEAN into its comprehensive strategic plan.[56]

A large percentage--if not the majority--of Soviet deployments in the Far East are targeted on the United States and its forces, not on the People's Republic of China. Perceiving the U.S. threat to be increasing, the Soviet Union is intent to build up its own forces in East Asia. Moreover, the geographical, historical, ideological, and foreign policy differences between the Soviet Union and China tend to reinforce the Soviet concept that the PRC is a long-term threat to Soviet interests. A fundamental concern of Moscow is that China might align with the United States, Japan, and Western Europe.[57]

---

[55] _Washington Post_, December 29, 1982, p. A4.

[56] Thomas Perry Thornton, "The USSR and Asia in 1983," _Asian Survey_, 24, 1 (January 1984), pp. 1-2.

[57] For an overview of Soviet perceptions of China, see Morris Rothenberg, _Whither China: The View from the Kremlin_ (Miami, FL: University of Miami, 1977).

Based upon extensive discussions in 1981 with Soviet specialists on Chinese affairs, Banning Garrett reported:

> China is a far greater military and political concern to the Soviet Union than is usually understood in the United States. This concern about the "Chinese threat" has been deepened by the emerging Sino-American military relationship, which has had a wide-ranging impact on Soviet leaders' perceptions of the Soviet Union's strategic environment and on their decision-making in both foreign policy and defense programs. The Soviets are especially concerned about the possibility of a two-front war, whether it results from the U.S. and NATO coming to China's aid or taking advantage of a war-weakened Soviet Union following a Sino-Soviet war, or from China opening a second front or seeking to gain from the aftermath of a U.S.-Soviet war.[58]

Garrett noted: "Soviet analysts express apprehension that Sino-American collusion against the Soviet Union is shifting the global 'correlation of forces' against the Soviet Union. Soviet analysts clearly viewed Sino-American military ties as intended as offensive pressure on the Soviet Union and aimed at forcing concessions from Moscow, distracting the Soviet Union from Europe and the U.S., and at 'overburdening' the Soviet and East European economies. The analysts also argue that U.S. policy is aimed at tying a faction of the Chinese leadership to the United States and at heading off possible Sino-Soviet reconciliation."[59]

Garrett believed the immediate military threat perceived by the Soviet Union as a result of Sino-American strategic cooperation was less important than its psychological impact on the Soviet leadership. Top Kremlin leaders felt Beijing might not fear a nuclear war because of the possibility of China's survival and the superpowers' destruction. The Russians were especially concerned about the prospects of U.S.-Chinese military coordination during wartime. Because of this concern, Garrett observed:

---

[58] Banning N. Garrett, <u>Soviet Perceptions of China and Sino-American Military Ties</u> (Arlington, VA: Harold Rosebaum Associates, June 1981), p. 3.

[59] Ibid., pp. 7-8.

The Soviet's two-front war dilemma--including the protracted war, post-nuclear threat from China--places far greater demands on any Soviet warwinning strategy than would a simple bipolar calculus of a U.S.-Soviet conflict. Soviet analysts say that the Soviet leadership's response to this situation has been to further increase the overall military buildup and to improve Soviet military capabilities in the Far East.[60]

Moscow believes that, in reaction to its 1968 invasion of Czechoslovakia, the buildup of Soviet forces along the Sino-Soviet border, and the 1969 military clashes, China is seeking to establish a de facto security alliance with the United States and its regional allies. This "anti-hegemony" united front is to be composed of the PRC, Japan, the United States, NATO, ASEAN, and ANZUS, as well as Pakistan and Egypt.
According to Richard Solomon, since the mid-1970s the USSR has attempted to build its own security coalition in Asia to counter this worst-case scenario. The Soviet coalition is based upon bilateral security treaties with Mongolia, Vietnam, India, Afghanistan, South Yemen, and Ethiopia. Solomon forecast that in the 1980s Moscow would seek to forestall the consolidation of Beijing's united front coalition

by trying to gain greater influence in Indonesia (which fears a growing Chinese presence in Southeast Asia), and by enticing the Japanese to invest in the development of the natural resources of the Soviet Far East. The Soviets will also attempt to pull North Korea to their side in the Sino-Soviet feud, probably by trying to influence a leadership succession struggle in Pyongyang. They will strengthen their military assets and base structure in Asia so as to neutralize the American military presence, intimidate the Chinese and Japanese, and weaken America's ties to its allies. Moscow will seek to create a sense of insecurity along the sea and air lines of communication by which the U.S. would reinforce its allies in time of war, and through which Japan and other countries gain access to Middle Eastern oil and other natural resources, and promote trade.[61]

---

[60] Ibid., p. 10.

[61] Richard H. Solomon, "Choices for Coalition-Building:

Donald Zagoria and other scholars have noted that the Soviet Union adheres to the principle of "total security." Moscow believes it must have at its disposal the military means to overcome the combination of all perceived threats. In Asia this would include the combined threat from the United States, Japan, South Korea, and China. Based upon this interpretation of Soviet motives, Zagoria told Congress in 1983:

> Given the Soviet commitment to total security, the absence of any sense of military sufficiency, their real and perceived disadvantages in the Asian theater, and the long Russian history of being involved in Asian military conflicts, there is likely to be a continuing Soviet military buildup in the Pacific motivated by a Soviet effort to neutralize what is perceived as an overall Western superiority.[62]

Zagoria suggested that the following would continue to be the USSR's goals in the Asia-Pacific theater:

1. A continuing and relentless effort to alter the present military balance in the Pacific.

2. Continuing efforts to weaken the Western alliance system led by the United States.

3. Continuing efforts to contain China, while at the same time seeking to improve relations with the PRC but without making major concessions.

4. A gradual improvement of relations with Japan through a combination of stick-and-carrot policies designed to loosen Japanese-U.S. ties and prevent a major Japanese rearmament.

The Soviet Presence in Asia and American Policy Alternatives" (Santa Monica, CA: Rand, April 1981), p. iv.

[62] Remaks of Donald S. Zagoria in U.S. House of Representatives, Committee on Foreign Relations, Subcommittees on Asian and Pacific Affairs and on Europe and the Middle East, The Soviet Role in Asia (Washington, D.C.: GPO, 1983), pp. 37-38.

5. Continuing efforts to prevent ASEAN from joining the United States in strategic cooperation, while at the same time consolidating the Soviet position in Vietnam.

6. Expanding efforts to play a more prominent role in the Asian security system through various confidence-building measures."[3]

Zagoria's third point was discussed in some detail by Harry Gelman during the same 1983 congressional hearings. Gelman noted that Sino-Soviet relations are conducted on two tracks. In secondary matters such as trade, sports exchanges, and student exchange programs, some progress in state-to-state relations have been made since 1981. On the more important security and strategic aspects of the relationship, however, little progress has been made. Among the issues falling into the latter category, Gelman mentioned: "the Soviet military buildup along the Sino-Soviet border, the Soviet Armored Forces in Mongolia that perpetually threaten the north China plain, the on-going Soviet strategic deployment of the Backfire bomber and the SS-20, the Soviet support for the Vietnamese in Cambodia, the Soviet military use of Cam Ranh Bay, and Soviet military effort to enhance their domination of Afghanistan."[4]

During the hearings, Kenneth Lieberthal predicted that Chinese demands that the Soviet Union pull back from Afghanistan, Vietnam, Mongolia, and from along the Sino-Soviet border will not be accepted. Lieberthal said: "these Soviet military assets, acquired over a period of time at great cost, are central to the larger Soviet regional strategy for counter-balancing U.S. forces in Asia, and for insuring Japan's vulnerability."[5] Some elaboration of the strategic value of Afghanistan, Vietnam, and Mongolia to the USSR is perhaps necessary.

Afghanistan is important to the Soviet Union because it gives "the Soviets an advance position that points in several directions."[6] Not only does Afghanistan provide one further link in Moscow's persistent efforts to encircle and contain China, the

---

[3] Zagoria, ibid., p. 38.

[4] Harry Gelman, ibid., pp. 343-344.

[5] Kenneth G. Lieberthal, ibid., p. 365.

[6] Helmut Sonnenfeldt, ibid., p. 30.

Soviet presence in Afghanistan gives the USSR considerable flexibility for possible future moves toward Iran and the Middle East, or toward Pakistan and the Indian subcontinent. Moreover, a presence in Afghanistan advances the Soviet Union one step closer to a warm-water port, in this case on the strategically important Indian Ocean.

Moscow began to move closer to Hanoi as early as 1964. In June 1978 Vietnam joined COMECON and in November of that year entered into a military alliance with the USSR. The PRC's efforts to "punish" Hanoi in February 1979 resulted in increased military cooperation between Vietnam and the Soviet Union. The use of Cam Ranh Bay, Danang, and the Kampuchean port of Kompong Sam has inserted the USSR into the regional affairs of Southeast Asia.[67]

The security advantages gained by the Soviets from the use of these bases far outweigh any potential concessions likely to be extended by the Chinese should the USSR acquiesce to PRC demands to stop supporting Hanoi. As Harry Gelman observed: "Thus far the Soviets have been unwilling to risk losing the bird they have in the hand--their present advantages in Indochina--for the uncertainties of the bird in the bush--the hypothetical Chinese gratitude."[68] Soviet troops in Mongolia are perhaps the most serious threat to China's security. Shigeo Hiramatsu described the threat in a September 1983 article in the *Journal of Northeast Asian Studies*:

> If Soviet military forces in Mongolia and the Trans-Baikal Military District were to make a direct attack on Shanhaiguan facing the Bay of Bohai from Inner Mongolia through Outer Mongolia, China would be quickly divided, and northeastern China would be cut off from "Inner China" south of Shanhaiguan. From Mongolia, moreover, Soviet troops would not only conquer Beijing within a few days but also invade the northeast part of China. Moving westward, they could destroy military facilities around Lanzhou and attack Xinjiang. Mongolia would be the best base for the Soviet army if the Soviet Union were to wage war, particularly a limited one, against China.[69]

---

[67] Paul Kelemen, "Soviet Strategy in Southeast Asia: The Vietnam Factor," *Asian Survey*, 24, 3 (March 1984), pp. 336-345.

[68] Gelman, *The Soviet Role in Asia*, p. 344.

An indication of the importance of Mongolia to the Soviet Union came in May 1983, when Ulan Bator expelled several hundred Chinese over strong PRC protests. Despite the fact that Moscow and Beijing were attempting to improve bilateral relations, the Soviet Union publicly supported Mongolia's actions.[70]

Because of these strategic advantages, Soviet leaders are unlikely to make concessions on Afghanistan, Vietnam, and Mongolia. The Kremlin has indicated a willingness to discuss mutual troop reductions along the Sino-Soviet border as a means of improving the ambiance of relations between the two countries. There is, however, evidence to suggest resistance to this among the Soviet military, who warn against the long-term Chinese threat and look with concern at possible Sino-American military cooperation.[71] Given the voice Soviet military leaders have in such affairs, it would appear that any USSR troop reductions along the border would be minimal. Such a policy would be consistent with the current program for building facilities to maintain forces there permanently.

3.4 KOREA AND JAPAN

Soviet and Chinese differences over Korea and Japan should also be briefly noted. Korea is strategically important to both the Soviet Union and the PRC. Neither Moscow nor Beijing can allow the other to dominate the peninsula. Recognizing this fact, North Korean leader Kim Il Sung has for many years skillfully balanced the influence of his two larger communist neighbors to preserve his independence and flexibility. In late May 1984, for example, the North Korean leader visited the Soviet Union for the first time in 19 years, holding extensive talks with Soviet President Konstantin Chernenko and other top Kremlin leaders. When the Chinese heard of Kim's pending visit to Moscow, they immediately dispatched Communist Party leader Hu Yaobang

---

[69] Shigeo Hiramatsu, "A Chinese Perspective on Sino-Soviet Relations," Journal of Northeast Asian Studies, 2, 3 (September 1983), p. 61.

[70] Washington Post, June 2, 1983, p. A24; New York Times, May 27, 1983, p. A6; and ibid., June 4, 1983, p. 3.

[71] See "Suggestive Developments in Soviet Relations with China," Soviet World Outlook, 7, 11 (November 15, 1982), pp. 5-7.

to Pyongyang to ensure that Kim's trip did not result in a shift in North Korea's position relative to China and the Soviet Union.[72]

Although both the USSR and China evince discomfort over many of Kim's policies--the October 1983 bombing in Rangoon, the personality cult built around the North Korean leader, and his intention of having his son succeed him as leader are examples--Moscow and Beijing cannot withdraw support from Pyongyang. Indeed, in the event of a conflict on the Korean peninsula, there is high probability that the Soviet Union and China would come to the aid of North Korea, even if Kim or his unpredictable son, Kim Jong Il, initiated the attack against the South. Since the United States is committed by treaty to come to the aid of Seoul should such aggression occur, both Moscow and Beijing carefully try to moderate Pyongyang's policies while at the same time preserve their own influence and limit the influence of the other with the North Korean leadership. The unpredictability of North Korea's leaders and the strategic importance of the peninsula will make any reconciliation of Soviet and Chinese interests over Korea extremely difficult to achieve.

The preservation of peace on the Korean peninsula and the limitation of Soviet influence in Pyongyang are objectives shared by the United States and China. Chinese Premier Zhao Ziyang discussed ways to achieve this objective with President Reagan during his trip to Washington in early 1984.[73] The United States offered its own plan during President Reagan's visit to China in April 1984.[74]

Chinese and Soviet economic and strategic interests also clash over Japan. Japan is the economic giant of the Far East, possessing capital and technological expertise critical to the development of both Siberia and China. Since economic development is essential to the long-term political stability of both communist governments, there is considerable competition to attract Japanese investment and assistance.

In this endeavor, China has been far more successful than the Soviet Union. Japanese businessmen are willing to invest in Siberia, but political considerations severely restrict their involvement with Soviet projects. The major bilateral issue between Japan and the USSR remains the Soviet occupation of the

---

[72] *Washington Post*, May 27, 1984, p. A18.

[73] For details of the plan presented by Zhao Ziyang, see *Los Angeles Times*, February 5, 1984, Part I, p. 1.

[74] *Washington Post*, June 6, 1984, p. A14.

"Northern Territories." These four islands in the Kurile chain off the Shiretoko peninsula of northern Hokkaido are viewed by Moscow as essential to the security of its strategic nuclear missile submarine fleet in the Sea of Okhotsk. Japan, however, considers the Soviet occupation, which dates from the end of the Second World War, as an infringement on its territorial integrity. Foreign Minister Masayoshi Ito once called the occupation "the largest unsettled issue" between Tokyo and Moscow.[75] Successive governments in Tokyo have linked Japan's participation in the development of Siberia with a satisfactory resolution of the Northern Territories issue. Nonetheless, the Japanese have left the door open for future economic cooperation. In February 1983 a 252-member trade delegation led by Chamber of Commerce and Industry President Shigeo Nagano visited Moscow to discuss overall business prospects.[76]

Despite periodic disagreements over issues such as Japanese textbook treatment of Japan's invasion of China during the Second World War, Sino-Japanese relations have been exceptionally cordial in recent years. Japanese businessmen have been hurt, as have other foreign investors, by China's economic retrenchments, but the long-term prospects for Sino-Japanese economic cooperation are excellent. Leading officials frequently exchange visits and offer glowing praise of their friendly relations. During his November 1983 trip to Japan, Hu Yaobang said:

> To live in lasting friendship is of great significance to the security and prosperity of both China and Japan, and it constitutes an important factor in the maintenance of peace and stability in the Asian-Pacific region and the removal of threats posed by the forces of war.[77]

During the visit of PRC Foreign Economic Relations and Trade Minister Chen Muhua in February 1983, the Chinese requested a massive Japanese loan totalling $5.6 billion. Between fiscal years 1979 and 1983, Japan provided China with about $1.3 billion in loans.[78] Chen

---

[75] *Japan Times*, January 27, 1981, p. 5. For the official Japanese government bulletin on "Japan's Northern Territories Day," see ibid., February 7, 1981, p. 2.

[76] *Kyodo*, February 25, 1983, in *FBIS-Asia & Pacific*, February 28, 1983, p. C1.

[77] *Washington Post*, November 24, 1983, p. A24.

also announced that China is planning to increase its foreign trade fourfold to $160 billion by the end of the century, with Sino-Japanese trade keeping the current level of one-quarter of the total.[79]

Strategically, Soviet and Chinese stakes in Japan are considerable. Neither communist country wants Japan to rearm heavily, although China is more supportive of a strong Japanese defense than is the Soviet Union.

A primary Soviet objective is to neutralize Japan through military and diplomatic pressures, thereby severing the United States from its chief security anchor in the Pacific. As Osamu Miyoshi of the Japan Center for the Study of Security Issues noted: "Soviet strategy is to contain Japan with the USSR's expanding security system in the Far East, promote Finlandization through military and diplomatic pressures, and eventually subordinate Japan to Soviet political control."[80]

The Soviet Union wants to Finlandize Japan because American forces there (and to some extent those in South Korea) can effectively neutralize much of the Soviet Pacific Fleet based at Vladivostok, Petropavlovsk, and other key naval bases through control of the Japanese straits. Prime Minister Yasuhiro Nakasone's defense policies, characterized by more active military cooperation with the United States, deeply concerns Moscow. Nakasone's reported comments about making Japan an "unsinkable aircraft carrier" capable of sealing the Japanese straits from Soviet use in time of war caused the Soviet Union to be particularly blunt in its warnings. Soviet Foreign Minister Nikolay Patolichev told the Nagano trade mission in February 1983: "the Japanese archipelago will sink in 20 minutes if attacked."[81]

---

[78] Kyodo, February 23, 1983, in FBIS-Asia & Pacific, February 23, 1983, p. C1.

[79] Kyodo, February 22, 1983, in FBIS-Asia & Pacific, February 23, 1983, p. C1.

[80] Osamu Miyoshi, "Toward a New U.S.-Japan Alliance: The Crucial Choices of the Eighties," Comparative Strategy, 2, 4 (1980), p. 283.

[81] Kyodo, February 24, 1983, in U.S. Government, Foreign Broadcast Information Service, Daily Report: Soviet Union, February 24, 1983, p. C1. (Hereafter, FBIS-Soviet Union.)

3.5 SOVIET STATEMENTS ON U.S.-PRC RELATIONS

In addition to building up its military to counter the potential threat of Sino-American strategic cooperation, the Soviet Union has sought to weaken the appeal of the relationship through propaganda. A recurrent Soviet theme is that the United States, while claiming to want friendly relations with China, actually behaves in a way harmful to PRC interests. According to Moscow, one objective of the United States is to obstruct close Sino-Soviet ties. Moscow Radio told its Chinese audience on February 21, 1983:

> The U.S. imperialists always have only one criterion in their attitude toward Soviet-Chinese relations, that is, the worse Soviet-Chinese relations are the better it is for the United States....The United States has done everything possible to aggravate the differences between the Soviet Union and China and to stand in the way of the normalization of Soviet-Chinese relations....China holds an important place in Washington's plan. While creating a terrifying atmosphere with their fabricated Soviet threat to China, the U.S. imperialists also try to imbue people with the idea that China can save itself from Soviet attack only by maintaining relations with the United States. To maintain such relations, the imperialists preach that China should not be too sensitive, even when the United States tramples on its sovereignty, infringes on its territorial integrity and injures the Chinese people's national dignity....
>
> U.S. imperialism has not abandoned its aggressive nature, nor has it abandoned its hostile schemes against China. The U.S. President's secret directive No. 59 is proof of this. According to this directive, American nuclear missiles are constantly aimed at more than 100 targets in China.[82]

The Soviet Union has been especially sensitive to efforts by the United States to strengthen the PRC militarily or to draw China into a closer strategic relationship. Referring to a November 1983 article in the Washington Post calling upon China to spend $200

---

[82] Moscow Radio, February 21, 1983, in FBIS-Soviet Union, February 24, 1983, pp. B1-B2.

billion to modernize its armed forces, Moscow Radio claimed that the imperialists had three objectives in mind:

> 1. The spending of such a tremendous sum on nonproductive military purposes would drain China of its financial resources and help only the imperialists. The poorer and weaker China is, the greater the chances for the imperialists to materialize their long-cherished ambitions of again making her an imperialist domain and restoring imperialist rule over her.
>
> 2. The collection of such a tremendous sum is good for U.S. arms dealers.
>
> 3. U.S. imperialists do not rule out the possibility that, after firmly tying China to the American war machine, China would oppose the Soviet Union as Washington has long wanted or, in other words, the two communist giants would both suffer as anticipated by people in Washington.[83]

A favorite Soviet theme is the Taiwan issue, which Moscow points to as an example of American insincerity in establishing friendly relations with China. Moscow Radio commented on February 28, 1983, that in the Shanghai Communique

> the U.S. side declared that it acknowledged that all Chinese on either side of the Taiwan Strait maintained there is but one China, that Taiwan is a part of China, and that the United States Government does not challenge that position. The United States promised to withdraw its forces from Taiwan as the tension in the area diminishes.
>
> However, subsequent facts have shown that the U.S. imperialists do not plan to return Taiwan Island at all. They have long regarded Taiwan was their own unsinkable aircraft carrier. They are unwilling to return Taiwan to the embrace of its owner--the People's Republic of China.[84]

---

[83] Moscow Radio, November 27, 1983, in FBIS-Soviet Union, November 30, 1983, pp. B1-B2.

Commenting on the trip of Secretary of State George Shultz to China in March 1983, Tass stated:

> Effectively creating a "two Chinas" situation, the United States continues to develop to the utmost economic relations and trade with Taiwan and still supplies modern weaponry to the Taiwan regime, and this is how Washington intends to act in the future, too....
>
> Despite all this, the U.S. leaders declare their desire to develop relations with the PRC, "but not to the detriment of Taiwan," as the U.S. President put it....It seems they want to develop these relations in their own way, in the interests of U.S. imperialism, on condition of keeping Taiwan under their own control and using it as one of their "unsinkable aircraft carriers."[85]

In commentary on a speech given by Secretary of Defense Caspar Weinberger in December 1983, the Soviet Union characterized U.S. policy as trying to establish a strategic relationship with China while maintaining close ties to Taiwan. Moscow Radio said:

> The far-reaching goal of U.S. policy toward China has two premises: One is that the United States wants China to take a stand as close as possible to its own or even to take the same stand on strategic issues in the world.
>
> In his speech at the National Press Club, Weinberger talked profusely about the strategic importance of U.S.-China relations and broadly hinted that the United States hopes China will take the road of not getting close to the USSR and other countries of the socialist camp. As can be seen, the first basic principle of the policy toward China by this biggest imperialist country is to create a confrontation between China and the socialist system in the world and to draw China onto the road of the U.S. global

---

[84] Moscow Radio, February 28, 1983, in *FBIS-Soviet Union*, March 8, 1983, p. B2.

[85] Tass, March 4, 1983, in *FBIS-Soviet Union*, March 9, 1983, p. B2.

strategy.

The second premise of the U.S. imperialist policy toward China is to maintain the so-called "special relations" with the anticommunist authorities in Taipei. In the eyes of the United States, the Taipei authorities have been and still remain a convenient tool for exerting pressure on the People's Republic of China and for intervening in the Chinese people's internal affairs....

We can easily see that the U.S. policy toward China was, is, and will continue to be a component of its anticommunist global strategy aimed directly at instigating disputes and conflicts among socialist countries and at undermining and disintegrating the socialist system in the world....

In planning and implementing the U.S. policy toward China, imperialist strategists cherish the illusion of having China strategically subject to the United States as the Chiang Kai-shek regime was in the past. This is borne out by the "two Chinas" policy pursued by the United States and by the increasing efforts it is making to improve its plan toward the People's Republic of China.[86]

Although the Taiwan issue has some propaganda value to the Soviets, Beijing is unlikely to be impressed by Soviet assurances of Moscow's support on the problem. In addition to offering little help to China during the 1958 Quemoy crisis, the USSR has hinted on occasion that it would like to see Taiwan separated from the mainland. Henry Kissinger noted that on April 3, 1969, Soviet Ambassador Dobrynin told him that "it seemed to many in the Soviet Union that Taiwan might well become an independent state."[87]

The possibility of some type of arrangement between Moscow and Taipei has also been noted by Beijing. Following Nixon's trip to China in 1972, ROC Foreign Minister S. K. Chow told reporters that the ROC was prepared to explore the possibility of establishing friendlier relations with the Soviet Union and other

---

[86] Moscow Radio, December 17, 1983, in FBIS-Soviet Union, December 19, 1983, pp. B1-B2.

[87] Kissinger, White House Years, p. 173.

communist countries. Also of interest in this regard was the visit of Soviet journalist Victor Louis to Taipei in 1968.[88] Taiwan's current policy is to reject any Soviet connection, and Beijing has said it might use force to prevent any involvement of Moscow in Taiwan's affairs.

Based upon this overview of the Sino-Soviet split and the strategic concerns of Moscow in East Asia, it would appear that the USSR, while desiring to improve relations with the PRC, nonetheless is limited in its flexibility. Soviet strategic competition with the United States and Moscow's historical fear of confronting a two-front war involving a strong western power (in this case the United States) and a modern Asian power (presently Japan and China) ensure that major Soviet concessions to the Chinese on Afghanistan, Vietnam, or Mongolia are highly unlikely. Troop reductions elsewhere along the Sino-Soviet border remain a possibility. But from the point of view of China's security concerns, these reductions would be symbolic only. Nonetheless, a reduction of tensions between the two communist powers is clearly in their mutual interests.

U.S. interests will continue to be affected by the Sino-Soviet dispute. The depth and complexity of the Sino-Soviet conflict are such that complete normalization of PRC-USSR relations will probably occur, if at all, only gradually over a period of time. There seems to be little likelihood of a return to a Sino-Soviet alliance, nor does a major conflict seem to be in the offering. What U.S. officials should note is that, barring a major change in policy in Washington which would alter the threat perceptions of Moscow and Beijing, there is little the United States can do to perpetuate or reduce the level of conflict between China and the Soviet Union. This becomes even more apparent when one considers that since 1980, when the United States began to seek a more active strategic relationship with the PRC, Beijing chose instead to improve its relations with Moscow as part of its "independent" foreign policy.

---

[88] James C. H. Shen, _The U.S. and Free China: How the U.S. Sold Out Its Ally_ (Washington, D.C.: Acropolis Books, Ltd., 1983), pp. 112-115.

4
China's Independent Foreign Policy

The decision by the Chinese to initiate an "independent" foreign policy began to evolve at approximately the same time as the 1980 U.S. presidential campaign, when Beijing downgraded the immediate Soviet threat to China. Li Xiannian told a visiting Italian journalist in September 1980 that Europe, not China, was the likely point of Soviet aggression.⁸⁹ A month later Deng Xiaoping noted the possibility of improved Sino-Soviet relations. In an interview with the editor of the Christian Science Monitor, Deng said:

> If the Soviet Union changes its global strategy and social-imperialist policy, Sino-Soviet relations can be changed right away, and there is no reason for us to wait for a few years. The Soviet Union must prove with concrete action that it has changed its global strategy and abandoned its hegemonism by reducing its one million troops (along the Sino-Soviet border) to at least the same number as that under Khrushchev (ten divisions.)⁹⁰

Two main factors contributed to the Chinese decision to pursue an independent foreign policy: the Soviet Union's willingness to reduce Sino-Soviet tensions, and the U.S. determination to deter further Soviet aggression in East Asia.

---

⁸⁹ Turin La Stampa, September 12, 1980, in FBIS-China, September 25, 1980, p. 7.

⁹⁰ Xinhua, November 24, 1980, in FBIS-China, November 24, 1980, p. L18.

- 58 -

Valuable insight into the reasoning behind
Beijing's decision to pursue an independent foreign
policy and to normalize relations with Moscow was
provided by a top secret CPC document obtained by
Japan's Foreign Ministry. As summarized in <u>Yomiuri
Shimbun</u>, the document cited the following factors in the
PRC decision:

>1. The two superpowers--the United States
and the Soviet Union--are contending with each
other in pursuit of hegemony. Militarily, the
Soviet Union stands in an offensive position
and the United States is relatively inferior.
The potential strength of the United States,
however, should not be underestimated.
>
>2. The United States normalized its
diplomatic relations with China. But it did
so for the purpose of compensating for its
military inferiority to the Soviet Union and
because it thought that normalization would be
of benefit to itself. In deciding on
normalization, the United States recognized
"one China" but it still continues its
commitment to Taiwan. This constitutes an
intervention in China's internal affairs and,
for the development of U.S.-China relations,
it is undesirable for the United States to
continue such a policy.
>
>3. The Soviet Union has lately been making
overtures to China for a rapprochement. This
is also intended for the Soviet Union's own
benefit. Although militarily it is relatively
superior to the United States, the Soviet
Union is isolated internationally and faces
economic difficulties domestically and,
therefore, it thinks that easing tension with
China will be of benefit to itself.
>
>4. In the final analysis, both the United
States and the Soviet Union are trying to use
China as a card in the process of seeking
hegemony. The fact that the Soviet Union
desires a rapprochement with China does not
alter the intrinsic nature of Soviet
hegemonism or big-power chauvinism.
Nevertheless, the Soviet Union was a friend of
China for a long time. An excessive
confrontation with the Soviet Union is
ill-advised for China as well.'[1]

An independent foreign policy also implied a distancing of China from the United States, particularly in the area of strategic cooperation. China's decision in this regard was made possible because of U.S. determination to oppose future aggression by the USSR in the wake of the Soviet invasion of Afghanistan.

Evidence of Chinese thinking along these lines was given by Huan Xiang, director of China's Institute for International Affairs, in an interview with Der Spiegel in late 1983. In response to questions contrasting Beijing's current "independent" foreign policy to the "coordinated measures" against Moscow advocated by Deng Xiaoping in 1979, Huan explained:

> What has changed is the international situation. In the early seventies the Soviet Union had very strongly expanded toward the outside militarily and had become a threat to everybody. For this reason China offered cooperation to each state that felt threatened by the Soviet Union.
>
> Near the end of the Carter administration's term and at the beginning of the term of the Reagan administration, the Americans determinedly and energetically put up a front against the Soviet Union politically and militarily in the struggle for superiority in nuclear armament, in the matter of the European intermediate-range weapons, in the Caribbean region, in the Middle East and, finally, also in Asia.
>
> This stopped the Soviet Union, and the rivalry of the two superpowers considerably intensified throughout the world. It seems that the Russians still do not feel strong enough to react to the U.S. offensive. In our view, a certain balance between the two has emerged, especially in the military field.[92]

China's independent foreign policy was set firmly in place by 1982. In response to several appeals from Kremlin leaders to improve Sino-Soviet relations, the PRC announced that it stood ready to work toward normalization at the Twelfth National Congress of the

---

[91] Yomiuri Shimbun, November 30, 1982, pp. 1-2.

[92] Der Spiegel, December 26, 1983, in FBIS-China, December 29, 1983, pp. A7-A8.

CPC in September. Hu Yaobang said:

> The relations between China and the Soviet Union were friendly over a fairly long period. They have become what they are today because the Soviet Union has pusued a hegemonist policy. For the past twenty years, the Soviet Union has stationed massive armed forces along the Sino-Soviet and Sino-Mongolian borders. It has supported Viet Nam in the latter's invasion and occupation of Kampuchea, acts of expansion in Indochina and Southeast Asia and constant provocations along China's border. Moreover, it has invaded and occupied Afghanistan, a neighbor of China, by force of arms. All these acts constitute grave threats to the peace of Asia and to China's security. We note that Soviet leaders have expressed more than once the desire to improve relations with China. But deeds, rather than words, are important. If the Soviet authorities really have a sincere desire to improve relations with China and take practical steps to lift their threat to the security of our country, it will be possible for Sino-Soviet relations to move toward normalization. The friendship between the Chinese and Soviet peoples is of long standing, and we will strive to safeguard and develop this friendship, no matter what Sino-Soviet state relations are like.'[93]

In October 1982 the PRC Embassy in Washington issued a press release explaining China's independent, non-aligned foreign policy:

> China opposes anyone who seeks hegemony, and at any place. This is the independent stand of China. On the Afghanistan and Kampuchean issues, both China and the United States oppose the armed invasions by the Soviet Union and the Soviet-backed Viet Nam. However, the United States met with opposition from both China and the Soviet Union in its support for Israeli aggression and for the racist regime in South Africa. As can be seen, this by no means indicates that China "enters into

---

[93] Hu Yaobang, "Create a New Situation in All Fields of Socialist Modernization," <u>The Twelfth National Congress of the CPC</u> (Beijing: Foreign Languages Press, 1982), pp. 58-59.

alliance" with the United States in one case and becomes a partner of the Soviet Union in another. But it does prove that first, China is independent of any superpower, and secondly, while the Soviet Union and the United States are contending with one another for world hegemony, China may, toward certain issues, adopt an attitude similar to that of one of the superpowers. But the "rendezvous" are carried out from different points of departure."⁴

In November 1982 Peng Zhen elaborated on the new foreign policy of the PRC. Peng said the policy "involves developing diplomatic relations and economic and cultural exchanges with various nations." According to Peng, the principles underlying these relations would be:

1. "the five principles of mutual respect for sovereignty and territorial integrity, mutual non-aggression, non-interference in each other's internal affairs, equality and mutual benefit, and peaceful coexistence"

2. "opposing imperialism, hegemonism, and colonialism"

3. "strengthening unity with the people of other countries"

4. "supporting the oppressed nations and developing countries in their just struggle to win and preserve national independence and develop their national economies"

5. "striving to safeguard world peace and promote the cause of human progress"

Peng Zhen noted, "Our adherence to these principles of foreign policy is dictated by the nature of our state and our social system." He promised, "We will also persist in the treating of all countries, big or small, as equals....China will never seek hegemony and will never allow any hegemonists to subdue it." Peng said this policy would allow China to open up to the outside world but maintain its independence."⁵

'⁴ Embassy of the People's Republic of China, Press Release No. 82/019, n.d., p. 4.

4.1 NORMALIZATION OF SINO-SOVIET RELATIONS

In speeches given in Soviet Azerbaijan in September 1982 and in Moscow in October, Soviet leader Leonid Brezhnev voiced the USSR's wish to see Sino-Soviet relations improve. Brezhnev's Moscow speech, delivered October 27 before Soviet military leaders just days before his death, was particularly important. After criticizing the United States for its "aggressive policy...adventurism, rudeness and undisguised egoism," Brezhnev said of Sino-Soviet relations:

> In this situation it is very important, of course, how our relations with other countries will shape up. Of no small importance are relations with China. We sincerely want a normalization of relations with that country and are doing everything in our power toward this end. No radical changes in the foreign policy of the People's Republic of China are to be seen so far. But the new things which appear must not be ignored by us.'⁶

In analyzing Brezhnev's speech, the Advanced International Studies Institute of the University of Miami suggested the Soviet leader had two objectives in mind when addressing the high-ranking military audience. First, the Soviet armed forces were wary of normalized Sino-Soviet relations and had continually warned of the Chinese threat and the danger of Sino-American military cooperation. Brezhnev argued that improved relations with the PRC could also improve the Soviet military situation with the United States. Second, the speech before the military might have been intended to prepare the way for a later proposal to reduce the level of troops along the Sino-Soviet border.'⁷

Tentative talks toward normalization were held in Beijing in October 1982 between Soviet Deputy Foreign Minister Leonid Ilyichev and Chinese Vice Foreign Minister Qian Qichen. The discussions had the effect, in the words of the Washington Post, of taking "the

---

'⁵ Xinhua, November 26, 1982, in FBIS-China, November 26, 1982, pp. K9-K10.

'⁶ The text of Brezhnev's speech may be found in New York Times, October 28, 1982, p. A7.

'⁷ "Suggestive Developments in Soviet Relations with China," Soviet World Outlook, November 15, 1982, pp. 5-7.

sting out of Sino-Soviet rivalry."[98]

In a significant gesture to the Soviets, China sent Foreign Minister Huang Hua to the November funeral of Brezhnev. Huang called the Soviet president, who during his life had received harsh criticism from Beijing, an "outstanding statesman." The first high-ranking Chinese official to visit the Russian capital in eighteen years, Huang said on the eve of his departure for Moscow:

> The Chinese people sincerely wish that there will be a genuine improvement in the relations between the two countries through the removal of obstacles and that these relations will return to normal step by step. While mourning the death of President Brezhnev, we hope that General Secretary Yuri Andropov and the Soviet party and government authorities make new efforts to promote the improvement of Sino-Soviet relations.[99]

Huang Hua was warmly received in Moscow by Andropov, and he spent more than ninety minutes in private talks with Soviet Foreign Minister Andrei Gromyko. While Huang was in Moscow, the editor of Pravda hinted that the Soviet Union might be willing to join in a mutual pullback of troops along the Sino-Soviet border. Viktor Afanasyev told Japanese journalists: "It is possible that the two sides might promise each other a reduction of military forces in border areas."[100] Upon his return to Beijing, Huang Hua said he was "optimistic" about the two countries achieving progress on substantive matters.[101]

The day after Huang returned to China, he was replaced as Foreign Minister by Wu Xueqian. No doubt this move angered Moscow, which had given the red-carpet treatment to the Chinese offical. As a possible sign that Huang may have responded too enthusiastically to Soviet overtures, other Chinese leaders signalled a retreat from the friendship displayed by Huang in

---

[98] Washington Post, October 27, 1982, p. A21.

[99] "Huang Hua on Sino-Soviet Relations Before Leaving for Moscow," Embassy of the People's Republic of China, Press Release No. 82/020, November 17, 1982, pp. 1-2.

[100] New York Times, November 18, 1982, p. A1.

[101] Xinhua, November 18, 1982, in FBIS-Soviet Union, November 18, 1982, p. B1.

Moscow. Zhao Ziyang told Thailand's Prime Minister Prem Tinsulanonda that improved Sino-Soviet relations depended entirely upon whether the Soviet Union removed its threat against China. Zhao listed these threats as the massive deployment of Soviet troops along the Sino-Soviet and Sino-Mongolian borders, Soviet occupation of Afghanistan, and Moscow's support of the Vietnamese occupation of Kampuchea.[102] The next day Deng Xiaoping told the visiting Thai Prime Minister: "We are still making contacts with the Soviet Union. But our consultations with the Soviet Union on the normalization of relations are based on one principle, namely opposition to hegemonism and preservation of world peace."[103]

On November 26 in his first extensive statement on foreign affairs, Yuri Andropov reaffirmed the Soviet Union's desire to improve relations with China. The new Soviet leader said:

> The Communist Party of the Soviet Union and the Soviet state sincerely wish for the development and improvement of relations with all socialist countries....This also refers to our great neighbor, the People's Republic of China. The ideas formulated by Leonid Ilyich Brezhnev in his speeches in Tashkent and Baku, the emphasis he put on common sense, on the need to overcome the inertia of prejudices, expressed the conviction of all our party, its desire to look ahead. We pay great attention to every positive response to this from the Chinese state.[104]

The Chinese responded a few days later: "We have noted the statement by Yuri Andropov on Sino-Soviet relations. We hope to see the new Soviet leadership make a new effort in eliminating the obstacles hindering the normalization of relations between the two countries."[105]

---

[102] "Chinese Premier on Sino-Soviet Relations," Embassy of the People's Republic of China, Press Release No. 82/021, November 21, 1982, p. 2.

[103] "Deng Xiaoping Meets Thai Prime Minister," ibid., p. 1.

[104] Excerpts from Andropov's speech may be found in New York Times, November 23, 1982, p. A13.

[105] AFP, November 25, 1982, in FBIS-China, November 26,

In early December 1982 Deputy Foreign Minister Qian Qichen told a group of visiting Austrian journalists that complete normalization of Sino-Soviet relations would be possible only if (1) "the threat to China's northeastern border," where the Soviet Union had stationed over 50 divisions, was eliminated; (2) Soviet troops were withdrawn from Afghanistan; and (3) the Soviet Union agreed to a solution of the Cambodian problem along Chinese lines--i.e., withdrawal of all Vietnamese troops and an international guarantee for a free and neutral Kampuchea. Qian went on to say, however: "It is hardly possible for the Soviet Union to solve all these problems at once, but even if there were changes with respect to one or another item this would lead to an improvement of relations."[106]

The Kampuchean problem seemed especially important to the Chinese. Beijing reportedly submitted a proposal to Soviet negotiator Leonid Ilyichev in October 1982 calling for a complete withdrawal of Vietnamese troops from Cambodia over a reasonable period of time in return for a gradual improvement in Sino-Vietnamese relations. Under the proposal, Cambodia would be neutral and nonaligned following the Vietnamese withdrawal. The Soviets refused to discuss the issue, arguing that China should talk directly to the Vietnamese on the matter.[107]

On December 26 a conciliatory message was sent by Beijing to Moscow in the form of a greeting to the Soviet people on the sixtieth anniversary of the founding of the Soviet Union. The message said in part: "China sincerely hopes to bring about gradual normalization and to establish good-neighborly relations between our two countries....Both sides must take practical steps to remove obstacles by means of consultations, applying joint efforts to achieve this goal."[108]

The Soviet Union on January 14, 1983, published an article strongly criticizing China for undermining Sino-Soviet detente by continuing to refer to unequal treaties and Russian seizure of Chinese territory.[109] Beijing responded in a commentary which claimed that the PRC "has solemnly declared on many occasions that China

---

1982, p. C1.

[106] Die Presse, December 7-8, 1982, in FBIS-China, December 7, 1982, p. C1.

[107] Washington Post, January 17, 1983, p. A17.

[108] New York Times, December 27, 1982, p. A1

[109] Ibid., January 15, 1983, p. 1.

has no territorial claims whatsoever on the Soviet Union nor does it demand the return of its territories ceded to czarist Russia under a series of unequal treaties."[110]

In February 1983 both sides maneuvered in preparation for the second round of Sino-Soviet talks scheduled for March. Once again, the PRC placed high priority on the situation in Kampuchea. Just prior to Qian Qichen's trip to Moscow on February 27, the Chinese released details of a five-point proposal on Cambodia submitted at the previous October 1982 meeting.[111] Repeating its insistence that China discuss the issue with the Vietnamese, the Soviet Union suggested instead border negotiations or mutual troop withdrawals as the first step in the reduction of tension. In its public statement, Moscow stressed: "normalization of Soviet-Chinese relations is in the interests of both the Soviet people and the Chinese people."[112]

In contrast to the Soviet desire to reach an early understanding on less substantive issues, the Chinese adopted a less eager stance. PRC officials told Secretary of State George Shultz during his February 1983 visit to China that they had little expectation of Soviet policy shifts on major issues dividing the two countries.[113] Wu Xueqian, in the first press conference between American journalists and a Chinese Foreign Minister in seventeen years, told reporters that "during the first round of negotiations, no identical views were shared by the two sides on major issues." Wu, who had replaced Huang Hua in November 1982, said it was not realistic to expect quick normalization of relations between the two sides and that before any progress could be made, the USSR had "to do one or two concrete things to remove the obstacles in the way of normalization."[114] Later, the Foreign Minister told a special envoy from Prime Minister Nakasone: "there will not at all be any dramatic change" in Sino-Soviet relations.[115]

---

[110] Ibid., January 24, 1983, p. A3.

[111] Details of the PRC proposal can be seen in "Text of Foreign Ministry Statement on Kampuchea," in FBIS-China, March 4, 1983, p. E1.

[112] Radio broadcast to China by Soviet sinologist Smirnov, February 20, 1983, in FBIS-Soviet Union, February 23, 1983, p. B2.

[113] Washington Post, February 7, 1983, p. A19.

[114] Ibid., February 11, 1983, p. A18.

The talks in Moscow between Qian and Ilyichev opened on March 1. After the first week, amid reports that the Soviets had refused to discuss the Kampuchean question, Russian troops in Afghanistan, or Soviet military forces in Mongolia on the grounds that they were "questions involving the affairs of a third country," Beijing criticized Moscow's position in the official organ Xinhua. The commentary said the Soviets were "inventing an excuse for not removing the obstacles on the road toward normalization of Sino-Soviet relations." Xinhua stated:

> China's requirement that these questions must be discussed during Sino-Soviet talks is not at all aimed at interfering in the "internal affairs" of other countries, but at getting rid of obstacles and promoting the normalization of Sino-Soviet relations. As the saying goes, whoever started the trouble should end it. If the Soviet Union really wants to improve Sino-Soviet relations, it should not continue to create excuses or act perfunctorily. Instead, it should take effective measures to eliminate the obstacles obstructing the normalization of Sino-Soviet relations.[116]

When the Moscow round of talks drew to a close, the only concrete agreement was that ten students from each country would be exchanged for the autumn 1983 semester.[117] Nonetheless, there were indications that substantive matters had been discussed. The Soviets reportedly proposed a mutual nonaggression agreement, but the Chinese turned it down on the grounds that such an agreement was inappropriate while obstacles remained between the two sides.[118] Qian also met for a lengthy exchange of views with Soviet Foreign Minister Gromyko. According to Tass, the Soviet official emphasized "the USSR's willingness to look for ways towards the normalization of relations with the PRC."[119] Upon his

---

[115] Kyodo, February 19, 1983, in FBIS-China, February 23, 1983, p. C2.

[116] Xinhua, March 6, 1983, in FBIS-China, March 7, 1983, pp. C1-C2.

[117] Washington Post, March 23, 1983, p. A18.

[118] Kyodo, March 19, 1983, in FBIS-Soviet Union, March 21, 1983, pp. B2-B3.

return to Beijing, Qian described his talks with
Ilyichev as being held in a "tranquil atmosphere," and
that while the discussions were "beneficial," "the
differences still remain."[119]

Diplomats observing the talks concluded that
Beijing saw no hurry to secure withdrawal of Russian
troops from along the Sino-Soviet border. Chinese
leaders recognized that the PRC's greatest asset to the
West--hence, its strongest bargaining chip in dealing
with both superpowers--was in China's ability to hold
down Soviet military forces along its northern frontier.
Since Moscow was unwilling to reduce its presence in
those areas of real security concern to
Beijing--Mongolia, Vietnam, and Afghanistan--the PRC saw
no reason to accept symbolic troop reductions in
marginally important sections of the Sino-Soviet border.
To do so would lessen China's strategic value to the
West, but not decrease the Soviet threat. Under the
circumstances, Beijing's interests could best be served
by gradually improving relations with the Soviet Union,
thereby reducing the immediate Soviet threat, and by
preserving the image of a strategically vital China in
the eyes of the West in order to maximize trade,
technology, and other benefits.[121]

Despite the cautious, incremental approach adopted
by both sides on substantive issues, Moscow and Beijing
continued to signal their desire to reduce bilateral
tensions. On March 10, 1983, for example, a PRC-USSR
commodity exchange agreement was signed in Moscow
boosting the level of Sino-Soviet trade in 1983 by more
than 150% over that of 1982. In the $1 billion package,
China promised to import Soviet steel products,
nonferrous metals, timber, chemical fertilizers, cement,
sheet glass, and chemical and machinery products. The
Soviet Union committed itself to purchase Chinese
minerals, meats and meat products, edible vegetable oils
and oil products, silks and satins, cotton, textiles and
clothing, light industrial products, tea, and animal
products.[122]

---

[119] Tass, March 21, 1983, in FBIS-Soviet Union, March 21, 1983, p. B3.

[120] AFP, March 22, 1983, in FBIS-China, March 22, 1983, p. C2.

[121] New York Times, March 22, 1983, p. A7.

[122] Xinhua, March 10, 1983, in FBIS-Soviet Union, March 11, 1983, p. B1.

Another symbolic step was taken in June 1983, when for the first time in twenty years the two countries opened trading stations along the Sino-Soviet border. The three stations reopened were at Heile in Heilongjiang Province and at Helgus and Tolgot in Xinjiang-Uygur Autonomous Region.[123]

Leaders in both countries continued to affirm their desire to normalize Sino-Soviet relations. During his May 1983 visit to Yugoslavia, Hu Yaobang told members of the press: "China sincerely wishes normalization of relations with the USSR. This meets the fundamental interests of the two countries and also the interests of peace and stability in the whole world."[124] In a similar vein, the USSR Supreme Soviet Presidium sent a congratulatory message to Li Xiannian upon his election to the office of PRC President in June 1983. The message said in part: "We express confidence that the normalization and improvement of Soviet-Chinese relations accord with the fundamental interests of the USSR and PRC peoples."[125]

Periodic signs of impatience arose, however. In April 1983 an authoritative commentary in Izvestiya harshly criticized the PRC for not reciprocating Moscow's "constructive approach" to Soviet-Chinese relations.[126] In June another Izvestiya article lashed out at the Chinese press, saying, "whereas Soviet mass information organs are striving to create a favorable atmosphere for the normalization of Soviet-Chinese relations, the same can in no way be said about the Chinese press."[127]

One of the major differences between Moscow and Beijing during this period was their respective approaches to normalization. The Soviet Union emphasized the need to improve the atmosphere of Sino-Soviet relations before substantive steps reducing Soviet deployments around China could be taken. China, on the other hand, stressed the need for immediate concrete actions on the part of Moscow to remove its

---

[123] Ansa, June 27, 1983 in FBIS-Soviet Union, June 28, 1983, p. B1.

[124] Tass, May 15, 1983, in FBIS-Soviet Union, May 16, 1983, p. B1.

[125] Pravda, June 22, 1983, in FBIS-Soviet Union, June 22, 1983, p. B1.

[126] New York Times, April 20, 1983, p. A11.

[127] Izvestiya, June 19, 1983, in FBIS-Soviet Union, June 20, 1983, pp. B1-B2.

threat to the PRC. In his statement before the Sixth
National People's Congress in June 1983, Premier Zhao
Ziyang noted that "a major issue that cannot be evaded"
is the Soviet removal of the "real threat to China's
security." Zhao said that Chinese proposals for
normalization were set forth in the Sino-Soviet
consultations which started in October 1982. Zhao
observed, "We are awaiting the Soviet side to prove its
good faith by deeds."[128]

The Soviet Union refused to make a fundamental
change in its security policy and instead stressed
incremental improvements in Sino-Soviet relations. In
August 1983 Andropov said in a Pravda interview that he
regarded "as abnormal the state of Soviet-Chinese
relations that existed for two decades." He added:

> Recently, some positive tendencies have become
> discernible in our relations....The present
> level of bilateral relations is, however, far
> from being one that should, in our view, exist
> between such big and, moreover, neighboring
> powers as the Soviet Union and the People's
> Republic of China. Much can be done in
> expanding trade, economic and scientific and
> technical cooperation, and in cultural, sports
> and other exchanges. Common efforts to work
> out and implement trustworthy measures along
> the Soviet-Chinese border areas would improve
> the atmosphere of bilateral relations to a
> great extent....

Andropov cautioned, however: "We have substantial
differences with China in approaches to some important
international problems and relations with certain
states."[129]

Showing impatience of their own, the Chinese let it
be known they were not looking for atmospherics.
Foreign Minister Wu Xueqian called Andropov's statement
"nice remarks," but went on to note that the
"substantial differences" referred to by the Soviet
leader were precisely what Beijing wanted to discuss.[130]
Hu Yaobang pointedly rejected the Soviet argument that
discussion of China's three demands for normalization

---

[128] Xinhua, June 6, 1983, in FBIS-China, June 6, 1983, p. K15.

[129] Xinhua, August 27, 1983, in FBIS-China, August 29, 1983, p. C1.

[130] Kyodo, August 28, 1983, in FBIS-China, August 29, 1983, p. C1.

involved third countries and therefore should not be topics for bilateral negotiations. The CPC head said:

> "Third countries" doubtless refers to Vietnam, Kampuchea, Afghanistan and Mongolia. We have never harmed these countries and will never harm them in the future. What is at stake and is threatened is our security. We have said and said again that we are willing immediately to start negotiations for the normalization of relations between China and Vietnam as soon as Vietnam withdraws its troops from Kampuchea. It would benefit everyone--Kampuchea, China, Vietnam itself. We have no designs either on Kampuchea or on Vietnam. As for Mongolia: against whom are the five Soviet divisions in Mongolia lined up? Obviously against China. A withdrawal of Soviet troops from Mongolia would be advantageous both to the USSR and to China and Mongolia. There is still less to be said about Afghanistan. How are we supposed to be harming Afghanistan's interests? It is up to the Afghan people, as masters of their own country, to decide their own affairs. The USSR must not intervene. Nor must anyone else. If the USSR withdraws its troops from Afghanistan, among other things it will be freeing itself of a major burden.[131]

Not surprisingly, given the fundamental differences between the two sides, the third round of talks between Ilyichev and Qian in Beijing in October 1983 did not resolve the outstanding issues. Both sides, however, appeared satisfied with the frankness of the negotiations. The Soviets reportedly presented a ten-point proposal designed to implement confidence-building measures, including the signing of a nonaggression pact, discussions on the troops massed along the Sino-Soviet frontier, and the creation of a nuclear free zone between the two countries.[132] According to the Wall Street Journal, the two sides agreed to double their trade, increase the number of exchange students on each side from 10 to 70, and to modernize Soviet-built factories in northern China.

---

[131] L'Unita, August 29, 1983, in FBIS-China, September 1, 1983, p. A1.

[132] AFP, November 2, 1983, in FBIS-Soviet Union, November 4, 1983, p. B1.

Sports and cultural exchanges were also to be expanded.[133]

By December 1983 Chinese experts on the Soviet Union were saying that, while Andropov wanted to improve relations with China, the Soviet leader did not intend to take any major steps toward removing the main obstacles to Sino-Soviet relations. The Chinese apparently had reconciled themselves to a slow, steady improvement of relations, but without substantive changes in Soviet policy.[134]

Andropov's death in February 1984 was seen by the Chinese as an opportunity to speed up the normalization process. In a gesture interpreted as treating "the Chinese as comrades and good neighbors, not adversaries or potential enemies," Moscow gave Beijing early notice of the passing of the Soviet leader.[135] The Chinese reciprocated with a good-will gesture of their own, sending Senior Vice Premier Wan Li to Moscow for Andropov's funeral. Wan was the highest-ranking Chinese official to visit the Soviet Union in more than two decades. In its message of condolence to the USSR, China said: "President Andropov had expressed on several occasions his desire to improve Sino-Soviet relations....It is the sincere desire of the Chinese government to see relations between the two governments normalized."[136]

In February 1984 it was announced that the two sides would increase their bilateral trade by 60% to $1.2 billion. The new trade protocol included for the first time a number of strategically important items such as Chinese rare earth metals needed in Soviet aerospace programs and Soviet-made precision tools needed for China's industrial modernization. It was also announced that Soviet First Deputy Premier Ivan Arkhipov would travel to Beijing in the spring to sign an agreement providing for the renovation of factories built by the USSR in China in the 1950s.[137] Arkhipov would be the most senior Soviet official visiting China since 1969.

---

[133] *Wall Street Journal*, October 21, 1983, p. 26.

[134] *Kyodo*, December 15, 1983, in *FBIS-China*, December 19, 1983, p. C2.

[135] *Los Angeles Times*, February 13, 1984, Part I, p. 1.

[136] *Ibid*.

[137] *Los Angeles Times*, February 13, 1984, Part IV, p. 2.

Despite these early signs that the Soviet Union under the leadership of President Konstantin Chernenko might be willing to hasten normalization of Sino-Soviet relations, hopes for meaningful Soviet concessions were soon dashed. In March 1984 the fourth round of consultations were held in Moscow. According to the Chinese, both sides "affirmed the recent tendency of increasing contacts between the two countries and agreed to further develop exchanges in the economic, trade, scientific, technological, sports, and cultural fields on the basis of equality and mutual benefit." Another round of talks was scheduled for October 1984 in Beijing. The Chinese went on to point out, however, that the

> three major obstacles to the normalization of Sino-Soviet relations still exist. That is, the Soviet Union still stations massive forces along the Sino-Soviet border and the Sino-Mongolian border, and the Kampuchean issue and the Afghan issue remain unsettled. Moreover, the deployment of a large number of SS-20 missiles by the Soviet Union in the Far East has also greatly upset our people. Without removing the three major obstacles, it is hard to expect any major development in Sino-Soviet relations.[138]

Beijing was surprised by the last minute cancellation of the scheduled visit in May of Deputy Premier Arkhipov. It was widely believed that the Kremlin cancelled the visit in protest of the favorable treatment given President Reagan on his April trip to the PRC. Arkhipov reportedly had been prepared to discuss Sino-Soviet nuclear power cooperation.[139]

By June 1984 Sino-Soviet relations had cooled somewhat. Bitter exchanges were made by both sides in the wake of renewed Sino-Vietnamese border clashes. In a statement following his talks with Vietnamese leaders in Moscow, Chernenko said that "the Soviet side resolutely condemned the hostile actions of the Chinese authorities against Vietnam." This was the first statement of the new Soviet leader attacking China by name on the Sino-Vietnamese issue.[140] In discussions

---

[138] <u>Ban Yue Tan</u>, May 10, 1984, in <u>FBIS-China</u>, June 11, 1984, p. A1.

[139] <u>Kyodo</u>, May 5, 1984, in <u>FBIS-China</u>, May 7, 1984, p. C1.

[140] <u>Xinhua</u>, June 12, 1984, in <u>FBIS-China</u>, June 12, 1984,

with Lao leaders a few days later, Chernenko "resolutely condemned China for its hostilities against Vietnam, Laos and Kampuchea."[141]

In an effort to prevent a deterioration of relations with the Soviet Union, Beijing sent Qian Qichen to the USSR in early July. On July 5 Qian returned from Moscow, saying he had discussed "quite a lot of problems" but made no progress on the major obstacles in Chinese-Soviet relations.[142]

In the wake of the hardening Soviet attitude, Beijing launched a series of verbal attacks of its own. In a July commentary in Beijing Review Chinese observers said, "It is unrealistic and impossible for Sino-Soviet relations to return to what they once were in history." The writers went on to condemn Chernenko's policies toward the PRC as being stubborn.[143]

4.2 FUTURE SINO-SOVIET RELATIONS

Given the many ups and downs in relations between Moscow and Beijing over the last 35 years, any prediction for future Sino-Soviet relations is highly speculative. What can be said with some confidence is that in the foreseeable future Sino-Soviet relations will remain lukewarm at best. The two nations almost certainly will not become allies as they did in the early 1950s, nor will they likely come into conflict as in 1969. Both countries will continue to perceive their interests as being served by a gradual improvement in bilateral relations, but distrust and resentment will remain on both sides.

It is doubtful the Soviet Union will make meaningful concessions on the three issues stressed by China. Soviet deployments along the Sino-Soviet and Sino-Mongolian border, the occupation of Afghanistan, and continued support given to the Vietnamese in exchange for basing rights in Indochina are too important from a larger strategic perspective for Moscow to give up. Likewise, the PRC will continue its pressure on Hanoi and maintain a dialogue with the

---

p. C1.

[141] Xinhua., June 27, 1984, in FBIS-China, June 27, 1984, p. C1.

[142] AFP, July 5, 1984, in FBIS-China, July 5, 1984, p. C1; and Washington Post, July 6, 1984, p. A25.

[143] Beijing Review, 28 (July 9, 1984), pp. 12, 31-32.

United States regarding military and strategic cooperation--much to Moscow's discomfiture. This situation is unlikely to change unless one or more of the major powers alters its fundamental foreign policy or strategic perceptions.

It is important for the United States to assess accurately the Sino-Soviet split, because it provides an indication as to how far Sino-American strategic cooperation might progress. It seems apparent, given the nature of the Sino-Soviet conflict, that Washington has little direct influence over the course of relations between China and the Soviet Union.[144] The deep-seated geographic and historical conflicts, the bitterness of the dispute between the Soviet and Chinese communist parties, and the conflicting national security objectives of the two sides are bilateral issues far beyond U.S. manipulation.

The next chapter will examine the parameters of Sino-American strategic cooperation and attempt to answer three fundamental questions of concern to U.S. policymakers: (1) Can Sino-American strategic cooperation be expanded? (2) Can China be drawn into a defense alliance with the United States, if Washington so desires? and (3) Can the United States improve China's defense capabilities, thereby increasing the PRC's value as a strategic counterweight to the Soviet Union in Asia?

---

[144] See Jonathan D. Pollack and Richard H. Solomon, "The Sino-Soviet Conflict and American Security Concerns" (Santa Monica, CA: Rand, January 1979).

5
Parameters of Sino-American Strategic Cooperation

5.1   THE SOVIET CARD

Beijing is aware of Washington's anxiety regarding the prospects of Sino-Soviet detente. However, the Chinese have been careful to insist that they will never play 'the Soviet card' against the United States, nor 'the U.S. card' against the Soviet Union. In talks with United Nations Secretary General Perez de Cuellar in August 1982, Foreign Minister Huang Hua said:

> The basic points of our foreign policy are unity with Third World countries and peoples, alliance with those countries and peoples who cherish peace and uphold justice, opposition to hegemonism in defence of world peace no matter what direction such hegemonism comes from. China will never cling to any superpower. China will never play the "U.S. card" against the Soviet Union, nor the "Soviet card" against the United States. We will also not allow anyone to play the "Chinese card."[145]

Instead, the PRC maintains there is no connection between Sino-Soviet and Sino-American relations. Qian Qichen told visiting Austrian journalists in December 1982:

> We do not want to play the Soviet card. But we do not wish to play the American card either. Nor will we permit anyone else to play China as a card. The relations between the United States and China on the one hand

---

[145] Xinhua, August 20, 1982, in FBIS-China, August 23, 1982, p. A1.

and those between the USSR and China on the other are not interconnected at all.[146]

During his September 1983 visit to the United States, Chinese Foreign Minister Wu Xueqian emphasized on several occasions the separation of Sino-American and Sino-Soviet relations. In a speech before the National Committee on United States-China Relations on September 28, Wu said:

> China always adheres to an independent foreign policy, never attaches itself to any big power or group of powers and never yields to pressure from any big power. China has always adhered to principles, neither playing the Soviet card to put pressure on the United States, nor playing the American card to put pressure on the Soviet Union.

Regarding the ongoing series of talks with the Soviet Union and their relationship to Sino-American relations, Wu commented:

We have begun consultations and dialogue at the vice foreign minister level with the Soviet Union, but our stand against its hegemonist policies has not changed. During the Sino-Soviet consultations, we demanded that the Soviet Union stop supporting Vietnam in the latter's aggression against Kampuchea, withdraw its troops from Afghanistan and reduce its troops in the area along the Sino-Soviet border and withdraw its troops from Mongolia, so as to eliminate the three major obstacles to the normalization of Sino-Soviet relations. If these obstacles are truly removed, leading to improved Sino-Soviet relations, then what is wrong with it? Isn't it also a good thing to do for peace and stability in the Asia-Pacific regions? We hold that how Sino-U.S. relations will develop will not depend on Sino-Soviet relations. In fact, among the incidents which strained Sino-American relations in the past few years, not a single case had any direct relationship with Sino-Soviet relations.[147]

---

[146] *Kurier*, December 7, 1982, in **FBIS-China**, December 7, 1982, p. C1.

[147] **Renmin Ribao**, September 28, 1983, in **FBIS-China**,

A Liaowang article of July 16, 1984, stressed that the essence of China's independent foreign policy was nonalignment, not equisdistance from the superpowers. The article said:

> Some people call China's policy of independence from the United States and the Soviet Union, and its nonalignment with them, "equidistance." It is not an appropriate interpretation. For China, which acts in accordance with principle, "equidistance" is out of the question. We cannot indiscriminately blame the United States and the Soviet Union equally for something...to balance our relations with them. In this fast changing world, it is impossible to ask China to improve its relations one step further with one as it improves its relations with the other one step further, or vice versa. To put it briefly, China will not seek "equidistance," whether in its bilateral relations with the United States or the Soviet Union, on a particular international issue or in its international relations in general.[148]

When one considers the importance to China of relations with the United States and the Soviet Union, Beijing's insistence that there is no connection between Sino-American and Sino-Soviet relations does not appear credible. The PRC position does make sense, however, under certain conditions such as those which define the present correlation of forces.

Beijing has calculated that, for the time being, U.S.-Soviet relations will remain strained, neither superpower will attack China, and both Washington and Moscow will continue to seek improved relations with the PRC. Beijing is taking advantage of this opportunity to speed up China's modernization and to secure from the United States and the Soviet Union concessions on issues which otherwise might remain intractable. Nonetheless, China's position remains precarious because the PRC is the weaker of the three powers and the one most susceptible to major shifts of policy.

Chinese leaders are playing three-party politics, a game in which they have had long experience. As Henry Kissinger observed during his negotiations with the Chinese:

September 28, 1983, pp. B6-B7.

[148] Xinhua, July 12, 1984, in FBIS-China, July 13, 1984, pp. A2-A3.

> For all their charm and ideological fervor, the Chinese leaders were the most unsentimental practitioners of balance-of-power politics I have encountered. From ancient time Chinese rulers have had to contend with powerful non-Chinese neighbors and potential conquerors. They have prevailed, often from weakness, by understanding profoundly--and exploiting for their own ends--the pyschology and preconceptions of foreigners.[149]

5.2   SINO-AMERICAN MILITARY COOPERATION

Generally speaking, China has chosen to emphasize the political aspects of Sino-American strategic cooperation, while the United States has sought to increase the military dimensions of the relationship. Washington's preoccupation with this aspect of Sino-American relations is understandable--and perhaps unavoidable--given its global responsibility to deter the Soviet Union.

Recognizing the potential deterrent value of Sino-American military cooperation, many in Washington have looked to the People's Liberation Army as a counterweight to Soviet deployments in Europe, Southwest Asia, and the Far East. During the 1978-1980 "honeymoon" period in U.S.-PRC relations, considerable optimism was generated about the possibility of modernizing the PLA with American assistance. Consolidated Guidance No. 8 estimated that $50 billion in U.S. military aid would be required to make the PLA an effective deterrent against the Soviet Red Army.[150] The same document viewed China as playing a "pivotal role" in the global balance of power and stated that it would be in the U.S. interest "to encourage Chinese actions that would heighten Soviet security concerns." The study suggested that the United States should help build up the PLA, because China would then be able to tie down Soviet forces in a war involving NATO. The Guidance said Washington should consider the possibility of military support to Beijing if a Sino-Soviet nuclear or conventional war broke out.[151]

---

[149] Henry A. Kissinger, White House Years, pp. 1087-1088.

[150] Cited in William T. Tow and Douglas T. Stuart, "China's Military Turns to the West," International Affairs, 57 (Spring 1981), p. 295.

Although hope for a "quick fix" of the PLA diminished in light of the magnitude of problems confronting the modernization of the Chinese armed forces, the idea of having China as an ally against the Soviet Union has persisted. For example, the Fiscal 1984-1985 Defense Guidance predicted that a Soviet invasion of Persian Gulf oil fields would ignite a "major conflict" between the United States and the USSR. In such a conflict, China was projected as an American ally against the Soviet Union.[152]

The legal groundwork permitting U.S. military aid to the PRC was initiated during the 97th Congress at the request of the Reagan Administration. The Administration asked Congress to amend the Foreign Assistance Act and the Agricultural Development and Assistance Act to permit China to receive U.S. economic and military assistance. Congress did not specifically remove the PRC from the list of communist countries unable to receive U.S. aid, but the House Foreign Affairs Committee in its FY 1983 bill gave the President waiver authority under certain circumstances. Title VI, Sec. 602 of the House bill read:

> Section 620 of the Foreign Assistance Act of 1961 is amended by adding at the end thereof the following:
>
> "(y) Nothwithstanding the provisions of subsection (f) of this section, the President may authorize the furnishing of assistance prohibited by that subsection if he determines and reports to the Congress that extending eligibility for such assistance is important to the security of the United States."

Subsection (f) of the 1961 Foreign Assistance Act stated: "No assistance shall be furnished under this Act, as amended, to any Communist country." The subsection went on to list the People's Republic of China as being a "Communist country."[153]

---

[151] Consolidated Guidance No. 8 was summarized in New York Times, November 4, 1979, p. A1.

[152] For highlights of the leaked document, see China Post, January 18, 1983, p. 1, citing UPI sources in Washington.

[153] The Foreign Assistance Act of 1961, with amendments, can be found in U.S. Congress, Senate, Committee on Foreign Relations, and House of Representatives,

The FY 1983 bill did not pass the Congress, so a similar provision was included as Title IX, Sec. 905 of the FY 1984 Foreign Affairs Committee bill. As of August 1984, this bill had passed the House and remained before the Senate for its consideration.

Permitting China to purchase American weapons was another initiative taken by the Reagan Administration to improve PRC military capabilities. In June 1981 Secretary of State Alexander Haig announced that China would be able to purchase weapons on a case-by-case basis. The Department of State explained U.S. arms sales policy to the PRC in this way:

> Our policy on arms sales to China...would allow China to purchase arms on a case-by-case, commercial basis like other friendly countries....To date we have not received any specific requests from the Chinese to purchase weapons. Our policy requires that Chinese requests undergo the same case-by-case review process used for requests from all countries. In evaluating all such requests we would consider a broad range of factors, including the level of technology requested and the impact such sale of a weapon system would have on U.S. security interests and on friends and allies in the region. While no weapons have been sold thus far, we would envision approval of defensive weapons sales in an evolutionary approach compatible with Chinese needs and our policy objectives and responsibilities in the region.[154]

Similarly, provisions for the sale of military-related technology have been adopted by the Reagan Administration to assist the PLA's modernization. In May 1983 Secretary of Commerce Malcolm Baldrige

---

Committee on Foreign Affairs, Legislation on Foreign Relations Through 1981, Vol. 1 (Washington, D.C.: GPO, March 1982).

[154] See answers to questions submitted for the record by Congressman Mickey Edwards to James L. Buckley, Department of State, on March 11, 1982, in U.S. House of Representatives, Committee on Appropriations, Subcommittee on Foreign Operations and Related Agencies, Foreign Assistance and Related Programs Appropriations for 1983, Hearings, Part 1 (Washington, D.C.: GPO, 1982), p. 223.

announced a significant change in U.S. policy on the sale of advanced "dual-use" technology (technology with both civilian and military applications). China was placed in export-controls category V, which applies to friendly and nonallied nations, including several countries in Europe. Under this category, exports of "dual-use" technology are approved unless concerned U.S. agencies veto a specific item. Under category P, in which China previously had been placed, items could not be sold unless individually approved.[155]

The change in technology transfer policy occurred after many months of heated debate within the Administration over the extent to which the United States should buildup China's strategic capabilities. The Pentagon in particular had objected to the sale to the PRC of sophisticated computers and ground satellite tracking stations because of their application to China's guided missile program.[156]

From late 1980 to mid-1983 the United States and China found little agreement on the extent of Sino-American military cooperation. The three-year "cooling off" period ended in September 1983, however, when Secretary of Defense Caspar Weinberger visited Beijing to resume the strategic dialogue and to establish a framework for military exchanges and for programs of cooperation in certain types of defense technology. The military areas defined for initial cooperation were antitank and antiair. The new goal of the Reagan Administration, as defined by James Kelly in June 1984, "is to have an enduring defense relationship which will move in measured steps. China has made it clear to us that it seeks no alliance. Neither is one needed or appropriate from our perspective. Rather, defense relations must mirror the slow but steady growth of the U.S.-China political and economic relationship."[157]

---

[155] *Washington Post*, June 21, 1983, p. A1.

[156] Jack Anderson wrote several columns discussing the debate within the Administration between Baldrige and U.S. Ambassador to China Arthur Hummel, who strongly favored the easing of restrictions on high-tech sales to China, and the Defense Department, which opposed the sale of advanced technology with direct military applications. See *Washington Post*, May 26, 1983, p. B21; ibid., May 30, 1983, p. C15; and ibid., July 17, 1983, p. C7.

[157] Prepared statement of James A. Kelly, "Defense Relations with the People's Republic of China," given before U.S. House of Representatives,

Despite the renewed dialogue, U.S. efforts to expand strategic cooperation beyond carefully defined boundaries have met Chinese rebuffs. Recent rejections occurred during Weinberger's trip to China in September 1983, Zhao Ziyang's visit to the United States in January 1984, President Reagan's visit to the PRC in April 1984, and Zhang Aiping's trip to Washington in June 1984. Just prior to Zhao's trip, for example, the Chinese journal <u>Observation Post</u> said that it was "wishful thinking" on the part of Washington that China would become an ally of the United States.[158]

Notwithstanding efforts to dispel the image of a strategic alliance with the United States, the PRC has indicated an interest in purchasing certain weapons and defense technologies from U.S. sources. During his trip to the United States in June 1984, Zhang Aiping and Weinberger discussed the sale of the Improved TOW anti-armor system and U.S. artillery technology, including ammunition. Lower level officials discussed anti-air systems, and some Chinese hinted that the PRC might like to purchase the F-16A or other advanced aircraft from the United States.[159]

Although it has approved in principle the sale of certain types of defensive weapons and technology to Beijing, the Reagan Administration exercises caution. Its objective is to improve PRC defense capabilities against the Soviet Union, but not to give China the ability to attack either the USSR or China's neighbors. Underlying the Administration's policy is the belief that a friendly, yet cautious approach to arms sales would be of benefit to both the United States and China. As to whether the PRC would turn these weapons against the United States or its allies in the future, the Administration argues:

> While there is a need for prudence against the possibility of a different Chinese orientation in the longer term, we must also recognize that China's future orientation will itself be influenced by China's experiences. Excessive caution out of fears of an unexpected change in that orientation might become a self-fulfilling prophecy. On the

---

Committee on Foreign Affairs, Subcommittee on Asian and Pacific Affairs, June 5, 1984, p. 2, ms.

[158] <u>Washington Post</u>, January 7, 1984, p. A9.

[159] <u>New York Times</u>, June 12, 1984, p. A3; and <u>Washington Post</u>, June 12, 1984, p. A13.

other hand, a more forthcoming policy could enhance Chinese perceptions of the long-term value of a friendly relationship with the West, reducing the risk of eventual confrontation as well as favorably affecting the near-term global balance of forces.[160]

5.3 PRC REJECTION OF CLOSE MILITARY TIES

There were several reasons why China rejected close military and strategic relations with the United States during the period from 1980 to mid-1984. In the first place, Beijing determined it was unrealistic for China to purchase advanced weapons from the West to modernize the PLA. The cost would be too high, even if the necessary quantity and quality of weapons could be obtained--which was itself in doubt. Moreover, having been badly hurt by the sudden Soviet withdrawal of assistance in 1960, Chinese leaders did not want to become dependent again upon foreign sources. The Chinese goal was self-reliance.

Second, the international correlation of forces were such that China no longer needed a close military relationship with the United States to preserve PRC security. Washington's military buildup and its determination to counter Soviet aggression improved PRC security as well as that of American allies in the region.[161]

Third, there was little incentive for China to expand military cooperation with the United States. The Soviet Union had demonstrated repeatedly that its reaction to increased threats was to build more arms and to dig in even more deeply around China's periphery. The Chinese determined that their best deterrent posture was gradually to improve relations with the Soviet Union, while at the same time preserving limited political, military, and strategic cooperation with Washington.

In spite of the arms-length relationship Beijing maintains with Washington in security matters, China still depends on the unofficial U.S. nuclear umbrella established during the Nixon Administration. Below the strategic nuclear threshold, the Chinese are aware of the severe limitations on U.S. assistance to the PRC.

---

[160] James A. Kelly, "Defense Relations with the People's Republic of China," p. 8.

[161] Der Spiegel, December 26, 1983, in FBIS-China, December 29, 1983, pp. A7-A8.

In case of serious Sino-Soviet confrontation, it is highly unlikely that the Congress or the American public would approve large-scale U.S. assistance to China--if only out of fear that such intervention might drag the United States into a nuclear conflict with the Soviet Union. Similarly, only the most desperate Chinese leader would intervene on the side of the United States in case of a war between Washington and Moscow.

Nonetheless, in the event of a nuclear conflict between the superpowers, there is a high probability that China--despite its "independent" foreign policy--would be targeted by one or both of the combatants. The possibility of China's intervention on the side of the USSR would have to be eliminated by the United States, and the potential of China's alliance with the West would have to be neutralized by the Soviet Union. Neither Washington nor Moscow would want to face an unscathed China in the aftermath of a nuclear war.

Because of the vital security interests involved, all three governments will remain highly sensitive to strategic alliances between the other two countries. Since military alliances are viewed as especially threatening, these will probably be avoided. The most stable relationship between the United States, the Soviet Union, and the PRC is roughly equilateral, in which each country pursues its own interests, does not ally with any of the other two, and maintains an adequate deterrence against an attack by any or both of its major competitors. This, in essence, appears to be the trend in the triangular relationship at this time.

In today's nuclear environment, the importance of strategic cooperation between the United States and the PRC is militarily marginal but psychologically profound. Because its value is primarily psychological, the benefits of Sino-American strategic cooperation can be purchased at a fairly low cost. Thus, for example, symbolic arms sales by the United States to China or small-scale military exchange programs can be levered into significant Soviet anxieties. There is also the possibility of low-level conventional or clandestine military cooperation in areas such as Afghanistan, Indochina, or Africa, where Soviet troops or those of its proxies are conducting operations detrimental to the interests of both Washington and Beijing. Beyond these limited spheres, however, Sino-American military cooperation is severely restricted. It can even be harmful to American and Chinese interests, if the Soviet response is to increase its own military preparations or to expand its overseas base structure.

5.4 FUTURE SINO-AMERICAN STRATEGIC COOPERATION

The above considerations would seem to lead to the following answers to the questions posed earlier in this study:

1. Can Sino-American strategic cooperation be expanded? Militarily speaking, it does not appear that strategic cooperation can be significantly increased. The reasons are in large part political. Beijing has elected to normalize relations with Moscow as a means of reducing tensions between them. Given Soviet sensitivity to possible Sino-American military-strategic cooperation, any move in that direction on the part of Beijing would likely spur Moscow to tighten, not relax, its ring of containment around China. At this stage of its modernization, the People's Republic of China needs a stable and peaceful environment. For this reason alone, the Chinese leadership is unlikely to jeopardize its domestic programs by deliberately increasing tensions with the Soviet Union. Moreover, the security advantages to be gained from closer military cooperation with the United States are limited.

Politically, Sino-American strategic cooperation is valued by both Washington and Beijing. Both want the Soviet Union to be uncertain about their intentions but not so threatened as to pursue military solutions. In a political sense, the United States and the PRC can cooperate on a wide range of international issues, particularly in Southeast Asia, Afghanistan, and possibly in Korea. China's encouragement to NATO and Japan to maintain their security relationship with the United States is also valuable. In other areas of the world such as the Middle East, Africa, and Latin America, the possibility for political cooperation is more limited. China defines itself as a developing nation whose interests coincide with those of the Third World. The United States is by definition an imperialistic, hegemonistic superpower sharing with the Soviet Union the responsibility for world turmoil. Political strategic cooperation can be increased, therefore, but only incrementally and under limited circumstances.

2. Can China be drawn into a defense alliance if the United States so desires? For a number of reasons this appears improbable. First, China is seeking more normal relations with the USSR. A defense alliance with the United States would destroy that hope and might well lead to a serious deterioration in Sino-Soviet relations. Second, a U.S.-PRC defense alliance would be very difficult to sell politically in the two countries. Few Americans would be willing to go to war to help China fight the Soviet Union. Similarly, PRC intervention on behalf of the United States would be unlikely unless China's interests were directly

threatened. Third, a defense alliance with China would risk severe USSR reprisal but not add to American--or Chinese--security. There is very little more the PRC can do to counterbalance the Soviet threat in Asia, and the United States already benefits from current efforts. Fourth, a Sino-American defense alliance would signal a major departure from the U.S. strategy of maintaining a defensive perimeter in East Asia centered on Japan and other U.S. allies, notably the Republic of Korea and the Philippines. Such a shift would cause great consternation among U.S. friends in Asia and precipitate substantial diplomatic difficulties for the United States.

3. <u>Can the United States improve China's defense capabilities, thereby increasing the PRC's value as a counterweight to the Soviet Union in Asia?</u> Over time, the United States probably can do a great deal to help China modernize the PLA. But the U.S. contribution will be constrained in varying degrees by: (1) congressional opposition to major military assistance programs; (2) limited availability of China's foreign exchange reserves; (3) the sheer magnitude of the modernization effort required; (4) political opposition in Beijing to close military relations with the United States; (5) the difficulty the PLA will have in absorbing the advanced technology central to modern Western armaments; and (6) the concerns of many U.S. allies in Asia who oppose military sales to the PRC. Indonesia and Malaysia are particularly concerned about U.S. efforts to strengthen China. To them, China looms as a future threat.

It is worth noting that Sino-American relations have warmed considerably following the mid-1983 decision by the Reagan Administration to relax controls on the export of high technology to China. Zhao Ziyang's trip to the United States in January 1984 and President Reagan's visit to China in April emphasized the economic and technological aspects of Sino-American relations.

It would seem, therefore, that the U.S. contribution to China's defense capabilities might be significant at the industrial-technological level, but that the limited quantities of weapons sold would have limited impact on the strategic balance of power in East Asia. Moreover, any increase in China's defense capabilities would likely be countered by further Soviet force enhancements in the region. Thus, U.S. efforts to improve the PRC's defense will probably not greatly increase Beijing's counterweight value, but may have a profound regional effect where the balance of force structure is as delicate as in the Taiwan Strait area.

In sum, the fundamental national security interests of both the United States and China are well served by normalized Sino-American relations. However, the allure of strategic cooperation with the PRC should not distort reality. China is unwilling to enter into a strategic relationship with the United States on any meaningful military scale. Moreover, such an alliance would not greatly increase U.S. security. Indeed, it might undermine peace and stability in East Asia due to the likely Soviet response. Both the United States and China serve to gain from the political and psychological dimensions of strategic cooperation. For this reason both countries should remain disposed to cooperate when their mutual interests are served.

Since Marxist-Leninist theory encourages contradictory tactical maneuvering to achieve long-range goals, the various zig-zags that have been witnessed in China's foreign policy can be expected to continue as PRC leaders adjust to shifts in the "correlation of forces" both internally and internationally.

Given these realities, the United States should carefully evaluate its plans for long-term strategic cooperation with the PRC. U.S. security in Asia should be based on American strength and the suppport of traditional allies in the region, not on optimistic projections of China as an ally vis-a-vis the Soviet Union. The possibility for PRC contributions to U.S. security interests will continue and should be taken advantage of when appropriate. Likewise, there is much the United States can do to enhance PRC security without increasing the threat to American friends in Asia. But two facts should be carefully noted: First, there are definite limits to Sino-American strategic cooperation; and second, the Taiwan issue has nothing whatsoever to do with the degree of strategic cooperation evinced by Washington and Beijing. The critical determinant remains the Soviet threat to the United States and China, and the considerations by leaders in both countries as to how best to deal with that threat given available resources and geopolitical realities.

Part II
The Role of Taiwan

6
Taiwan Today: An Overview

6.1   BACKGROUND

The territory under direct control of the government of the Republic of China includes the island of Taiwan (roughly 13,800 square miles), the Pescadores (or Penghu, 49 square miles), the Quemoy (Kinmen) and Matsu groups located off the Fujian coast (78 square miles), and several smaller islands around Taiwan itself. The 14,000 square miles is roughly equal to the area of West Virginia. Taiwan is centered on the Tropic of Cancer and is heavily mountainous. Sixty peaks are over 10,000 feet in elevation. About 25% of Taiwan is a rich alluvial plain located along the west coast. The vast majority of Taiwan's 18.7 million people live on this plain. With an average population density of 520.4 persons per square kilometer, the island is the second most densely populated land in the world.
    China first claimed Taiwan during the latter part of the Ming Dynasty (1368-1644), but the Manchu or Ching Dynasty (1644-1911) was the first to rule and administer the island from the mainland. In 1662 Cheng Chen-kung (Koxinga) overcame the Dutch outpost on the island (then known as Formosa) and established a temporary haven for the last remnants of the Ming. His efforts succeeded until 1683, when his successors turned the island over to the Ching. In 1895, following the Sino-Japanese War, China ceded Taiwan to Japan. Tokyo administered the island until the end of the Second World War, at which time Taiwan and Penghu were turned over to the Republic of China. Until that time neither the communists nor the KMT had much interest in Taiwan. Mao Zedong told Edgar Snow in 1936 that Korea and Taiwan should be independent of both Japan and China. Mao said: "We will extend them our enthusiastic help in their struggle for independence."[162]

---

[162] Edgar Snow, <u>Red Star Over China</u> (New York: Modern

- 91 -

The Republic of China was founded on the mainland under the leadership of Dr. Sun Yat-sen, who engineered at least ten attempts during the period 1895 to 1911 to overthrow the decadent Manchu Dynasty. Following the collapse of imperial China in 1911, Dr. Sun struggled to unite the country but met with little success. Before he died in 1925, Dr. Sun established the Kuomintang (KMT), or Nationalist Party, and appointed Chiang Kai-shek as head of the Nationalist army. The KMT's ideological base remains Dr. Sun's San Min Chu I, or Three Principles of the People. These are defined by the ROC government in terms of Abraham Lincoln's concept of government of, by, and for the people.

By 1928 General Chiang Kai-shek had managed to bring most of China under Nationalist control, but the seeds of the Communist Party of China (CPC) had also taken root. Campaigns against the communists led to the famous Long March in 1934. From 1937 to 1945 the KMT and the CPC cooperated to a degree against the Japanese occupation of the mainland. Following the war, the two sides resumed their struggle for supremacy, despite efforts by the United States to bring the factions together in a negotiated settlement. By late 1949 the Nationalists had been defeated, and Chiang Kai-shek withdrew to the island of Taiwan with approximately 1.2 million members of his government and army.

The Taiwanese, those who had lived on the island before 1945, at first welcomed the Nationalists as liberators. Within a short time, however, the exploitative actions of the Nationalists soldiers who arrived in 1945 alienated the Taiwanese. Severe riots occurred in 1947, and thousands of Taiwanese were killed. When President Chiang Kai-shek became aware of the situation, he punished those responsible and instituted policies designed to improve the life of the Taiwanese. Although friction between the mainlanders (who today comprise about 15% of Taiwan's population) and the Taiwanese remains an underlying social problem, it has abated with time and through the efforts of both groups to work out their differences. The offspring of mainlanders and Taiwanese have identical views on most issues.

Taiwan's fall to the communists seemed imminent in early 1950, and the U.S. government decided not to intervene in that outcome.[163] With the North Korean

---

Library, 1944), p. 96.

[163] An excellent overview of U.S. involvement with Taiwan can be found in Ralph N. Clough, Island China (Cambridge, MA: Harvard University Press, 1978). Also see Frederick H. Chaffee, et.al., Area Handbook

invasion of South Korea in June 1950, however, the
United States dramatically changed its policy.
President Truman interposed the Seventh Fleet into the
Taiwan Strait to prevent either party to the Chinese
civil war from widening the Korean conflict. Truman's
decision was also prompted by concern that Communist
China might attempt to use Taiwan to threaten the U.S.
position in Japan. In his statement of June 27,
President Truman explained:

> The attack upon Korea makes it plain beyond
> all doubt that communism has passed beyond the
> use of subversion to conquer independent
> nations and will use armed invasion and war.
> It has defied the orders of the Security
> Council of the United Nations issued to
> preserve international peace and security. In
> these circumstances, the occupation of Formosa
> by Communist forces would be a direct threat
> to the security of the Pacific area and to the
> United States forces performing their lawful
> and necessary functions in that area.
>
> Accordingly, I have ordered the Seventh
> Fleet to prevent any attack on Formosa. As a
> corollary of this action, I am calling upon
> the Chinese Government on Formosa to cease all
> air and sea operations against the mainland.
> The Seventh Fleet will see that this is done.
> The determination of the future status of
> Formosa must await the restoration of security
> in the Pacific, a peace settlement with Japan,
> or consideration by the United Nations.[164]

With the entry of the PRC into the Korean conflict,
U.S. hostility toward the Beijing regime became firm
policy. As part of its strategy to contain Communist
China, Washington increased political, economic, and
military ties to the Republic of China. The greatly
expanded U.S. economic and military aid programs to the
ROC were reinforced in 1954 by the U.S.-ROC Mutual
Defense Treaty. The treaty, signed in response to a
concerted PRC effort to gain control of the offshore
islands in September 1954, said in part:

---

for the Republic of China (Washington, D.C.: GPO, 1969).

[164] American Foreign Policy, 1950-1955: Basic Documents, II (Washington, D.C.: GPO, 1957), p. 2467.

> Desiring to declare publicly and formally their sense of unity and their common determination to defend themselves against external armed attack, so that no potential aggressor could be under the illusion that either of them stands alone in the West Pacific Area,
>
> Each party recognizes that an armed attack in the West Pacific Area directed against the territories of either of the Parties would be dangerous to its own peace and safety and declares that it would act to meet the common danger in accordance with its constitutional processes....
>
> The Government of the Republic of China grants, and the Government of the United States accepts, the right to dispose such United States land, air and sea forces in and about Taiwan and the Pescadores as may be required for their defense, as determined by mutual agreement.

The territory defined under the agreement included the island of Taiwan and the Pescadores, but did not include the several offshore islands occupied by the Nationalists, notably Kinmen and Matsu. The exclusion of the offshore islands reflected disagreement in Washington over whether the United States should risk going to war with the PRC over these islands. Following the evacuation with U.S. assistance of Nationalist forces on the offshore islands of the Tachens, the U.S. Congress on January 29, 1955, passed the Formosa Resolution giving the President the authority to defend Kinmen and Matsu if he felt it necessary for the security of Taiwan and the Pescadores. The Senate and House of Representatives resolved:

> That the President of the United States be and he hereby is authorized to employ the Armed Forces of the United States as he deems necessary for the specific purpose of securing and protecting Formosa and the Pescadores against armed attack, this authority to include the securing and protection of such related positions and territories of that area now in friendly hands and the taking of such other measures as he judges to be required or appropriate in assuring the defense of Formosa and the Pescadores.[165]

Although the extension of U.S. assistance to the ROC in case of a Chinese attack against the offshore islands of Kinmen and Matsu was left deliberately vague, in practice American support given to Taiwan in the Quemoy crises of 1954, 1958, and 1962 defined U.S. security interests as generally including the defense of these islands. On June 27, 1962, President Kennedy stated that he supported the positions taken by the previous administrations in 1954 and 1958, and reaffirmed the policy that "we would defend Quemoy and Matsu if there were an attack which was part of an attack on Formosa and the Pescadoes."[166]

In 1957 the United States announced that it would deploy Matador missiles on Taiwan capable of hitting parts of the mainland with both conventional and nuclear warheads.[167] Under American protection, and with conscious decisions by the ROC government to implement major land reform, to expand the role of free enterprise, and to increase democratic participation, Taiwan emerged as a viable and distinctive society in its own right.

Taking advantage of its strong economic growth and friendly ties with the United States, Japan, and other free nations, Taiwan became one of the most stable and prosperous societies in all of Asia. The United States ended all economic assistance to the ROC in 1965 and phased out all military aid in the mid-1970s. Taiwan has been frequently cited as an ideal example of a successful developing nation which other Third World countries should emulate.

---

[165] United States Statutes at Large, LXLX (Washington, D.C.: GPO, 1955), p. 7.

[166] See "President Kennedy's Statement on the Taiwan Strait, June 27, 1962," Current History, 43 (September 1962), p. 178.

[167] Alice Langley Hsieh, Communist China's Strategy in the Nuclear Age (Englewood Cliffs, NJ: Prentice Hall, 1962), pp. 104-105.

6.2   ECONOMIC CONDITIONS

In the 35 years since the ROC moved to Taiwan, the island has achieved remarkable success economically.[168] In large measure, this success can be attributed to sound economic strategies adopted by the ROC government, which put into place its first four-year plan in 1953.

Throughout the 1950s, heavy emphasis was placed on agriculture. An effective land reform program was implemented, which had the important effects of stimulating agricultural production, improving rural living standards, and compensating former landlords. Many landlords in turn used their compensation to invest in domestic industries. At the same time that agricultural reform was introduced, labor-intensive import-substituting industries were developed to help conserve foreign exchange and to provide needed jobs. Food, textiles, and building materials were given development priority during this early period.

The 1960s saw a shift in strategy, with the enactment of legislation designed to attract foreign and domestic investment capital to key industries. Export-oriented industries were encouraged, such as electronic goods and home appliances. With the advantage of Taiwan's low-labor costs, these goods began to find their way into world markets. New agricultural products were developed and the export of these farm products encouraged.

In the 1970s a new stage of economic development was entered. Government policies began to emphasize a shift from labor-intensive to basic and heavy industries, such as iron and steel, shipbuilding, and machine tools. A process of backward integration was adopted by establishing petrochemical intermediate goods industries. Large sums were spent on the elimination of transport bottlenecks and the building of infrastructure such as new ports, airports, and highways. Rural development and farmer income also received high priority.

The economic strategy adopted by the government for the 1980s calls for the restraining of energy-intensive industries and the development of strategic industries with low energy use, such as computers and other forms

---

[168] Numerous books have been written about Taiwan's economic "miracle." Two of the most useful are Shirley W. Y. Kuo, et.al., _The Taiwan Success Story: Rapid Growth with Improved Distribution in the Republic of China, 1952-1979_ (Boulder, CO: Westview Press, 1981); and James C. Hsiung, ed., _The Taiwan Experience: 1950-1980_ (New York: Praeger Publishers, 1981).

of advanced electronics. This will require a transformation of the island's industrial structure. Production technology and modern management techniques are being adopted to offset rising labor costs and to increase productivity. Labor-intensive industries are being encouraged to automate their production processes. Taiwan's educational institutions are placing great emphasis on science and technology to provide the highly skilled manpower necessary to carry out this transformation. At the same time, more effort is being made to ensure that social development parallels the island's economic development.

As the result of these largely successful development strategies, rapid economic growth has been sustained for over 30 years. During the 1950s, the annual increase in gross national product (GNP) averaged 8.2%. During the 1960s, GNP growth averaged 9.2%. A 10% growth was registered during the 1970s, despite two oil-price shocks. Due to the international recession of 1981 and 1982, the growth of Taiwan's economy slowed considerably. But in 1983, with the recovery of world trade and the introduction of domestic policies designed to buoy export growth and to stimulate fiscal and monetary conditions, Taiwan's GNP jumped 7.1%, to U.S. $49.75 billion. Taiwan's per capita GNP in 1983 was $2,673--one of the highest in Asia.[169]

For many years, export expansion has been the engine of Taiwan's economic growth. In 1983 the export of goods and services amounted to $25.12 billion, or 55.2% of Taiwan's gross domestic product (GDP). Imports totalled $20.29 billion, or 46.4% of GDP. These percentages were among the highest in the world. In fact, Taiwan is the leading developing nation in trade.

The most important trading partners of Taiwan in 1983 were the United States, Japan, Saudi Arabia, Hong Kong, Federal Republic of Germany, and Kuwait. Table 5 shows the pattern of trade with these countries.

---

[169] Unless otherwise noted, these and other statistical data on Taiwan's economy have been taken from Statistical Yearbook of the Republic of China: 1983 (Taipei: Directorate General of the Budget, Accounting and Statistics, 1983); Urban and Regional Development Statistics: ROC, 1983 (Taipei: Housing and Urban Development Department, Council for Economic Planning and Development, October 1983); Economic Development, Taiwan, Republic of China (Taipei: Council for Economic Planning and Development, April 1984); and "Essential Statistics on Taiwan, Republic of China" (Taipei: Council for Economic Planning and Development, April 1984).

TABLE 5

Major Trading Partners of Taiwan, 1983

Country	Imports	%	Exports	%	Balance
U.S.A.	$4.6	22.9	$11.3	45.1	+$6.7
Japan	$5.6	27.5	$ 2.5	9.9	-$3.1
Saudi Arabia	$1.9	9.5	$ 0.8	3.0	-$1.1
Hong Kong	$0.3	1.5	$ 1.6	6.5	+$1.3
W. Germany	$0.7	3.4	$ 0.9	3.4	+$0.2
Kuwait	$1.1	5.6	$ 0.2	0.9	-$0.9

Figures are in U.S. billion dollars. Percentages are of total trade.

Taiwan's principal exports in 1983 were, in order of value, textile products ($5 billion), electrical machinery and apparatus ($4.9 billion), metal products and machinery ($2.3 billion), plastics and products ($1.8 billion), timber products and furniture ($1.2 billion), and transportation equipment ($1 billion). Principal imports were crude oil ($4.1 billion), electrical machinery and apparatus ($2.4 billion), machinery and tools ($2 billion), basic metals ($1.8 billion), chemicals ($1.8 billion), and transportation equipment ($1 billion).

The characteristics of Taiwan's trade reflect the island's production structure, which has evolved since the 1950s from an agriculturally based economy to that of a newly industrialized country. In 1983 93% of Taiwan's exports were industrial products, while 69% of its imports were raw materials.

During 1983 industry accounted for 49.8% of gross domestic product, while services amounted to 42.8% and agriculture 7.4% of GDP. Taiwan's employment structure reflected these percentages: 41% of the labor force worked in industry, 40% in services, and 19% on farms. The unemployment rate was quite small: 2.67% for men and 2.76% for women. Underemployment, however, is an area of concern. Taiwan's labor force is one of the most highly educated in the world.

The people of Taiwan annually save about 30% of their gross income. This exceptionally high ratio, coupled with the rapid rate of economic growth in general, has given Taiwan a gross domestic capital formation of around 30% of GNP during the past decade.

The government has adopted policies designed to attract foreign investment as well. Between 1952 and

1983, U.S. businesses invested nearly $1.2 billion in Taiwan. Overseas Chinese invested $1.1 billion, Japanese enterprises invested $0.9 billion, and European businesses invested $0.4 billion. Nearly 29% of all foreign and Overseas Chinese investments have gone into electronic and electric products industries. Foreign investment accounts for only 3-5% of gross domestic capital investment. Although foreign-invested firms account for a small percentage of the total national output, they produce a significant proportion of Taiwan's exports. Overseas investment is encouraged because of the high technology, management skills, and competition introduced into Taiwan by foreign firms.

Price stability is an important government policy. The decade of the 1970s saw a rather rapid rise in prices, reflecting the spiraling costs of oil and other raw materials. But in 1983 urban consumer prices rose by only 1.8%, while wholesale prices declined 1.2%. The inflation rate for 1983 was -1%.

Unlike most developing countries, a fair system of income distribution has accompanied Taiwan's economic growth. In 1952 the income of the wealthiest 20% of Taiwan's households was 15 times that of the lowest 20%. In 1983 the figure was 4.3 to 1, one of the most equitable distributions in the world.

Prior to 1980 Taiwan's central government ran an annual budget surplus. Since that time, however, there has been a small deficit. In 1983 that figure was 2.4% of GNP, or about $1.1 billion out of a total budget of $13 billion. Table 6 shows the planned budget for FY 1983.

Because of Taiwan's highly successful economic policies, the citizens of the ROC enjoy a relatively high standard of living. In 1983 34% of average family spending went for food, 28% for housing, 21% for education and recreation, 7% for beverages and tobacco, 5% for clothing, and 5% for transportation. Life expectancy increased from 58.6 years in 1952 to 72.7 years in 1983. Daily calory intact increased from 2,078 to 2,749. Per capita living space more than doubled during the same period. Virtually every household had electricity and a television set. Almost 60% of all households owned a car.

Although statistics are important indicators of Taiwan's economic strength, other observations must be made to put the overview into perspective. It will take roughly ten to fifteen years for Taiwan to restructure its economy. In the process there are numerous short-term and long-term problems to overcome. In the short-term, Taiwan must eliminate the problem of counterfeiting foreign industrial products and curtail the occasional practice of dumping its products in order to gain a larger percentage of the overseas market.

TABLE 6

Central Government Budget, FY 1983

Revenues

Revenues from Taxes.................243
Surplus of Public Enterprises
  and Public Utilities............... 36
Fees................................. 12
Proceeds from Sales of Properties
  and Recalled Capital............... 8
Proceeds from Issues of Public Debts 20
Miscellaneous Revenues............... 12
Surplus Previous Fiscal Year......... 6
Total Revenues......................338

Expenditures

General Administration............... 16
Defense and Foreign Affairs.........144
Education, Science and Culture...... 35
Economic Construction and
  Communication...................... 63
Social Welfare....................... 53
Obligations.......................... 7
Aid to Local Governments............ 14
Miscellaneous Expenditures.......... 6
Total Expenditures..................338

Unit: NT billion dollars. NT$40 = US$1

Product quality must be improved substantially, and greater efforts have to be expended to lower the trade surplus with the United States.

Over the long-term, Taiwan must develop knowledge-intensive industries such as advanced computers, electronics, lasers, and microbiology to remain competitive in the world market. Rather than merely duplicating what others have done, Taiwan's industries must move into a creative phase of high technology in which they contribute directly to the development of new products. Automation will play an increasingly important role in Taiwan's industry, but this will require substantial improvement in educational and technical training institutions. International financial services is also an area into which Taiwan should move to ensure its continued integration with the world's economy. Taipei has taken steps in this direction by establishing a money market in 1976 and adopting a floating exchange system in 1978. There are 30 branches of foreign banks operating in Taiwan at present and more are applying each year. The government also recognizes that additional efforts must be made to diversify overseas markets as a means of avoiding protectionist measures being adopted by countries such as the United States in response to pressure from domestic manufacturers.

The ROC government is adopting policies designed to accomplish most of these objectives. The trend is toward the liberalization of trade to give greater flexibility to Taiwan's businessmen. Tariffs are being reduced and other protectionist measures removed. The three key ingredients responsible for Taiwan's economic success--the free enterprise system, outward looking policies, and achievements in technology--continue to receive emphasis. Export expansion will continue, but with improved products and with a constant eye on the dangers of protectionism in key markets.

Because of the importance of the U.S. market--Taiwan is the fifth largest export market for the United States and the sixth largest import market--great efforts are being made to lower the U.S. trade deficit. Since 1978, eight "Buy American" missions have been sent to the United States, purchasing a total of $6.7 billion in agricultural and industrial products which might have been bought elsewhere.[170] ROC economists point out that in 1983 Taiwan spent 13% of its GNP, or $6 billion, to help the United States recover from its economic recession and to help reduce Taiwan's trade surplus.[171]

The ROC is presented with both opportunities and risks as a result of uncertainties generated by China's scheduled takeover of Hong Kong in 1997. Numerous businesses are relocating in Taiwan or establishing branches there. Taiwan is setting up offshore banking services to replace part of those presently located in the Crown Colony. The ROC is also establishing itself as a major storage, transportation, and marketing center for the entire Pacific Basin to absorb part of the expected Hong Kong loses. On the negative side, an undetermined amount of Taiwan's trade with Hong Kong might be adversely affected by the mainland's takeover. In the summer of 1984 Taiwan established an ad hoc committee to study these and other problems relating to

---

[170] *Free China Journal*, January 15, 1984, p. 4.

[171] Remarks made in conference on "U.S.-ROC Relations: Economic and Strategic Dimensions," April 30, 1984, Taipei, Taiwan.

the 1997 transition.

ROC economists predict that Taiwan will be able to maintain a 7% growth rate for the foreseeable future. The main factors contributing to this forecast are a high educational level for Taiwan's work force, the island's capital surplus, and the wealth of technology available to Taiwan from domestic and foreign sources.

It is important to note that most Taiwan economists say that economic modernization can only occur as Taiwan develops socially and politically. To become a newly industrialized country requires that Taiwan also move foward in its evolution toward a more open, mobile, and pluralistic society. This brings into focus the close interrelationship between Taiwan's economic prosperity and the island's political stability.

6.3   POLITICAL SYSTEM

Since coming to Taiwan in 1949, the government of the Republic of China has persisted in its claim to represent all of China, of which Taiwan is one province. In keeping with that claim, the ROC government maintains a full array of central governing bodies transported to the island just prior to the Nationalist's collapse on the mainland. Taiwan's provincial government, Taipei and Kaohsiung special municipalities, and various levels of local administration are kept separate from and subordinate to the central bodies.

Under the 1947 Constitution, the people are given four powers: suffrage, recall, initiative, and referendum. The government's administrative power is vested in five branches (Yuan): Executive, Legislative, Judicial, Control, and Examination. Heading the government is a President, elected by the popularly elected National Assembly. The National Assembly also elects the Vice President and amends the Constitution.

The Executive Yuan, whose head (Premier) is appointed by the President and approved by the Legislative Yuan, is responsible for policy and administration. The heads of the various ministries of the Executive Yuan (communications, economic affairs, education, finance, foreign affairs, interior, legal affairs, and national defense), plus certain other officials, form the ROC cabinet.

The Legislative Yuan is the nation's main lawmaking body. Its members are popularly elected and have the responsibility to oversee the activities of the Executive Yuan. The Judicial Yuan is the highest judicial organ of the Republic. The Control Yuan is a traditional Chinese government organ which monitors the efficiency of public service and investigates instances of corruption. Its members are also elected. The Examination Yuan, another traditional Chinese organ, functions as a civil service system. It attends to the recruitment of personnel through competitive examinations and oversees personnel matters such as service performance records, promotion, salaries, and retirement.

Just prior to the retreat to Taiwan, national elections were held on the mainland in accordance with the Constitution. Some 3,045 members were elected to the National Assembly, 773 to the Legislative Yuan, and 180 to the Control Yuan. The loss of the mainland prevented subsequent elections (every six years for the National Assembly and Control Yuan, and every three years for the National Assembly) from being held. The enactment in April 1948 of the Temporary Provisions Effective During the Period of Communist Rebellion set aside the mandated elections and gave the President extraordinary powers, including the right to declare martial law. As subsequently amended by the National Assembly, the Temporary Provisions enabled those elected on the mainland to hold their seats indefinitely in the central government on Taiwan.

This has created the peculiar situation whereby democracy has proceeded apace at the local and provincial levels of government on Taiwan, but the elected bodies at the central government level have tended to be ineffective. At the present time the National Assembly has fewer than 1,400 members and the Legislative Yuan less than 400. Active members number considerably fewer. To invigorate the central government's elected bodies and to reflect Taiwan's vital importance to the ROC, several supplemental elections have been held on the island.

Real political power on Taiwan rests in the hands of the President of the ROC and the Chairman of the ruling Kuomintang political party. Both positions are currently held by Chiang Ching-kuo, the son of former President Chiang Kai-shek. President Chiang Ching-kuo has proven to be an exceptionally able leader.

Taiwan's political system is dominated by the KMT. Two minor and insignificant parties exist: the Democratic Socialist Party and the Young China Party. Since the formation of new political parties is forbidden under the Temporary Provisions, those opposing the government do so as independents or nonpartisans, known as Tangwai. Independent candidates consistently win about 25% of the votes.

The ROC government is firmly opposed to the Taiwan independence movement. Minister of the Interior Lin Yang-kang, himself a Taiwanese, said in October 1983: "it is an illusion that Taiwan can become an independent nation." Lin listed several reasons why: First, "If

Taiwan should become independent, the 26 million Overseas Chinese will stop supporting us." Second, the notion that Taiwan would be recognized by foreign nations if it should declare independence is a delusion. Third, "Peking would have a good excuse for attacking Taiwan...on the excuse that it was trying to 'suppress a revolt.'" And fourth, if Taiwan declared independence the one billion people on the mainland would lose hope for achieving the freedom, prosperity, and democracy attained by the ROC on Taiwan.[172]

On February 25, 1983, Premier Sun Yun-suan described the long-term goals of the ROC government:

> We shoulder a double mission: to reconstruct the bastion of national revival and recover the mainland. We must make adequate preparations and redouble our effort so as to strengthen national construction based on the three principles of the people and also reinforce our subjective strength for recovery of the mainland....Our goals include:
>
> 1. We must safeguard the Constitution and the constitutional system to promote democracy, honor the rule of law, and establish a society in which everyone abides by the law, maintains discipline and carries out his duty. In abiding by the law, we shall maintain the spirit of democracy; in observing discipline, we shall maintain social order; and by doing our duty, we shall safeguard the criteria of freedom.
>
> 2. To recover the mainland is our resolutely fundamental national policy. It will never change. To the Chinese Communists, peace talk is merely another form of war. We shall never fall into their trap. We must give special attention to rooting out any view of compromise and sessionism that violates the Constitution and national policy. We must wipe out the fallacies of "Taiwan independence," a movement whose supporters have forgotten their ancestral origins. In so doing we shall ensure the purity and stability of our bastion of national revival.

---

[172] *China Post*, October 21, 1983, in *FBIS-China*, October 31, 1983, p. V1.

3. China must be unified, independent, democratic, free, progressive, open and peaceful. The distribution of its wealth must be equitable. The China of the Chinese people must be the Republic of China unified under the three principles.[173]

In his 1984 report to the Legislative Yuan, Premier Sun reconfirmed the government's central policies as "consolidating our bastion for national revival and creating the opportunity of recovering the mainland."[174]

6.4 RECENT POLITICAL DEVELOPMENTS

Although Taiwan's political system remains essentially a one-party authoritarian system, a number of developments have occurred recently which indicate that the system is becoming more democratic.

An important trend has been the policy of President Chiang Ching-kuo to use his power of appointment to liberalize the central government and to make it more representative of the Taiwanese majority on the island. A fortnight after the November 1981 Taiwan provincial elections, the cabinet was reshuffled and a number of new appointments were made. Almost all the appointees were Taiwanese and considered young by Chinese standards. Those Taiwanese appointed included: Chiu Chuang-huan, Vice President of the Executive Yuan (Vice Premier); Lin Yang-kang, Minister of the Interior; Lien Chan, Minister of Transportation and Communications; Lin Chin-sheng, Minister without Portfolio; and Chen Chi-lu, Chairman of the Cultural Development Commission. In addition, Lee Teng-hui was promoted from Taipei City Mayor to Governor of Taiwan Province; Shao En-hsin was moved from Taipei County Magistrate to Taipei City Mayor; and Chen Shao-shan was promoted from Deputy Commander in Chief of the Army to Commander of the Taiwan Garrison Command.

In February 1984 Lee Teng-hui was elected Vice President of the ROC. As such, he is constitutionally in line to succeed President Chiang, although real power could shift to the premiership in the event of a change in the presidency.

---

[173] Premier Sun's statement of policy to the Legislative Yuan can be found in China Post, February 26 and 27, 1983, pp. 4-5.

[174] Ibid., February 25, 1984, pp. 2-3.

At the same time as Lee's election, the Central Standing Committee of the KMT increased the number of its Taiwan representatives. Of the 31 members of the new Committee, 12 or 39% were Taiwanese. Five of the eight newly elected members were born on Taiwan. The Presidium of the KMT contains the most senior political figures of the Party. Of the 12 members in February 1984, four were Taiwanese.

In the central government there are Taiwanese in important decision-making positions. Those Taiwanese appointed to the June 1984 cabinet included: Lin Yang-kang, Vice Premier; Wu Po-hsiung, Minister of Interior; Shih Ch'i-yang, Minister of Justice; Lien Chan, Minister of Communications; and Kao Yu-shu, Chang Feng-shu, and Kuo Wei-fan, Ministers without Portfolio. Chiu Chuang-huan became Governor of Taiwan Province.

Since the population of Taiwan is 85% Taiwanese and the KMT's membership is approximately 70% Taiwanese, it can be argued that Taiwan's representation in the decision-making bodies of the central government and the KMT is still inequitable. Nonetheless, the trend toward a more equitable distribution of power seems to be firmly rooted in the political process. The Vice President, Vice Premier, 40% of the ministers on the cabinet, and 40% of the members of the KMT Central Standing Committee are Taiwanese. These numbers are a significant improvement over the past, and they will no doubt increase in the future.

The same movement toward a more equitable distribution of power can be found in Taiwan's election process. Democracy was begun at the grass roots level as early as October 1950. Elections for county and city council seats, magistrates and mayors, and Taiwan Provincial Assembly seats were held in 1950, 1951, 1952, 1954, 1957, 1958, 1960, 1961, 1963, 1964, 1968, 1972, 1974, and 1977. Beginning in 1977, true competition began to emerge between the KMT candidates and non-partisans. Prior to that election, the voters were given a wide range of choice between various KMT candidates. Competition between the KMT and those who ran independently increased substantially during the provincial and local elections of November 1981, January 1982, and June 1982. Voter turnout was over 70%. The KMT won 77% of the Provincial Assembly seats, 74% of the Taipei City Council seats, 76% of the Kaohsiung City Council seats, 85% of city and county council seats, and 96% of town and village mayorships.[175]

---

[175] See John F. Copper and George P. Chen, <u>Taiwan's Elections: Democratization and Political Development in the Republic of China</u> (Baltimore, MD: University of Maryland School of Law, 1984.)

National elections have posed a dilemma for the central government. The ROC maintains that it represents all of China; therefore, its elected offices must reflect this official view. The Temporary Provisions, enacted by the General Assembly on the mainland in April 1948 and subsequently amended on Taiwan in 1960, 1966, and 1972, permit those elected on the mainland to hold their offices without reelection. Supplementary elections have been held on Taiwan to invigorate the Legislative Yuan and National Assembly and to reflect the reality of the limited territory under de facto control of Taipei.

Supplementary elections were first held in 1969, when 15 new delegates representing Taiwan Province and Taipei special municipality were elected to the National Assembly, plus 11 to the Legislative Yuan, and two to the Control Yuan. These additional delegates comprised about 1%, 3%, and 3% respectively of the three elected organs of the central government. The process was repeated in 1972 and again in 1975 for the Legislative Yuan. In 1972, 53 members were added to the National Assembly, 51 to the Legislative Yuan, and 15 to the Control Yuan. In 1975, 52 more were added to the Legislative Yuan. Some 87% of the newly elected representatives to the Legislative Yuan--the most important of the legislative bodies--were Taiwanese. About 73% of the victors in these elections were KMT candidates.

The national election of 1980 was highly significant and should be considered a watershed event in Taiwan's politics. Progressive elements in the government and various opposition groups worked together to evolve a set of ground rules which would permit greater and more meaningful competition and discussion of issues. Still unable to form new political parties, the Tangwai nonetheless organized into a loose political association and formulated a political platform stressing the need to increase democracy on Taiwan.

The election was free and hotly contested. Government policies were assailed on many accounts, and the candidates were left free to discuss or advocate any position except two: the advocacy of communism or Taiwan independence. Voter turnout was about 66%. The KMT officially backed only 42 candidates for the National Assembly and 38 for the Legislative Yuan, but won 63 seats in the National Assembly (or 82% of the contested seats) and 56 seats in the Legislative Yuan (80% of those contested). The Tangwai did not make a very good showing in terms of the percentage of their candidates winning, but individual Tangwai candidates were among the top vote getters in the elections.

On December 3, 1983, Taiwan's fifth supplementary election was held. Competing for 71 seats in the

Legislative Yuan were 171 candidates.[176] Again the Tangwai took the central government to task on such issues as democracy, greater political participation for Taiwanese, human and civil rights, freedom of speech, lifting martial law, and the status of the ROC in the international community. Many Tangwai also criticized the government for special privileges, allowing pollution to get worse, and doing nothing about traffic, flooding and other social problems, and for not controlling economic crimes.

KMT candidates stressed the economic progress that had been made under the Party's leadership; the need for an evolutionary rather than revolutionary change in the political system; the threat from the PRC and the need to remain united; and the need for the government and people to transcend ethnic and other differences in the face of the major international and domestic problems confronting Taiwan. The KMT conducted a rather sophisticated campaign, utilizing many electioneering devices common to better run campaigns in the United States.

Of the 171 candidates filing for the 71 seats, 58 were nominated by the KMT and 77 entered as independents. The KMT captured 62 seats, 6 went to Tangwai, and 3 went to others. Some 6,891,160 people voted, or 63.17% of the eligible population. Although the KMT captured 87% of the available seats, it won only 73% of the total popular vote. The Tangwai and other candidates won 26% of the popular vote but landed only 13% of the seats. Of the victorious candidates, 66 were Taiwanese and 5 were mainlanders.

In general, the victorious KMT candidates were moderates. However, most of the Tangwai winners could be categorized as "progressives" or "radicals." The KMT was highly organized and efficient, but the Tangwai split into several factions which tended to undermine the moderate independents and to polarize dissatisfied voters around a few radicals. The moderate Tangwai had advocated reform from with the system, while the radicals had urged a reform of the system itself.

Taiwan, then, is in the midst of an important political evolution. The dominant trends which can be identified are toward more democracy, a more equitable distribution of power between the Taiwanese and the mainlanders, and a rejuvenation of the central government's elected bodies through the introduction of younger, more highly educated public servants.

---

[176] Information on the election can be found in *Free China Review*, December 1983; and *ibid.*, February 1984.

This process is being encouraged and abetted by President Chiang Ching-kuo and the Koumintang. It is unlikely that it will be curtailed, although the pace of the evolution will probably remain deliberate and incremental. Nonetheless, there are important implications for the future of Taiwan inherent in the process currently underway. First, it will create a closer bond of shared interests between the Taiwanese and the mainlanders on the island, and most especially between their children. At the present time, only about 9% of Taiwan's population has ever been on the mainland. Second, it will further widen the already considerable gap betwen the lifestyles of the people on Taiwan and those on the mainland, making reunification a more delicate political issue. And third, it will improve the image of Taiwan in the eyes of the world community, thus strengthening Taipei's case for international recognition as a separate political entity (although not necessarily a separate country) from the PRC.

The political evolution currently underway on Taiwan is in the U.S. interest, because Taiwan is demonstrating the advantages of a free enterprise system and participatory democracy to many Third World nations. There are dangers to the evolution, however. The PRC may decide to derail Taiwan's democratization for its own interests. In addition to various military, political, economic, and diplomatic pressures Beijing can bring to bear on Taipei, there are persistent rumors that PRC agents in the United States and elsewhere are in contact with radical elements of the Taiwan Independence Movement (Tai-tu). Tai-tu extremists, with or without PRC assistance, may turn to terrorism on Taiwan as a means of preventing the merger of Taiwanese and mainlander interests on the island. The resulting polarization of Taiwan's society would benefit no one, save the radical elements who seek to create an independent Taiwan and remove from the island all vestiges of the mainlanders and the KMT. Moreover, there are rightist elements within Taiwan who are also dissatisfied with the democratization process. Therefore, although the evolution of Taiwan's political development seems to be in a direction favorable to U.S. interests, there are a number of threats to that evolution which could destabilize Taiwan and present the United States with a major foreign policy problem in the future.

6.5 FOREIGN POLICY

The decision by the United States in June 1950 to interpose the Seventh Fleet in the Taiwan Strait and to maintain relations with the Republic of China gave the ROC government an opportunity to recover from its disastrous defeat on the mainland. Taipei's diplomatic situation picked up considerably in 1952, when the ROC concluded a peace treaty with Japan and resumed diplomatic relations with a number of countries in Europe, Asia, Latin America, the Middle East, and Africa. In 1954 the United States and the ROC signed a Mutual Defense Treaty, formally incorporating Taiwan into the U.S. security alliance system built around the periphery of Asia. During the Vietnam conflict, Taiwan proved its usefulness to the United States by serving as an important logistics and repair station for U.S. air, ground and naval combat units.

The decade of the 1970s, however, saw a number of diplomatic setbacks for Taiwan. Beginning with Canada's shifting of relations from Taipei to Beijing in October 1970, dozens of nations shifted recognition from the ROC to the PRC. Henry Kissinger's secret trips to China starting in June 1971, Taipei's withdrawal from the United Nations that same year, the issuance of the Shanghai Communique in February 1972, and the severance of diplomatic relations with Japan a few months later were severe blows to Taiwan's international prestige. The low point of the decade occurred on December 15, 1978, when President Jimmy Carter announced that on January 1, 1979, the United States would terminate its diplomatic relations with the ROC and recognize the government of the People's Republic of China as the sole legal government of China.

Today, Taiwan maintains diplomatic relations with 24 countries. Trade or cultural offices are staffed in 40 countries, and 21 countries have offices in Taiwan. Taiwan has a membership in 644 international organizations. Those countries with which the ROC maintains diplomatic relations are: Bolivia, Costa Rica, Dominican Republic, Dominica, El Salvador, Guatemala, Haiti, Holy See, Honduras, Malawi, Nauri, Nicaragua, Panama, Paraguay, St. Christopher and Nevis, St. Vincent and the Grenadines, Saudi Arabia, Solomon Islands, South Africa, South Korea, Swaziland, Tonga, Tuvalu, and Uruguay.

Taiwan's "substantive" relations with other countries are carried out through many diversified channels, including political, economic, social, educational, cultural, scientific, and technological exchanges. Relations between Taipei and East Asian and Pacific countries are reinforced with conferences and specific agreements in areas of mutual interest. The most important official relationship is maintained with South Korea. Contact with West Asian countries is maintained through medical and technological exchanges, trade, and frequent high-level exchange visits. Relations between the ROC and Saudi Arabia are especially close. Important diplomatic relations are also maintained between the ROC and South Africa. Trade missions help to maintain contact with other African nations. Unofficial relations with the countries of Europe are increasing. Numerous European banks have opened branches in Taiwan. Other types of contact occur through cultural, economic, and trade offices, technical cooperation agreements, frequent exchange visits of high-ranking officials, and cultural and sports exchanges.

The area of greatest ROC diplomatic success has been Latin America. Thirteen of the 24 nations with which Taiwan maintains diplomatic relations are in Latin America. High-level exchange visits are common and numerous agreements have been signed. Among the most important of these have been technical programs in which Taiwan assists various Latin American countries develop fisheries, agricultural products, and basic industries. Taiwan's own highly successful development makes the island's economic model an influencial one in Latin America.

The foreign policy of the ROC is based on "four firm and unchangeable principles." These are:

> 1. The system of the state of the Republic of China as established under Article 1 of the Constitution will never be changed. Article 1 of the Constitution reads: "The Republic of China, founded on the Three Principles of the People, shall be a democratic republic of the people, to be governed by the people, and for the people."
>
> 2. The overall goals of anti-Communism and national recovery of the Republic of China will never be changed.
>
> 3. The Republic of China will remain always with the democratic bloc and its dedication to the upholding of righteousness and justice and safeguarding peace and security of the world will never be changed.
>
> 4. The resolute stand of the Republic of China in never compromising with the Chinese Communist rebel group will never be changed.[177]

Because of the diplomatic setbacks experienced by Taipei in recent years, many ROC foreign policy experts, particularly the younger generation, criticize the moralistic tone of Taiwan's foreign policy and advocate a more realistic, flexible policy. Although this debate is ongoing, Taiwan's current foreign policy remains strongly bipolar in separating the democratic and communist camps. Premier Sun's report to the Legislative Yuan in February 1984 summarized Taiwan's present emphasis in international affairs:

> The central task of our current diplomatic endeavors are based on our national policies of adhering to the democratic camp and remaining anti-Communist. We shall continue strengthening our ties with friendly nations. We shall promote substantive relations with friendly states that have no formal ties with us. We shall at all times do our best to expose Chinese Communist evils, strike back at Chinese Communist united front intrigues and seek further understanding and support of the international community.[178]

The two most important governments with which Taipei must deal are the United States and the People's Republic of China. Unofficial relations between the people of the United States and the people of Taiwan are governed by the Taiwan Relations Act (TRA), signed into law by President Carter in April 1979. The TRA has important provisions specifying U.S. regional interests and policy toward Taiwan. The Act provides for the continuation of commercial, cultural, and other relations between the two societies; arms sales to meet Taiwan's defense needs; the legal status of Taiwan and its citizens in the United States; mutual investments; the establishment of the American Institute in Taiwan (AIT) to handle business previously managed by the American embassy; reporting procedures to Congress to see that the Act is fully implemented; and other matters.

As its counterpart to AIT, Taiwan established the Coordination Council for North American Affairs (CCNAA). AIT has offices in Taipei and Kaohsiung, while the CCNAA

---

[177] *Republic of China: A Reference Book* (Taipei: United Pacific International, Inc., July 1983), p. 293.

[178] The text of Premier's 1984 report to the Legislative Yuan may be found in *China Post*, February 25, 1984.

maintains offices in Washington, Atlanta, Chicago, Boston, Honolulu, Houston, Los Angeles, New York, San Francisco, and Seattle. In October 1980 AIT and CCNAA agreed to extend to each other's personnel the privileges, exemptions, and immunities normally given to diplomatic personnel. Most U.S. and ROC observers feel that, under the TRA, the conduct of unofficial relations through AIT and CCNAA have been generally satisfactory, although problems do exist.

Taiwan now ranks as the United States' sixth largest trading partner. But in recent years the United States has experienced chronic trade deficits. In 1983, for example, the U.S. trade deficit was $6.7 billion, up $2.7 billion from 1982. In part, the dramatic increase was due to the quick economic recovery of both Taiwan and the United States from the world-wide recession of 1981-1982. But there were other causes as well. AIT is pressing for the removal of certain trade practices and regulations which present obstacles to U.S. exports. Taiwan is gradually removing these obstacles, and at the same time pledging to purchase from U.S. companies a majority of the components necessary to complete the island's new major project activity. The value of these large construction projects--including a subway system for Taipei, upgrading and expansion of CCK International Airport, construction of nuclear power plants 7 and 8, and major computer and energy related projects--is expected to reach $2.5 billion by 1989.

Counterfeiting of U.S. products by Taiwan's businessmen is another problem in U.S.-Taiwan relations. The negative image this practice has created for Taiwan in the United States has been recognized by Taipei and steps are being taken to correct the situation.

The most important problem in U.S.-Taiwan relations, however, centers on the Taiwan issue in U.S.-PRC relations. The United States has determined that its fundamental national interests are served by the preservation and advancement of its relations with China. The basic U.S. position, set forth in the 1972 Shanghai Communique, the 1979 joint communique establishing relations with the PRC, the Taiwan Relations Act, and the August 17, 1982 communique on arms sales to Taiwan, is as follows:

1. The United States recognizes the People's Republic of China as the sole legal government of China.

2. The United States acknowledges the Chinese position that Taiwan is part of China and states that the future of Taiwan is a matter for Chinese on both sides of the Taiwan Strait to decide.

> 3. The only U.S. interest is that the matter be decided by peaceful means.
>
> 4. At the same time, the United States remains committed to maintain the full range of unofficial contacts between the people of the United States and the people of Taiwan, as set forth in the TRA.

Not surprisingly, Taiwan is very concerned over U.S.-PRC relations and frequently complains that Washington sacrifices ROC interests in order to further relations with Beijing. A common perception in Taiwan is that U.S. officials do not know how to deal with the communists on the mainland. As one September 1983 editorial noted regarding Secretary of Defense Caspar Weinberger's attempts to get the Chinese to enter into a closer strategic relationship with the United States:

> We often feel that during negotiations, Western officials, who do things according to formal logic and accepted norms of international relations, are no match for the communists who are accustomed to using dialectical tactics at the negotiating table. We do not believe that in the present circumstances the Chinese Communists would change their so-called independent foreign policy of not allying with any particular big power or bloc of big powers. Firmly we do not believe that the Chinese Communist regime will join the anti-Soviet strategic group headed by the United States....[179]

During President Reagan's April 1984 trip to China, there was deep concern in Taiwan that the President had fallen prey to the illusion that the Chinese communists were actually good people and could be used against the Soviet Union. As government spokesmen James Soong said: "The biggest danger of President Reagan's visit is the perception that a good Communist can be used to check a bad Communist."[180]

As the remaining chapters in Part II demonstrate, there are several aspects of U.S. unofficial relations with Taiwan which anger authorities in Beijing. The most important of these include arms sales to Taiwan and

---

[179] Chung Kuo Shih Pao, September 30, 1983, in FBIS-China, October 5, 1983, p. V1.

[180] Washington Post, May 18, 1984, p. A18.

actions which seem to the PRC to reflect a "two-China" or "one China, one Taiwan" policy on the part of the United States.

Taipei is taking steps to balance the trade deficit with the United States and to stop counterfeiting. However, the government of the ROC firmly rejects the notion that Taiwan is an issue in Sino-American relations. The real issue, it claims, is whether China in the future will be free or communist. As Premier Sun told participants in the Eleventh Sino-American Conference on June 10, 1982:

> The Republic of China on Taiwan...does not constitute an issue. We believe the real issue is that of mainland China--the issue of whether the people there should forever continue to live under Communist rule. To the free world, the common issue we face is the "China issue"--the issue of preference for a strong and hostile Communist China or a peace-loving non-Communist China. If a non-Communist China is to be preferred, the free world should obviously allow the people on the two sides of the Taiwan Straits to make their own choice. In other words, we should leave the problem of China's future to the decision of the Chinese people as a whole.[181]

The government of the ROC maintains that since a successful model for a modern Chinese society has already been built on Taiwan, world attention should be focused not on whether Taiwan will unify with the mainland, but rather on the broader problem of how to persuade Beijing to adopt a developmental strategy along the lines of that proven on Taiwan.

Authorities on Taiwan recognize the importance of the United States to the island's security, economic prosperity, and continued participation in the international community. They emphasize, however, that Taiwan is important enough to justify being considered on its own merits, rather than always linked to U.S. and other countries' relations with the mainland. From the point of view of those living on the island, Taiwan has a right to exist as an international entity because of its population, size, role in international affairs, economic strength, relations with other countries, cultural and historical past, and political and social progress.

---

[181] The text of Premier Sun's remarks can be found in "The China Issue and China's Reunification" (Taipei: Government Information Office, 1982).

To a certain extent, Taiwan's importance to the United States has been recognized in the Taiwan Relations Act. In the TRA U.S. political, security, and economic interests are tied to peace and stability in the region. The document also expresses the interest of the United States in human rights on Taiwan and in any threats which might arise to the security or the social or economic system of the people of Taiwan. The fact that Taiwan is the sixth largest trading partner of the United States and that over $6 billion in U.S. equity and loan investments are located on the island enhances Taiwan's value to American citizens. An intangible but important value of Taiwan to the United States is its role model for developing nations. Taiwan's land reform program, free enterprise economic system, equitable distribution of wealth, and now its positive political evolution--all prove to the Third World that the way of freedom is superior to collectivist or totalitarian approaches to national development.

What the people of Taiwan want most from the United States is time and opportunity to prove the superiority of their system over that of the communists on the mainland. Taiwan wants continued U.S. support through the sale of defensive weapons and through the championing of Taipei's right to participate in international organizations. The sale of arms is important both for security reasons and for the psychological confidence such tangible expressions of American concern bring to the people of Taiwan. U.S. support of Taiwan's right to participate in international events and forums boosts morale on the island and allows the long-term processes now underway on both Taiwan and the mainland to evolve naturally to the place where a resolution of their differences can occur.

6.6   THE IMPORTANCE OF TAIWAN

A great deal of controversy has arisen over the importance of Taiwan. In the United States, for example, various scholars and government officials have viewed Taiwan as being either vital to the defense of the Western Pacific region or of no consequence to the region's defense. The following discussion outlines the various levels of value which could be placed on Taiwan by the principal governments involved with the island's future.

In a strategic sense, Taiwan's value stems from the fact that it sits astride two of the most important sea lanes in the Western Pacific: the Bashi Channel between Taiwan and the Philippines and the Taiwan Strait, separating the island of Taiwan from the mainland.

Taiwan is also the largest island in the Western Pacific between Japan and the Philippines. Its position could be used effectively by a major power in a number of ways, including:

   --interdiction of the sea lanes connecting Japan with Southeast Asia and the Middle East

   --use of the threat of interdiction to gain concessions from Japan or influence Tokyo's foreign policy

   --projection of force against the Chinese mainland

   --projection of air and naval force into the open Pacific

   --projection of force into Northeast or Southeast Asia

   --monitoring or disruption of superpower air and naval transits between Northeast and Southeast Asia

From the point of view of the United States, Taiwan is best suited as a strategic basing area for strikes against mainland China. Since China is no longer considered an enemy, Taiwan's strategic value to the United States has diminished considerably since the Vietnam War. However, the prevailing U.S. perception of Taiwan's strategic value rests on several assumptions which, if changed, would alter the U.S. view. These include continued access to bases in Japan and the Philippines, the absence of conflict in the region, and a friendly China.

But the most important reason American analysts downgrade the strategic value of Taiwan is that the island is currently controlled by a friendly government eager to cooperate with the United States. If Taiwan were controlled or used by a major hostile power, the island's bases and strategic position would be of major concern to U.S. planners.

From the perspective of the Soviet Union, Taiwan's strategic value is also minimal at present. Numerous Soviet air and naval patrols pass close to Taiwan. In 1981-1982, for example, there were 127 Soviet naval ships transiting the eastern and western waters adjacent to Taiwan. In 1981 there were 45 TU-95 sorties and 142 IL-62 sorties, while in 1982 there were 41 TU-95 sorties and 170 IL-62 sorties passing through Taiwan's air identification zone. But since Taiwan is not permitted to play a role in western security plans, Moscow has little to fear from Taiwan's armed forces.

The Soviet Union also recognizes the importance of Taiwan to Beijing. While Sino-Soviet rapprochement remains a possibility, Moscow is highly unlikely to attempt to woe Taipei. The strategic value of the island in countering both China and U.S. forces in East Asia is obvious to the Soviets, however. Moscow will probably keep its options open in regards to future use of the island should relations with the PRC deteriorate significantly, or should Taiwan's authorities reach out in desperation for Soviet assistance in order to survive.

In the past Japan has defined the importance of Taiwan second only to that of South Korea in terms of its national security. As long as Taiwan remains in friendly hands and Sino-Japanese relations are progressing smoothly, Tokyo will remain quiet on the Taiwan issue. Nonetheless, geographic realities and sizable Japanese investments on Taiwan cannot be ignored. Japan will continue to have a major interest in who controls the island.

Taiwan plays a rather minor strategic role from the perspective of ASEAN. However, the Taiwan issue has become important symbolically to these nations--as it has to South Korea--because it is a weather vane of U.S. commitments to its friends in the Western Pacific region. Moreover, PRC actions toward Taiwan are seen as signals of China's peaceful or hostile intentions toward Southeast Asia. In case of conflict or a major shift in Taiwan's foreign policy, ASEAN's concerns would become more visible. Southeast Asia has not forgotten that the island of Taiwan played a vital role in the Japanese invasion of the region during the Second World War.

There is little doubt about the strategic importance of Taiwan to both Taipei and Beijing. From the Chinese point of view, Taiwan is part of the territory of China. Further, it is the gateway to the Pacific, an island which must be secured if China in the future is to maintain a blue water fleet and play a major maritime role in East Asia. Above all, Taiwan must be kept out of the hands of the superpowers, either of whose presence on the island would constitute a direct threat to the mainland. The Chinese on both sides of the Strait are also aware of the importance of the island in terms of China's relations with Japan. Taiwan blocks Japanese southern expansion and conveniently places China in a strong bargaining position with Tokyo should the need arise in the future.

To the Nationalist on Taiwan the island is vital to the continued existence of the Republic of China, the Kuomintang, and the hope of Chinese everywhere that China's future will not be under the yoke of communism.

In February 1983 Premier Sun Yun-suan spoke of Taiwan's strategic value from the perspective of the ROC:

> Taiwan Province of the Republic of China is strategically very important. It is a vital link in the island defense chain in the Western Pacific. It controls the Taiwan Straits and the Bashi Channel. It is the pivot between Northeast Asia and Southeast Asia. It sits astride the transportation lanes for vital commodities--in peacetime as well as in wartime. It is a major outpost for the free world and the United States in countering the expansionism of the Russian navy in the Western Pacific. For such major reasons, we have frequently pointed out that both the ROC and the U.S. will benefit if they can stick together, and that both of them will suffer if they stand apart.[182]

Taiwan also has political value to governments dealing with the PRC. Those wishing to antagonize Beijing can make gestures of support to Taiwan. Those wanting to improve relations with the PRC have but to distance themselves from Taipei to gain an appreciative nod from mainland China. The United States, Japan, the Soviet Union, South Korea, ASEAN, Australia, Western European countries, and other nations have at one time or another used Beijing's sensitivity over Taiwan to signal either approval of or alienation from PRC policies. Taiwan's role in this form of international communication will likely continue until the reunification issue is resolved.

Taiwan's political importance is more substantive to the Chinese. Like most cultures, China stresses the principle that there should be but one emperor under heaven. Conflicting claims between two or more rival governments for the right to rule all of China have been frequent historically, but never tolerated if one of the contenders could muster the force or subtlety necessary to overcome its competitors. Invariably, the use of arms has been the deciding factor in who would rule the Middle Kingdom. In many respects the conflict today between the communists in Beijing and the Nationalists in Taipei is similar to the great struggles of the past between rival factions seeking to gain ascendency over China. The CPC must establish control over Taiwan and eliminate the KMT as a rival for national power if the communists are ever to be able to claim true legitimacy

---

[182] Free China Review, 33, 3 (March 1983), p. 5.

in the eyes of the Chinese people. The KMT, on the other hand, must achieve victory over the communists if it is to retain its claim of representing the country. Given their fundamental ideological differences, it will be difficult for either party to give up its efforts to overcome the other.

The fact that the current generation of leaders in both Chinese governments played important roles in the bitter civil war on the mainland adds yet another dimension to this political problem. Senior leaders in Taipei and Beijing want to be remembered in Chinese history as having completed the great task of national reunification or, failing that, at least having been true to their principles to the very end. Family honor and the judgment of history rests upon their shoulders in a way little understood in the West, but highly influencial in the Chinese context.

Another dimension of the political competition between the two Chinese governments involves the Overseas Chinese community. Both Taipei and Beijing appeal to Chinese nationalism and national interests to plead their cases. Both expect tokens of support from the Overseas Chinese in the form of visits, contributions to family members still living on the mainland or on Taiwan, membership in pro-PRC or pro-ROC Chinese associations, and--from those with exceptional talent and skills--periodic returns to the China of their choice for professional contributions to national development.

In terms of domestic politics, the existence of a rival Chinese government offers a rallying point for factions critical of those in power. Every Chinese administrator, as a basic requirement for survival, must be able to demonstrate how he has advanced the cause of his government over that of its rival. Leaders in Beijing and Taipei are severely limited as to how far they can go in offering conditions of reconciliation to the other. Because of its superior national power, the PRC has a tremendous advantage in this respect and has been able to offer more generous and reasonable sounding proposals for reunification than the ROC. Nonetheless, the basic issues of which government is the central government and which system is the national system defy easy compromise.

Both China and Taiwan spend a tremendous amount of resources countering the other's propaganda and trying to eliminate subversive elements. Ideological purity is a virtue highly extolled by Chinese governments. Taipei has more to fear from subversion than Beijing. But the communist leaders do not dismiss the latent threat the Nationalists pose to their rule. Perhaps most troubling to the CPC is the prospect of the KMT coming to the aid of one or more domestic factions battling the central communist government in time of turmoil. Western observers tend to dismiss such speculation, but from the Chinese perspective history has proven conclusively that no government is safe from natural or manmade disaster.

Economically and culturally, Taiwan is also very important to the Chinese. Taiwan is one of the world's outstanding examples of democracy and free enterprise at work within a developing society. This lesson has not been lost to Chinese on the mainland. The question confronting the CPC leadership is not whether to emulate Taiwan's economic system, but rather to what degree it can be duplicated without placing at risk socialism in the PRC. Culturally, the ROC on Taiwan has attempted to preserve the rich heritage of China's past. This stands in marked contrast with earlier periods of communist rule in which ancient Chinese treasures and customs were systemically destroyed. Until recently, Overseas Chinese came to Taiwan, not the mainland, to enjoy true Chinese culture.

But perhaps the greatest importance of Taiwan from an historical sense is the success the island has had in modernizing without westernizing. For over 150 years the mainland has attempted to solve this fundamental problem. Under the Four Modernizations, Beijing has come face-to-face with the difficulties inherent in lifting China into the twentieth century through western techniques, but at the same time preserving a Chinese sense of identity. The lessons Taiwan has learned in this endeavor since the end of World War Two and the skills acquired by the managers of the island's transformation into a developed nation are badly needed by China. Far-sighted statesmen in both Taipei and Beijing will not lightly sacrifice these assets which can contribute to China's future greatness.

7
The Security of Taiwan

Fundamental to improved U.S.-PRC relations has been the perception in the United States that China would not utilize force against Taiwan and that should Beijing change its peaceful policy, Washington would be able to respond quickly enough to prevent the island from being overrun. This perception has been reinforced by a series of threat assessments made by concerned U.S. agencies. The assessments, generally composed of an evaluation of China's military capabilities and political intentions, have concluded that Beijing will not attack Taiwan in the foreseeable future. Typical of the conclusions reached in the official assessments were the remarks of Assistant Secretary of State John Holdridge in March 1982, when he told members of Congress:

> Tensions in the Taiwan Strait are at a 30-year low. We are quite certain that Taiwan is under no imminent threat of attack, and we believe we would have considerable lead-time--perhaps as much as five years--if there should be a shift in Beijing's intentions.[183]

It is important to note, however, that official U.S. assessments of the threat posed by the PRC to Taiwan have tended to emphasize the intentions side of the threat assessment equation, not military capabilities. Since outside evaluations of intentions are highly subjective and easily changed, most

---

[183] U.S. House of Representatives, Committee on Appropriations, Subcommittee on Foreign Operations, Foreign Assistance and Related Programs, Appropriations for 1983, Part 4, 97th Cong., 2d sess. (1982), p. 326.

assessments of threats to national security focus on capabilities. Attempts by U.S. agencies to stress the PRC's intentions and to minimize its military capabilities may, therefore, be politically motivated in order to smooth the development of U.S.-China relations.

7.1   PRC MILITARY THREAT

As Table 7 demonstrates, a comparison of the total military capabilities of the PRC and Taiwan shows an overwhelming superiority on the part of the mainland.[184] In several categories--all strategic nuclear forces, submarine chasers, naval bombers and fighters, and air force bombers--China has a total monopoly. In other key areas--total armed forces, total troops, infantry divisions, total naval personnel, submarines, fast attack craft, air force personnel, total combat aircraft, and fighters/interceptors--the PRC has a 10:1 advantage over Taiwan. Fairly close numbers can be found for frigates, patrol escorts, minesweepers, and fighters than can operate in a ground attack mode. Taipei is superior to Beijing in only one category: destroyers. Clearly, in any all-out conflict between the two Chinese governments, Taiwan would be defeated. The cost to the PRC, however, would likely be very substantial.[185]

The probability of such a full-scale conflict is small, however, because of the political nature of the Chinese disagreement, Beijing's need to deploy a large percentage of its armed forces along the Sino-Soviet and Sino-Vietnamese borders, and the possibility of U.S. intervention on the side of Taiwan. What is of more immediate concern in the assessment, therefore, must be the order of battle of forces located on Taiwan and in

---

[184]   See The Military Balance, 1982-1983 (London: International Institute of Strategic Studies, 1982), pp. 78-81; 94.

[185]   Perhaps the best assessment of the PRC threat to Taiwan is Edwin K. Snyder, A. James Gregor, and Maria Hsia Chang, The Taiwan Relations Act and the Defense of the Republic of China (Berkeley, CA: University of California, Institute of International Studies, 1980). See also Martin L. Lasater, Taiwan: Facing Mounting Threats (Washington, D.C.: The Heritage Foundation, 1984); and Martin L. Lasater, The Security of Taiwan: Unraveling the Dilemma (Washington, D.C.: Georgetown University, CSIS, 1982).

TABLE 7

PRC-ROC Military Forces

	PRC	ROC
Population	1,024,890,000	18,200,000
Total regular forces	4,000,000	464,000
Nuclear forces		
ICBM	4+	none
IRBM	60+	none
MRBM	50+	none
Army		
Total troops	3,250,000	310,000
Armored divisions	12	2
Infantry divisions	119	22
Navy		
Total men	360,000	38,000 plus 39,000 marines
Submarines	103 conventional 2 nuclear; 1 nuclear w/SLBM	2 conventional ASW plus 2 on order
Destroyers	10 w/Styx SSM	23 (9 w/ASROC; 5 w/ Gabriel SSM) + 1 on order
Frigates	29 (16 w/SSM)	9
Large patrol ships	8	5
Missile craft	230 w/SSM	49 w/SSM
Coastal craft	709	23
Submarine chasers	88	none
Minesweepers	23	14
Large landing ships	61	29
Amphibious types	449	21
Naval Air Force		
Bombers	150	none
Fighters	600	none
Air Force		
Total men	490,000	77,000
Total aircraft	5,300	485
Bombers	700	none
Fighter/bombers	500	422
Fighter/intercept.	4,000	19
Reconnaissance	130	44

the military regions opposite Taiwan. These regions are Guangzhou, Fuzhou, and Nanking.

Table 8 lists the ground forces available to both sides in the Taiwan Strait region.

TABLE 8

Main Ground Forces

	PRC	Taiwan
Personnel	535,000	340,000
Infantry Divisions	24	22
Armored Vehicles	2,150	2,350
(tanks)	(1,700)	(2,000)
Rocket Launchers	1,000	100
Artillery	1,450	1,750
Antitank Guns	1,450	2,300

    Estimates of the number of divisions required to successfully invade Taiwan range upward of 40 or more. In hearings prior to the enactment of the Taiwan Relations Act, the Senate Foreign Relations Committee was told that during WWII it had been estimated that 300,000 American troops would be required to defeat the 32,000 Japanese soldiers on Taiwan.[186] Given the fact that PRC and ROC ground forces are in rough parity in the Taiwan Strait region, there is little likelihood of an invasion attempt by Beijing in the foreseeable future. Any movement of troops large enough to constitute an invasion threat would be perceived by U.S. and ROC intelligence, giving Washington and Taipei ample opportunity to coordinate an adequate response.

    A less reassuring assessment emerges in terms of China's naval threat to Taiwan. As Table 9 shows, Taiwan is at a severe disadvantage in the key categories of submarines, missile craft, and coastal craft. The PRC's advantage could be quickly increased by reinforcements from the North Sea and South Sea fleets.

    The naval threat to Taiwan can be divided into three components: surface fighting ships, submarines, and amphibious invasion. The area of least concern to Taiwan is a PRC amphibious invasion, although improvements in this category are being made through the training of additional Marine-type units, the acquisition of surface-skim craft, and the introduction of helicopters in amphibious operations. It has been estimated that PRC naval vessels, plus motorized junks,

---

[186] "Legislative History, P.L. 96-8" (Taiwan Relations Act), U.S. Code Congressional & Administrative News, No. 4 (June 1979), 96th Cong., 1st sess., p. 661.

TABLE 9

Large Naval Vessels

	PRC East Sea Fleet	Taiwan
Submarines	40	2
Destroyers	2	23
Frigates	16	9
Patrol Ships	5	5
Missile Craft	90	49
Coastal Craft	290	23

would be able to transport 100,000-150,000 troops to Taiwan at any given time.[187]

ROC naval officers are concerned about the PRC surface fleet, particularly the many smaller, missile equipped vessels which would pose a formidable threat to Taiwan's larger, slower and more vulnerable destroyers. Since neither navy is equipped with adequate electronic countermeasures, and the missiles utilized by the two sides (the Russian-style Styx on the part of the PRC and Israeli-style Gabriel on the part of Taiwan) are roughly equivalent in range, an exchange between the surface fleets would likely be determined by the number of ships and missiles brought into play. In this equation, Taiwan is at a distinct disadvantage.

An even greater threat to Taiwan is posed by Beijing's numerous submarines. Only 9 of the 12 "Gearing"-type destroyers in the ROC navy have been equipped with anti-submarine rockets (ASROC); the remainder are armed with anti-submarine torpedoes of approximately the same range as the torpedoes carried by China's submarines. Taiwan's anti-submarine warfare (ASW) capabilities are being upgraded on a priority basis, but, as World War Two demonstrated, a large submarine fleet can wreak havoc on an island economy such as Taiwan's.

The submarine threat to Taiwan is serious. Taiwan's economy is totally dependent upon trade. If that trade could be cut for a number of months, or even substantially reduced, the island might be brought to its knees. Adding to Taiwan's vulnerability in this respect is the fact that over two-thirds of the island's trade goes through the ports of Kaohsiung and Taichung.

---

[187] <u>Ibid</u>.

Both of these ports face the Taiwan Strait and are vulnerable to a PRC blockade. Taiwan's other ports--Keelung, Hualien, and Suao--are more protected, but they would have great difficulty handling the volume of imports necessary to sustain the island during a blockade.

Some analysts feel that Beijing could effectively impose a blockade on Taiwan merely by claiming that one was in effect. Shipping companies serving Taiwan would immediately face a prohibitively high increase in insurance rates. The possibility of loss of ship, cargo, and crew would be sufficient to deter many international carriers regularly visiting Taiwan. Taiwan's own flag carriers are not sufficient to take up the slack at this time.

Reinforcing the naval threat to Taiwan is the air threat to the island. Whichever side controls the airspace over the Taiwan Strait dominates the seas in the region as well. Table 10 provides an estimate of the operational aircraft within 600 nautical miles of Taiwan.

TABLE 10

Air Forces

	PRC	Taiwan
Bombers	215	0
Fighter-bombers	100	0
Fighters	1,100	370
Reconnaissance	60	5

ROC sources report that within 750 nautical miles of Taiwan the PRC has deployed 358 bombers, 2,855 fighters, 410 transport planes, 209 helicopters, and 134 other military planes. Adding to the threat is the fact that additional air reinforcements can be flown in on short notice. A large number of PRC bases are within 250 nautical miles of Taiwan, or five to seven minutes flying time. These bases have been pre-stocked with fuel, spare parts, and munitions, and are maintained in a high state of readiness. The number of planes presently stationed there, however, is relatively small.

Taipei sees as one of its main military threats a multiphased PRC attack designed to exploit China's quantitative advantages and to nullify Taiwan's qualitative advantages. Waves of fighters and fighter-escorted light bombers would be timed to overburden the constantly recycling ROC fighter force. Although Taiwan expects a high win ratio in air-to-air combat in its favor, attacks against ROC airfields and the loss of aircraft, crews, and munitions would eventually exhaust Taiwan's inventory. At this point, the PRC would dominate the Taiwan Strait and airspace over Taiwan itself, and would be in a position to decimate Taiwan's surface navy, to bomb key installations or population centers, or to prepare for an invasion.

The above threats apply to the main island of Taiwan. It goes without saying that Kinmen and Matsu, because of their proximity to the mainland, would be even more vulnerable to air and sea attack, amphibious invasion, or blockade.

In terms of present military capabilities, therefore, Beijing could use force against Taiwan with a high probability of success in a number of scenarios. Because of its large quantitative superiority in terms of fighters, bombers, surface missile boats, and submarines, the PRC could attack the offshore islands, overwhelm ROC air and naval forces, or enforce a blockade of Taiwan itself. An invasion of Taiwan or the offshore islands might be prohibitively expensive, but such an invasion might not be necessary to bring Taipei to the negotiation table on PRC terms. In addition to the conventional threat scenarios, there is growing concern in Taipei that the PRC may use medium-ranged missiles with high-explosive warheads to attack the island's five airfields, two principal ports, and selected beaches before deploying its air, naval, and amphibious forces.

The military threat to Taiwan will likely increase in the future. Contributing to this assessment are the following factors: (1) the PRC has determined that the modernization of the PLA is a national priority; (2) China, because of its larger defense industry and budget, is able to outproduce Taiwan in terms of both weapons quantity and quality; and (3) Beijing is being given access to advanced weapons and technology from the West, whereas Taiwan faces a dwindling supply of sources because of the concern of other nations that such transfers would damage relations with the PRC.[188]

---

[188] See Martin L. Lasater, "The PRC's Force Modernization: Shadow Over Taiwan and U.S. Policy," Strategic Review, 12, 1 (Winter 1984), pp. 51-65.

To meet the current and foreseeable threat, Taiwan is emphasizing three defense priorities. As stated by Premier Sun in February 1984, these are:

-- improve the psychological preparedness of the military officers and men

-- pursue a strategy of "strategically long-drawn and tactically quick-ending," by increasing our firepower but reducing our manpower requirement through the "elite forces" policy

-- develop national defense science and technology in order to strengthen the "independent and self-sufficient defense system."[189]

Perhaps the most important efforts by Taiwan to increase its military strength are to purchase advanced weapons from abroad and to build sophisticated arms domestically. Significant progress--and problems--are being met in both endeavors.

The United States is the source of about 90% of all arms purchased by Taiwan. Since the signing of the August 17, 1982 U.S.-PRC joint communique on arms sales to Taiwan, the quantitative and qualitative levels of weapons sold to Taipei have been sufficiently high to enable the ROC to proceed with its force modernization program. However, two key weapons systems are presently denied Taiwan by the United States: the Harpoon anti-ship missile, and an advanced replacement fighter for the F-5E, Taiwan's principal interceptor. There is adequate technical justification for the sale of both systems to Taiwan, but political considerations--Beijing's anticipated reaction--have prevented the sales from being consummated.

Taiwan needs the Harpoon because of the PRC's vast numerical advantage in missile boats and other surface vessels which can be deployed in the Taiwan Strait. A more advanced fighter is required because of China's 10:1 numerical superiority in the air and because the PRC is introducing a more advanced fighter of its own.

Taiwan has suffered setbacks in the acquisition of advanced weapons from sources other than the United States. The Dutch government, which previously had agreed to sell Taiwan two conventionally powered submarines, announced in December 1983 that it would not permit Taiwan to purchase four additional submarines on

---

[189] *China Post*, February 25, 1984, p. 2.

the grounds that China was too important to offend a second time.[190]

Because of the difficulty in acquiring advanced weapons from abroad, Taiwan determined in 1982 to move forward in the design and production of its own sophisticated arms. The most important of these is an advanced fighter, presently being built on the island with the assistance of foreign contractors. Although the ROC has committed more than $1 billion to the production of this aircraft, it probably will not be deployed until after 1990. Taiwan is experiencing difficulties in achieving certain technological breakthroughs necessary to make the plane capable of countering China's MiG-23 and MiG-25 threats. Moreover, many of the key components such as engines, radar, avionics, and missile guidance systems must be obtained abroad on an item-by-item basis. The integration of these various components is a difficult, expensive task.

7.2 PRC INTENTIONS

The political intentions of the PRC toward Taiwan are clear: Beijing intends to establish control over the island at some time in the future. How and when are tactical decisions based upon several considerations. One of the most important of these is Taipei's response to China's proposals for reunification.

PRC policy toward Taiwan has varied between intense hostility and generous proposals for reunification subject to almost any condition Taipei would ask. The last ten years have seen two distinct periods. From 1975 to 1979, the PRC advocated the "liberation" of Taiwan, at times strongly implying the use of force to accomplish that objective. Since the normalization of U.S.-PRC relations, however, Beijing has stressed the return of Taiwan to "the embrace of the motherland" through various peaceful methods of reunification. A brief review of PRC statements since 1975 will illustrate the essentially tactical nature of Beijing's approach to reunification.

In January 1975, for example, Zhou Enlai told the Fourth National Party Congress: "We are determined to liberate Taiwan. Fellow-countrymen in Taiwan and people of the whole country, unite and work together to achieve the noble aim of liberating Taiwan and unifying the motherland."[191] In September Deng Xiaoping said: "We

---

[190] See _Xinhua_, December 29, 1983, in _FBIS-China_, December 29, 1983, p. G1.

are determined to liberate Taiwan and accomplish the great cause of reunifying our motherland."[192]

In 1976 officials called for "the defense of our great socialist motherland and the liberation of our sacred territory of Taiwan province."[193] In June 1976 People's Daily editorialized:

> Taiwan Province is a sacred territory of the People's Republic of China. The people there are our kith and kin. The liberation of Taiwan is China's internal affair which nobody has the right to interfere with. We will liberate Taiwan because this is the common desire and sacred duty of the people of all nationalities of our country. All schemes hatched to create "two Chinas," "one China, one Taiwan" or "one China, two governments" will be doomed to failure.[194]

Similar themes were voiced by Chinese officials during the period of Hua Guofeng's leadership in 1977. Wei Guoqing told a rally in Canton in June 1977: "We will be able to race against time and the enemy and work as quickly as possible, do a good job of preparing against an aggressive war and be prepared to liberate Taiwan at any time."[195] In September Huang Hua stated at the United Nations: "Taiwan is China's sacred territory. The Chinese people are determined to liberate Taiwan and accomplish the great undertaking of unifying our motherland. When and how to liberate Taiwan is entirely China's internal affair, which brooks no foreign interference whatsoever."[196]

In March 1978 Hua Guofeng told the Fifth National Party Congress: "The Chinese People's Liberation Army must make all the preparations necessary for the liberation of Taiwan. We are determined to realize the

---

[191] New China News Agency (NCNA), January 20, 1975, in FBIS-China, January 20, 1975, p. D26.

[192] NCNA, September 20, 1975, in FBIS-China, October 2, 1975, p. D2.

[193] Li Zhimin, NCNA, April 10, 1976.

[194] FBIS-China, June 26, 1976, p. A12.

[195] FBIS-China, June 8, 1977, p. H10.

[196] NCNA, September 29, 1977, in FBIS-China, September 30, 1977, p. A10.

behest of Chairman Mao and Premier Zhou and, together with our Taiwan compatriots, accomplish the sacred task of liberating Taiwan and unifying the motherland."[197] In September Vice Premier Li Xiannian told a visiting Japanese Sokagakki delegation: "Whether by peaceable means or by force, we must consider the liberation of Taiwan from an overall strategic standpoint."[198]

A major change in PRC rhetoric occurred just prior to the normalization of relations with the United States. Chinese statements dropped references to the "liberation" of Taiwan and adopted a much softer appeal. On December 16, 1978, Hua Guofeng said: "It is the common desire of the people of China, our Taiwan compatriots included, that Taiwan should return to the embrace of the motherland and the country be reunited."[199]

7.2.1 Beijing's Peaceful Offensive

The December 1978 period marked the beginning of a series of "peaceful" initiatives by the PRC. The objective of the new tactic was to bring Taiwan to the negotiating table through two interrelated appeals: first, to Taiwan's authorities by convincing them that Beijing was sincere in wanting to reunite peacefully under mutually acceptable conditions; second, to the United States and other countries by making Taiwan appear unreasonable in its continued refusal to negotiate. The latter would hopefully result in increased isolation for Taiwan and added pressure on its authorities to agree to talks with Beijing. The New Year's Day Message to Taiwan Compatriots on January 1, 1979, laid the foundation for China's new approach. The message said:

> It is our fervent hope that Taiwan returns to the embrace of the motherland at an early date so that we can work together for the great cause of national development....The responsibility for reunifying the motherland

---

[197] NCNA, March 6, 1978, in FBIS-China, March 7, 1978, p. D31.

[198] Kyodo, September 19, 1978, in FBIS-China, September 19, 1978, p. A1.

[199] NCNA, December 16, 1978, in FBIS-China, December 18, 1978, p. A5.

rests with each of us. We hope the Taiwan
authorities will place national interests
paramount and make valuable contributions to
the reunification of the motherland.[200]

The Message suggested that Taiwan and the mainland arrange for mutual visits and tours, establish postal and transportation services, set up various academic and cultural exchanges, and open up trade. On the same day of the Message's release, Beijing announced that it was ceasing the alternate day shelling of Kinmen "in order to convenience civilians and armymen on Taiwan, Penghu, Jinmen and Mazu islands who wish to visit their relatives and friends and make tours on the mainland and to facilitate shipping and production activities in the Taiwan Straits."[201]

Despite the change in tone, the threat of the use of force remained. Several statements were made by PRC officials during this period which implied that Beijing's peaceful approach to reunification had its limits. In January 1979 Deng Xiaoping told a U.S. Senate delegation led by Senator Sam Dunn that Beijing would consider the use of force against Taiwan if its authorities refused indefinitely to enter into negotiations or if there were an "attempt by the Soviet Union to interfere in Taiwanese affairs."[202] In referring to Taiwan, Deng told another congressman a few days later, "the Chinese people are very patient but their patience is not limitless."[203] Deng Xiaoping told Hedley Donovan of *Time* magazine that "ten years is too long a time" to wait for reunification.[204] In May 1979 Liao Chengzhi told a press conference:

We will strive for a settlement of the Taiwan
question through peaceful means. But, if some
countries arm Taiwan in their own interests,
and make the Taiwan authorities become
self-conceited and disregard the common wish

---

[200] NCNA, December 31, 1978, in FBIS-China, January 2, 1979, p. E1.

[201] NCNA, December 31, 1978, in FBIS-China, January 2, 1979, p. E8.

[202] AFP, January 9, 1979, in FBIS-China, January 9, 1979, p. A4.

[203] Yomiuri Shimbun, January 15, 1979, in FBIS-China, January 18, 1979, p. B2.

[204] Washington Star, January 29, 1979, p. 1.

of the entire Chinese people, then we cannot assure definitely not to use means other than peaceful ones.[205]

In June Liao said in Nagasaki:

> We hope to solve the Taiwan question by peaceful means. But, if anyone should arm Taiwan with guns and artillery and cause the Taiwan authorities to feel a parochial arrogance and blatantly ignore the common aspiration of all the Chinese people for the return of Taiwan to the motherland, then we cannot guarantee that we shall not take other than peaceful ways.[206]

Threats to use force against Taiwan if ROC authorities do not negotiate have been frequently reiterated. Beijing Review in January 1981, for example, said: "If we are driven by the Taiwan authorities' adament refusal to resort to non-peaceful means to solve the issue, that is entirely China's internal affair which the United States has no right to meddle in."[207]

7.2.2 Ye Jianying's Nine-Point Proposal

Despite these warnings, Beijing's peace proposals have gained international recognition. The most widely acclaimed was that offered by Ye Jianying on September 30, 1981. The "Nine-Points" of Ye Jianying were:

> (1) In order to bring an end to the unfortunate separation of the Chinese nation as early as possible, we propose that talks be held between the Communist Party of China and the Kuomintang of China on a reciprocal basis so that the two parties will cooperate for the third time to accomplish the great cause of national reunification. The two sides may first send people to meet for an exhaustive

---

[205] Xinhua May 21, 1979, in FBIS-China, May 24, 1979, p. D8.

[206] Xinhua, June 5, 1979, in FBIS-China, June 6, 1979, p. D2.

[207] Beijing Review, January 12, 1981, p. 9.

exchange of views.

(2) It is the urgent desire of the people of all nationalities on both sides of the Straits to communicate with each other, reunite with their relatives, develop trade and increase mutual understanding. We propose that the two sides make arrangements to facilitate the exchange of mails, trade, air and shipping services, and visits by relatives and tourists as well as academic, cultural and sports exchanges, and reach an agreement thereupon.

(3) After the country is reunited, Taiwan can enjoy a high degree of autonomy as a special administrative region and it can retain its armed forces. The Central Government will not interfere with local affairs on Taiwan.

(4) Taiwan's current socio-economic system will remain unchanged, so will its way of life and its economic and cultural relations with foreign countries. There will be no encroachment on the proprietary rights and lawful right of inheritance over private property, houses, land and enterprises, or on foreign investments.

(5) People in authority and representative personages of various circles in Taiwan may take up posts of leadership in national political bodies and participate in running the state.

(6) When Taiwan's local finance is in difficulty, the Central Government may subsidize it as is fit for the circumstances.

(7) For people of all nationalities and public figures of various circles in Taiwan who wish to come and settle on the mainland, it is guaranteed that proper arrangements will be made for them, that there will be no discrimination against them, and that they will have the freedom of entry and exit.

(8) Industrialists and businessmen in Taiwan are welcome to invest and engage in various economic undertakings on the mainland, and their legal rights, interests and profits are guaranteed.

(9) The reunification of the motherland is the responsibility of all Chinese. We sincerely welcome people of all nationalities, public figures of all circles and mass organizations in Taiwan to make proposals and suggestions regarding affairs of state through various channels and in various ways. Taiwan's return to the embrace of the motherland and the accomplishment of the great cause of national reunification is a great and glorious mission history has bequeathed on our generation. China's reunification and prosperity is in the vital interest of the Chinese people of all nationalities--not only those on the mainland, but those in Taiwan as well. It is also in the interest of peace in the Far East and the world. We hope that our compatriots in Taiwan will give full play to their patriotism and work energetically for the early realization of the great unity of our nation and share the honor of it. We hope that our compatriots in Hong Kong and Macao and Chinese nationals residing abroad will continue to act in the role of a bridge and contribute their share to the reunification of the motherland. We hope that the Kuomintang authorities will stick to their one-China position and their opposition to "two Chinas" and that they will put national interests above everything else, forget previous ill will and join hands with us in accomplishing the great cause of national reunification and the great goal of making China prosperous and strong, so as to win glory for our ancestors, bring benefit to our posterity and write a new and glorious page in the history of the Chinese nation."[208]

Ranking PRC leaders made it clear that Ye's statement was the most comprehensive and important proposal on reunification to date. The next day, Zhao Ziyang told visiting Italian officials that Ye's series of proposals were "the most important moves in that direction in the past two years."[209] A short time later, Deng called the proposal "a fair and reasonable

---

[208] Ye's Jianying's statement occurred in an interview with <u>Xinhua</u> on September 30, 1981. It can be found in <u>FBIS-China</u>, September 30, 1981, p. U1.

[209] <u>Ansa</u>, October 1, 1981, in <u>FBIS-China</u>, October 2, 1981, p. G2.

principle and policy concerning the return of Taiwan to the motherland and the realization of China's peaceful reunification that we have put forward in the light of the actual situation."[210]

7.2.3 Taiwan's Rejection of the Nine-Point Plan

Ye's proposals were rejected outright by Taipei because of the underlying assumption that the ROC government was, at most, a regional as opposed to a national government. The following point-by-point rebuttal of the PRC's proposal was made by Taiwan officials:

> (1) The problem is not talks but two different ways of life. The Republic of China wants China to be united under a system which is free, democratic and in the interests of the people. Unification under Communism is forever unacceptable. Peaceful unification under conditions of freedom is the common will of the Chinese people everywhere. Moreover, previous talks between the KMT and CPC have resulted in communist treachery; the communists seek to gain through negotiations what they cannot gain on the battlefield.
>
> (2) Peking is proposing the free exchange of mail, trade, visits, and services when these do not exist on the mainland. How can they offer Taiwan--which already enjoys these things--what the communists deny their own people? In essence, there is little that Taiwan would gain from these arrangements.
>
> (3) Not only are the communists refusing to acknowledge the legitimacy of the Republic of China, but they are proposing that Taiwan retain "a high degree of autonomy as a special administrative region." As shown in the case of Tibet, where Peking offered similar promises but later brutally imposed communism, the autonomy offered by the PRC is worthless. Besides, Taiwan currently enjoys freedom and has its own armed forces. The proposal gives the ROC nothing but takes away what it already has.

---

[210] Xinhua, October 2, 1981, in FBIS-China, October 5, 1981, p. G2.

(4) A similar argument is made here. Why should Taiwan take the chance that its social-economic structure will be left intact under the communists? To think that Peking would not eventually impose socialism on the island is naive. When that occurs, the high standard of living enjoyed by the people on Taiwan will be lost. It is far better that Taiwan prosper to demonstrate valid methods of modernization which one day can be applied to development on the mainland.

(5) It is unrealistic to expect that leaders of a democratic system such as that which exists on Taiwan could effectively function in a communist state where policy is dominated by those following Marxism-Leninism. Any posts given to current ROC leaders would be ceremonial at best.

(6) Taiwan doesn't need Peking's economic assistance. In truth, the communist leaders would like to share in Taiwan's economic prosperity.

(7) Again, it is unrealistic to expect that Peking will offer the people of Taiwan rights and privileges which are not enjoyed by the people on the mainland. Freedom of movement would have catastrophic results within the system of control on the mainland; it cannot be tolerated, nor promised with true intent.

(8) Although it is true that Taiwan's businessmen are similar to fellow tradesmen around the world in looking for investment potential, the fact is that foreign and Overseas Chinese investments on the mainland have not proven to be very profitable. Far more money is to be gained from investments on Taiwan.

(9) It is hard to take the communist proposal seriously when the freedom to make suggestions for the direction of government on the mainland is strictly forbidden. Any criticism of communist policy or suggestion for change in leadership is punishable. These inconsistencies lead one to conclude that Ye's proposals were not meant seriously to be considered by Taipei; rather, they were intended to influence opinion in the United States and elsewhere in order to further

increase pressure on the Republic of China to accommodate Peking.[211]

Of the various objections raised by Taipei, perhaps the most serious is the belief that Beijing will eventually impose a communist system on the island should it gain control--despite whatever assurances Ye or other PRC officials give at this time. There are indications from high-ranking Chinese sources that this might well be the case. In February 1979, for example, Liao Chengzhi, head of the Office of Overseas Chinese for the PRC, told a meeting of the National Association of Overseas Chinese:

> After China has achieved peaceful unification the long-term road for Taiwan will be the socialist road. Under the leadership of a single, proletarian political party, there is no reason why one segment should have a socialist system while the other follows the capitalist road. However, the main problem at present is how can we first realize the peaceful unification of China and end the state of disunity that has endured for thirty years. Party Central has spelled out that our task with regard to Taiwan under the present situation is to achieve the goal of peaceful unification through negotiation.[212]

Over the long-run (spoken of in terms of 50 years in the case of Hong Kong), Beijing has no choice but to communize Taiwan once Nationalist control has ended. Not to do so would jeopardize the principles on which the CPC claims its legitimacy. These principles were contained in the CCPCC Resolution on the Founding of the PRC issued June 30, 1981. In setting forth the goals of the CPC, the resolution stated:

> The objective of our Party's struggle in the new historical period is to turn China step by step into a powerful socialist country with modern agriculture, industry, national defense and science and technology and with a high level of democracy and culture. We must

---

[211] Paraphrased from "China's Reunification: Is the 'Nine-Point Proposal' a Yesable Solution" (Taipei: China Mainland Research Center, May 1982).

[212] Liao's speech was translated in *Inside China Mainland*, November 1981, p. 12.

also accomplish the great cause of reunification of the country by getting Taiwan to return to the embrace of the motherland. The fundamental aim of summing up the historical experience of the thirty-two years since the founding of the People's Republic is to accomplish the great objective of building a powerful and modern socialist country by further rallying the will and strength of the whole Party, the whole army and the whole people on the basis of upholding the four fundamental principles, namely, upholding the socialist road, the people's democratic dictatorship, the leadership of the Communist Party and Marxism-Leninism and Mao Zedong thought. These four principles constitute the common political basis of the unity of the whole party and the unity of the whole people as well as the basic guarantee for the realization of socialist modernization. Any word or deed which deviates from these four principles is wrong. Any word or deed which denies or undermines these four principles cannot be tolerated.

Unanimously, the government and people of Taiwan do not want to see the island communized or their life-style changed under a communist system. Regardless of whether the individual is mainlander or Taiwanese, member of the KMT or Tangwai, conservative or progressive, no one on the island wants to see the PRC extend its control over Taiwan. In fact, should Taipei enter into negotiations with Beijing at this time, there is a very real possibility that social and political unrest would ensue. Taiwan's fundamental policy of "no negotiations, no compromise, and no contact with the Peiping regime,"[213] is not only a popular policy, but one that could not be changed without great risk to the political fabric of the island.[214]

---

[213] China News Agency (Taipei), January 27, 1983, in FBIS-China, January 27, 1983, p. V1.

[214] See Martin L. Lasater, "Taiwan's View of the Confrontation with the Mainland," American Asian Review, 1, 3 (Fall 1983), pp. 27-45.

7.2.4 Special Administrative Regions

Efforts by Beijing to get Taiwan to the negotiation table have continued since the introduction of Ye's proposals. In early December 1982 the new PRC Constitution included among its provisions Article 31, providing for "special administrative regions" within China:

> The state may establish special administrative regions when necessary. The rules and regulations in force in special administrative regions shall be instituted by the National People's Congress in legal form in accordance with their specific conditions.[215]

Peng Zhen, who explained the draft constitution to the National People's Congress, said the article was designed for Taiwan, Hong Kong, and Macao. Peng said that China was highly unequivocal on the principle of safeguarding its sovereignty, unity and territorial integrity, but highly flexible as regards to specific policies and measures.[216]

In recent months, the top PRC leadership has sought to use the medium of Overseas Chinese visiting the mainland to communicate its views on reunification. In May 1983, for example, Hu Yaobang told Pennsylvania State University professor Parris Chang that the reunification of the Chinese mainland will be achieved before 1991 and that Taiwan will become China's special administrative region.[217]

In some cases, the PRC has used Chinese-American scholars to amplify or expand the proposals being offered Taipei. One notable instance was the June 26, 1983, discussion between Deng Xiaoping and Seton Hall professor Winston Yang.[218] In his summary of Deng's

---

[215] *New York Times*, November 27, 1982, p. 1.

[216] *Xhongguo Xinwen She*, November 28, 1982, in *FBIS-China*, November 30, 1982, p. K19.

[217] *Hsia Pao*, June 28, 1983, in *FBIS-China*, June 28, 1983, p. W1.

[218] The official version of the conversation was reported in *Xinhua*, July 29, 1983, in *FBIS-China*, August 1, 1983, pp. U1-U2. Winston Yang's version can be found in his article, "Deng Xiaoping's Latest Concept on Peaceful Reunification," *Chishih Nientai*, August 1, 1983, in *FBIS-China*, August 4, 1983, pp. W1-W6.

remarks, Dr. Yang quoted Deng as saying, "the CPC sincerely wants to cooperate with Taiwan and has no intention to weaken and isolate Taiwan." Deng said: "Our many practices are not directed at Taiwan but at the 'two Chinas' policy of the United States." The Chinese leader told Yang that Taiwan could use the name "China--Taibei" to retain its seat in the Asian Development Bank as a member of the organization together with China. According to Professor Yang, Deng Xiaoping put forward the following scheme for China's unification:

1. After reunification, Beijing will not dispatch its Army to Taiwan, nor will it send officials to take over, to take part in, or to oversee Taiwan's "internal affairs." Beijing will not concern itself with the personnel affairs in Taiwan's administrative structure and will not bother about the troop movements in Taiwan. (But he did not agree with the proposition of "Taiwan people governing Taiwan," because it has an implication of "Taiwan independence.")....Taiwan can maintain its economic system, its way of living, and its party, government, Army, and intelligence agency. The mainland and Taiwan will coexist peacefully. He said: "We will never harm even a single blade of grass or a tree on Taiwan." He also said that this arrangement should remain unchanged for at least 100 years. If disputes occur in the course of implementing the reunification terms, both sides can seek solutions through consultation. The most important thing is that neither side will conduct anything causing harm to the other side in its own territory. Taiwan's Army will have the right to buy weapons from other countries to consolidate its self-defensive ability.

2. After reunification, Taiwan will enjoy independent legislative rights and can basically maintain its existing laws. On the principle of not violating the Constitution, Taiwan's legislature has the right to enact its own laws which act as the foundation for Taiwan's administration.

3. After reunification, Taiwan will have its independent jurisdiction and judicial organs. The laws and acts on the mainland will not be applied to Taiwan. The court of

last instance for Taiwan should be set in Taiwan rather than in Beijing.

    4. After reunification, Taiwan will maintain certain rights to handle foreign affairs. It can handle its foreign economic relations independently. The Taiwan authorities can issue special passports to Taiwan people and grant entrance visas to foreigners. It can even have the right to sign some agreements directly with other countries.

    5. After reunification, Taiwan can still use its special flag and use the title of "China, Taiwan."

    Deng's proposals to Yang were considered especially important because they implied that Taiwan could maintain its current way of life, its form of government and economy, its armed forces (including limited purchases of arms from abroad), and some type of relations with other countries. According to the official Chinese version, Deng said: "the mainland will station neither troops nor administrative personnel in Taiwan," Taiwan "may exercise independent jurisdiction and the right of final judgment need not reside in Beijing," and "seats in the central government will be reserved for Taiwan." The PRC leader emphasized that he was proposing talks between two political parties (the KMT and CPC) and not negotiations between central and local authorities.

    Taiwan's freedom would be limited, however. Deng said that "complete autonomy is simply out of the question," "only the PRC is entitled to represent China in the international arena," Taiwan's government would be a local government only, Taiwan's armed forces must "not constitute a threat to the mainland," Taiwan's exclusive rights must "not impair the interests of the unified state," and "foreign interference absolutely will not be permitted."

    In a speech given in Chicago in October 1983, Chinese Foreign Ministry Wu Xueqian referred to Deng's proposals, saying "they were put foward after full consideration had been given to the long term and fundamental interests of the entire Chinese people, including our compatriots in Taiwan, and to peace and stability in the Asian-Pacific region." Wu told his American audience: "we do not ask for U.S. assistance in achieving the reunification of Taiwan with the mainland, but we ask the United States to refrain from obstructing in our effort."[219]

7.2.5 The Hong Kong Model

In 1983 the PRC made it clear that it would assume sovereignty over Hong Kong in July 1997 when the current lease on the New Territories expires. Ji Pengfei, head of China's Hong Kong and Macao Affairs Office, listed in October 1983 the following basic features of the "high-degree" of self-rule Hong Kong would experience after 1997:

--The maintenance of Hong Kong laws and the spirit of the rule of law--"with exceptions of those laws connected with the colonial rule."

--The judgement of the highest courts in Hong Kong will be final and Hong Kong will have the final court of appeal.

--China will be responsible for Hong Kong's defense but will not station troops in Hong Kong.

--China will be responsible for Hong Kong's external affairs but Hong Kong will have the full right to manage them.

--In immigration matters, over which Hong Kong will have full control, Hong Kong will be allowed to issue its own identity cards and passports to enable its residents to continue to travel freely.

--Hong Kong will be able to manage its trading relations with other countries, including the management of trade quotas it has negotiated with them.

--There will be no change in Hong Kong's free enterprise policy and residents will continue to enjoy property rights. Capital will be allowed to flow freely in and out of Hong Kong and foreign and Chinese capital will receive identical protection.

--Except for the highest posts, expatriates will be allowed to continue to work in public and private establishments and enjoy various civic rights.

---

[219] Xinhua, October 15, 1983, in FBIS-China, October 17, 1983, p. B1.

--In the initial stages of self-rule, local representative organizations will be asked to nominate, after consultations among themselves, Hong Kong's governor, who will then be appointed by China.

--The Chinese Government will not impose taxes in Hong Kong.[220]

From the outset of negotiations between China and Great Britain, observers drew the parallel between Beijing's model for Hong Kong's future and its proposals to Taiwan. Indeed, PRC officials frequently referred to the various plans being discussed for Hong Kong as also applicable to Taiwan. In May 1984 a high-ranking, but unnamed, Chinese leader said: "China's policy toward the Taiwan and Hong Kong issues is that in a period to come, there will be two systems within one China." The official stated that the practice of capitalism in Taiwan and Hong Kong will not hamper their reunification with the socialist mainland. He also noted that there were similarities and differences in the two issues: "What they have in common is that both Taiwan and Hong Kong will become special administrative regions in the future, retaining their current systems and ways of life and enjoying a high degree of autonomy. However, the two have different backgrounds. Hong Kong will be taken back from foreigners, but Taiwan is different. Of course, a satisfactory solution of the Hong Kong issue will make it easier to solve the Taiwan issue."[221]

In his report to the National People's Congress on May 15, 1984, Zhao Ziyang repeated the "one country, two systems" formula for Hong Kong and Taiwan. Regarding the Taiwan issue, the Premier said: "We hold that provided the Kuomintang and the Communist Party of China share a common language on peaceful reunification, everything else can be negotiated. It is better to solve the Taiwan question sooner than later." In the same report, Zhao stated that upon the resumption of the exercise of sovereignty over Hong Kong, China would adopt a series of special policies "to maintain Hong Kong's stability and prosperity." These policies, the Premier said, will remain unchanged for fifty years. Zhao said:

---

[220] *South China Morning Post*, October 15, 1983, in *FBIS-China*, October 17, 1983, pp. W1-W2.

[221] *Wen Wei Po*, May 1, 1984, in *FBIS-China*, May 1, 1984, pp. W5-W6.

> a Hong Kong special administrative region will
> be established in accordance with Article 31
> of our Constitution. It will be administered
> by the local inhabitants and will enjoy a high
> degree of autonomy. The existing social and
> economic systems and lifestyle will remain
> unchanged and the laws currently in force will
> remain basically the same. Hong Kong will
> retain its status as a free port and as an
> international financial and trade center. It
> will maintain and develop economic relations
> with foreign countries, regions and relevant
> international organizations. Due regard will
> be paid to the economic interests of Britain
> and other countries in Hong Kong.[222]

Many experts believe that Beijing's insistence that the future of Hong Kong be resolved at this time is related to the PRC's efforts to reach an early reunification agreement with Taiwan. If such a strategy is true, it may backfire. The logical response of Taiwan--although it remains unspoken--is to wait until 1997 to see if China keeps its promises. Perhaps as a way of eliminating this argument, Zhao Ziyang told newsmen in Copenhagen in June 1984 that China intends to resolve the Taiwan question before 1997.[223]

Deng Xiaoping's June 1984 public reprimand of Huang Hua and Geng Biao, who had previously promised that China would not send troops to Hong Kong after 1997, did little to reassure observers of PRC intentions not to meddle in Hong Kong's internal affairs following the withdrawal of the British. Deng said on Hong Kong television: "I want to refute a rumor. What Huang Hua and Geng Biao said was absolute rubbish. What they said about stationing troops in Hong Kong is not the view of the central authorities."[224]

The July 2, 1984, issue of *Liaowang* carried an article detailing Deng's comments on Hong Kong's future to leading Chinese businessmen from the Crown Colony. Deng said:

> We have time and again stated that after our
> government resumes exercising sovereignty over
> Hong Kong in 1997, the present socioeconomic

---

[222] *Xinhua*, May 31, 1984, in **FBIS-China**, June 1, 1984, p. K20.

[223] *Japan Times*, June 10, 1984, p. 4.

[224] *Cheng Ming*, June 1, 1984, in **FBIS-China**, June 5, 1984, p. W3.

> system there will continue; the laws currently
> in force will remain basically unchanged; the
> lifestyle will continue in its present form;
> its status as a free port and international
> trade and financial center will also remain
> unchanged; and it will be able to continue to
> maintain and develop economic relations with
> other countries and regions. We have also
> stated time and again that apart from
> stationing troops there, Beijing will not
> dispatch cadres to work in the government of
> the Hong Kong special administrative region,
> and this policy will not change, either. We
> will station troops there for the purpose of
> defending our national security, and not for
> interfering in the internal affairs of Hong
> Kong. Our policy toward Hong Kong will remain
> unchanged for 50 years, and we mean what we
> say.

Deng Xiaoping then added a peculiar caveat: "We discussed the policy for two systems in one country for several years. It is now approved by the NPC. Some people worry whether this policy will change. I say it will not change. The core of the matter is whether this policy is correct or not. If it is correct it will not be changed. If it is not correct it may change."

Deng said that the policy of two systems in one country had been designed to take into consideration the actual conditions in China, Hong Kong, and Taiwan. Regarding the problem of Taiwan, Deng asked:

> What is the solution to this problem? Is it
> for socialism to swallow up Taiwan, or for the
> "Three Principles of the People" preached by
> Taiwan to swallow up the mainland? The answer
> is that neither can swallow up the other. If
> the problem cannot be solved peacefully then
> it must be solved by force. This would do
> neither side any good. Reunification of the
> country is the aspiration of the whole nation.
> It if cannot be reunified in 100 years, then
> it will be reunified in 1,000 years. In my
> opinion, the only solution to this problem is
> to practice two systems in one country.[225]

---

[225] Xinhua, June 30, 1984, in FBIS-China, July 2, 1984, pp. E1-E2.

7.3 TAIWAN'S REUNIFICATION POLICY

As noted, Taipei consistently rejects Beijing's proposals for reunification, refusing even to discuss the issue publicly with communist authorities.[226] Something of the flavor of Taiwan's rejections can be seen in the following question-and-answer exchange between President Chiang Ching-kuo and Newsweek magazine in October 1982:

Q. Why has the Republic of China rejected the Communist's 'Nine-Point Plan'?

A. Because these are just their frequently used gimmicks. Their ultimate goal is to communize us and deprive us of our freedom. While our compatriots on the mainland, intensely persecuted under the Communist tyranny, are beating their brains to escape the Iron Curtain for freedom, we shall never be so stupid as to jump into the Communist trap.

Q. Under what conditions would it be possible to begin talks and/or negotiations on the peaceful reunification of China?

A. In the Communist lexicon, negotiations are another type of war. When the Chinese Communists cannot subdue us with guns, they will turn to negotiations to divide our ranks and create opportunities for our destruction. China's reunification is possible only when the Communist regime and system have disappeared from the mainland.

Q. Even if political reunification talks are not possible, do you see any circumstances under which direct trade between the Republic of China and the mainland might be permitted?

---

[226] There are persistent reports that Taipei and Beijing do communicate privately and indirectly. Certainly, both sides are aware of what the other is saying. Liao Chengzhi told a Japanese reporter in December 1981 that Ye's nine-point plan was handed to Taiwan four years earlier and that "contact has already been established." Sankei Shimbun, December 25, 1981.

> A. The Communist system poses as the biggest obstacle to free trade. Therefore, the existence of the Chinese Communist regime is the only obstacle to direct trade between the two sides of the Taiwan Straits. The Chinese Communists have tried to use trade as a bait to lure us into buying their political poison.[227]

President Chiang Ching-kuo told Der Spiegel in May 1983 that the Republic of China "had held several peace talks with the Chinese Communists and learned a bitter lesson. Therefore, since 1949, we have made up our minds not to talk with them again." Chiang said:

> The ultimate aim of the Chinese Communists in proposing "peace talks" is to communize Taiwan, Penghu, Kinmen and Matsu. This is not only unacceptable to the 18 million people in Free China but is also detested by the Chinese abroad and on the Chinese mainland. Free China's success in implementing democracy and in pursuing economic development has enabled the people as a whole to enjoy the blessings of freedom, progress and prosperity in Taiwan. All Chinese have therefore pinned their hopes on Free China.[228]

Although it receives little attention in the international press, Taiwan has its own proposals for national reunification. The focus of Taipei's proposals, however, is quite different from that underlying Beijing's. Whereas the PRC seeks to find a way to incorporate Taiwan and its government into a provincial relationship with the mainland, Taiwan concentrates on the fundamental question of the form of government a reunited China should have. A July 1983 ROC commentary on Deng's proposals delivered through a visiting scholar noted that the PRC leader "purposely omitted saying what form of government a reunited China will have. That is the focus of the issue." The commentary went on to explain Taiwan's position:

---

[227] China Post, October 27, 1982, p. 4.

[228] "President Chiang Ching-kuo's Interview with an Editor of Der Spiegel, May 16, 1983" (Taipei: Government Information Office, June 1983), pp. 8-9.

> The Republic of China does not reject national reunification, nor does Taipei insist that the Kuomintang must be in control of a reunited China. The fact is that the government of the Republic of China on Taiwan has been persistently working toward China's national reunification. The difference is that Taipei aims at achieving a reunited China under a democratic system.
>
> To the Chinese Communist leadership, however, reunification with Taiwan means subjugation of the island province's 18 million people under communism....It is not a question of a quarrel between two political parties. At stake is the future of China, a question of whether Chinese people will have democratic government or remain slaves under a totalitarian regime forever.[229]

The most well-known statement of Taiwan's views on reunification was given by Premier Sun on June 10, 1982, before participants in the Eleventh Sino-American Conference. Premier Sun said:

> Regarding "Chinese reunification," the two sides have advanced different views. Free China calls for Chinese reunification under the Three Principles of the People, whereas the Chinese Communist regime has advanced through...Yeh Chien-ying a nine-point proposal for so-called peaceful reunification which is actually intended to communize free China.
>
> In advocating the reunification of China on the basis of the Three Principles of the People, we are not trying to embarrass the Chinese Communist regime....In recent years, the Chinese Communists have often expressed their respect for Dr. Sun Yat-sen.
>
> The reunification of China is the common aspiration of the Chinese people. For the last more than 30 years, the government and people of the Republic of China have worked to reunify China and restore freedom to the Chinese people on the mainland.

---

[229] Taipei International Service, July 27, 1983, in FBIS-China, July 29, 1983, pp. V1-V2.

> We believe that Chinese reunification should be based on the free will of the Chinese people as a whole....The Chinese Communists...should give up the "four fundamental principles" as quickly as possible and take steps to change their way of life. If the political, economic, social and cultural gaps between the Chinese mainland and free China continue to narrow, the conditions for peaceful reunification can gradually mature. The obstacles to reunification will be reduced naturally with the passage of time.[230]

Since Taiwan is concerned that any sign of willingness to negotiate may undermine its international standing and cause domestic unrest, the PRC has been able to monopolize the highly visible reunification issue with more specific proposals. As a result, Taipei has been cast into an image of an unreasonable and stubborn participant in the reunification talks. To a large extent, this has been the cause of Taiwan being referred to as an "issue" and an "obstacle" in Sino-American relations. From a long-term perspective, Taiwan's survival might well depend on how well its leaders are able to resolve this basic dilemma: how to appear reasonable on the reunification issue, yet remain secure against PRC negotiation tactics designed to end the ROC's legitimacy at home and abroad.

The U.S. position on the reunification issue is a sensitive one. At the time of the initiation of the normalization process, the United States openly favored a "two Chinas" solution and supported Taiwan's right to claim independence as a separate nation. Richard Nixon in his memoirs noted that as early as August 1971 "we had...indicated our support of the concept of the 'two Chinas,' Chiang Kai-shek's Republic of China on Taiwan and the Communist People's Republic of China, each to have membership" in the United Nations. Regarding the U.S.-Chinese discussions over references to Taiwan in the Shanghai Communique, the former President said:

> Taiwan was the touchstone for both sides. We felt that we should not and could not abandon the Taiwanese; we were commited to Taiwan's right to exist as an independent nation. The Chinese were equally determined to use the communique to assert their unequivocal claim to the island.[231]

---

[230] "The China Issue and China's Reunification" (Taipei: Government Information Office, 1982).

U.S. policy on the reunification issue today is deliberately vague, stressing only that the solution must be a peaceful one. Assistant Secretary of State Paul Wolfowitz told the House Foreign Affairs Committee following President Reagan's April 1984 trip to China:

> With regard to the question of Taiwan's future, which was raised by the Chinese on several occasions. The President stated clearly to the Chinese, as he and others in his Administration have done before, that we will honor our commitments, that we expect the Chinese to honor theirs, and that within such a framework this issue is one for the Chinese on both sides of the Straits to resolve by themselves. Our sole and abiding concern, the President reiterated, is that any resolution be a peaceful one.[232]

Whether the PRC and ROC will be able to narrow their differences in the future is uncertain. The issue is so sensitive politically within both systems that significant compromise is very difficult. Deng Xiaoping and Chiang Ching-kuo may have the power and respect necessary to bring the two sides together, but even their flexibility is limited because of their personal beliefs and the political environment in which they must function. Succeeding leaders will likely have less personal power than either of these individuals, so a consensus for greater compromise would have to evolve from within the respective political systems. Although such a consensus could emerge in the future, it will not be easy in either the PRC or Taiwan. Therefore, despite its desire to avoid the use of force, Beijing may feel in time that it has no choice but to employ military means to bring Taiwan under its control. The island is much too important to China to allow it to become independent.

---

[231] Richard M. Nixon, RN: The Memoirs of Richard Nixon (New York: Grosset and Dunlap, 1978), pp. 556, 570.

[232] Prepared Statement of Paul Wolfowitz given before U.S. House of Representatives, Committee on Foreign Affairs, Subcommittee on Asian and Pacific Affairs, June 5, 1984, p. 5, ms.

8
The Taiwan Issue

Throughout the Indochina War, Taiwan was an important forward logistics and R&R center for American forces. Beginning around 1970, however, Taiwan's military value to the United States diminished as a result of the American retrenchment from Asia and the easing of tensions between Washington and Beijing.

8.1   THE SHANGHAI COMMUNIQUE

From the outset of discussions aimed at normalization of U.S.-PRC relations, it was clear that Taiwan would be an issue over which little agreement could be found. Nonetheless, by the time President Nixon made his historic trip to China in February 1972, the PRC had decided to make Taiwan a secondary issue and to concentrate instead on the larger strategic interests of the two countries. Henry Kissinger recorded that, during Nixon's visit, Mao

> delicately placed the issue of Taiwan on a subsidiary level, choosing to treat it as a relatively minor internal Chinese dispute; he did not even mention our military presence there....Neither then, nor in any subsequent meeting, did Mao indicate any impatience over Taiwan, set any time limits, make any threats, or treat it as the touchstone of our relationship. 'We can do without them for the time being, and let it come after 100 years.' 'Why such great haste?' 'This issue is not an important one. The issue of the international situation is an important one.' 'The small issue is Taiwan, the big issue is the world.' These were Mao's thoughts on Taiwan as expressed to us on many visits. (These were also the view of Chou En-lai and Teng

Hsiao-ping.) But Mao, like Chou and Teng, spent very little time in our talks on this issue.[233]

Zhou Enlai told President Nixon just prior to his departure from China on February 28, 1972: "We, being so big, have already let the Taiwan issue remain for twenty-two years, and can afford to let it wait there for a time."[234]

The most important document of this era was the Shanghai Communique of February 28, 1972, which set forth the major principles governing relations between the United States and the People's Republic of China. The communique acknowledged:

> There are essential differences between China and the United States in their social systems and foreign policies. However, the two sides agreed that countries, regardless of their social systems, should conduct their relations on the principles of respect for the sovereignty and territorial integrity of all states, non-aggression against other states, non-interference in the internal affairs of other states, equality and mutual benefit, and peaceful coexistence. International disputes should be settled on this basis, without resorting to the use or threat of force. The United States and the People's Republic of China are prepared to apply these principles to their mutual relations.
>
> With these principles of international relations in mind the two sides stated that:
>
> --progresss toward the normalization of relations between China and the United States is in the interests of all countries;
>
> --both wish to reduce the danger of international military conflict;
>
> --neither should seek hegemony in the Asia-Pacific region and each is opposed to efforts by the other country or group of countries to establish such hegemony; and

---

[233] Henry A. Kissinger, *White House Years* (Boston: Little, Brown & Co., 1979), p. 1062.

[234] *Ibid.*, p. 1087.

> --neither is prepared to negotiate on behalf of any third country or to enter into agreements or understandings with the other directed at other states.
>
> Both sides are of the view that it would be against the interests of the peoples of the world for any major country to collude with another against other countries, or for major countries to divide up the world into spheres of interest.

Regarding Taiwan, the two sides set forth their individual views which continue to guide their respective policies today:

> The Chinese side reaffirmed its position: The Taiwan question is the crucial question obstructing the normalization of relations between China and the United States; the Government of the People's Republic of China is the sole legal government of China; Taiwan is a province of China which has long been returned to the motherland; the liberation of Taiwan is China's internal affair in which no other country has the right to interfere; and all U.S. forces and military installations must be withdrawn from Taiwan. The Chinese Government firmly opposes any activities which aim at the creation of "one China, one Taiwan," "one China, two governments" or advocate that "the status of Taiwan remains to be determined."
>
> The U.S. side declared: The United States acknowledges that all Chinese on either side of the Taiwan Strait maintain there is but one China and that Taiwan is a part of China. The United States Government does not challenge that position. It reaffirms its interests in a peaceful settlement of the Taiwan question by the Chinese themselves. With this prospect in mind, it affirms the ultimate objective of the withdrawal of all U.S. forces and military installations from Taiwan. In the meantime, it will progressively reduce its forces and military installations on Taiwan as the tension in the area diminishes.

The two sides were able "to agree to disagree" over Taiwan because of important changes in both the United States and the PRC. The first and most important of these was that the top leadership in the two countries no longer viewed the other as an immediate threat. Second, both governments considered the Soviet Union as the most dangerous enemy to be contained, yet felt inadequate to deter the USSR unilaterally. Third, important domestic political events were at work. In the case of China, Lin Biao and his supporters had just been purged, giving the moderate wing of the CPC under Zhou Enlai an opportunity to press for improved relations with the United States. In Washington, President Nixon was looking foward to the 1972 election and wanted a major foreign policy victory to ensure his successful reelection. And fourth, a remarkable congruence of national leaders--Nixon and Kissinger, Mao and Zhou--were able to break out of traditional modes of thinking about Sino-American relations and to adjust their nations' policies to new international realities.

8.2 NORMALIZATION OF SINO-AMERICAN RELATIONS

In the intervening years between the setting up of liaison offices in Beijing and Washington in February 1973 and President Jimmy Carter's announcement of normalized relations with the PRC on December 15, 1978, a number of problems arose in Sino-American relations. Coincidentally with the rehabilitation of Deng Xiaoping in the spring of 1973, the PRC set three conditions for the normalization of relations with the United States: (1) termination of official relations with the Republic of China, (2) termination of the 1954 U.S.-ROC Mutual Defense Treaty, and (3) withdrawal of American troops and military installations from Taiwan. These conditions came as a surprise to many Americans, who had expected the Chinese to remain flexible on the Taiwan issue. In addition to the dampening effect of these demands, the pace of normalization slowed as a result of the strains placed upon the Nixon Administration by the Watergate investigations. When President Gerald Ford sent Kissinger to Beijing in October 1975, he found Deng to be inflexible and stern, thus closing the door to improved Sino-American relations under the Republicans.

In January 1976 Zhou Enlai died, ushering in a period of radical influence which prevented any further move on the part of China toward normalization. Following the death of Mao in September 1976 and the subsequent arrest of the Gang of Four by Hua Guofeng, Deng was once again rehabilitated. The resurrection of political and economic pragmatism in China provided an opportunity which the United States, now under the leadership of Jimmy Carter, sought to exploit. Carter, who entered the presidency determined to normalize relations with China,[235] sent Secretary of State Cyrus

Vance to Beijing in September 1977 to propose that an American embassy be established in Beijing and a liaison office in Taipei. The Chinese considered this to be step backward in Sino-American relations. Vance having been rebuffed, the pivotal contact with the Chinese during the Carter Administration became national security advisor Zbigniew Brzezinski. Brzezinski visited China in May 1978 to lay the groundwork for diplomatic recognition.

During the Huang Hua-Leonard Woodcock talks held in Beijing to work out the details, the United States did not press the Chinese for a pledge of nonuse of force against Taiwan, although the American side did state its intention of continuing to supply defensive arms to Taipei. President Carter also informed the Chinese that the United States would maintain the Mutual Defense Treaty with Taiwan until it was terminated according to its provisions and insisted that Beijing not contradict U.S. statements that the Taiwan issue should be settled peacefully and with patience. According to Carter, in late November 1978 the CPC Central Committee met to consider his proposal for normalization, along with two other key issues: the final consolidation of Deng Xiaoping's control and possible military action against Vietnam.[236]

The Chinese agreed to Carter's conditions on Taiwan. At the same time as normalization, the PRC softened its rhetoric directed toward Taipei and initiated a series of proposals designed, on the surface at least, to unite China under peaceful conditions. Carter noted that during Deng Xiaoping's visit to the United States in January 1979, the Chinese leader said that "the only two circumstances under which they would not resolve the issue peacefully and be patient were if there was an extended period of no negotiation or if the Soviet Union entered Taiwan."[237]

On December 15, 1978, the United States and the People's Republic of China announced they would exchange diplomatic recognition on January 1, 1979. In his televised statement to the American people, President Carter reaffirmed the principles agreed to by the United States in the Shanghai Communique and emphasized that "the Government of the United States of America acknowledges the Chinese position that there is but one

---

[235] See Jimmy Carter, Keeping Faith: Memoirs of a President (New York: Bantam Books, 1982), pp. 186-211.

[236] Ibid., p. 197.

[237] Ibid., pp. 209-210.

China and Taiwan is part of China."[238]
The President went on to address the future of American relations with Taiwan. He said:

> I wish also tonight to convey a special message to the people of Taiwan...with whom the American people have had and will have extensive, close, and friendly relations. This is important between our two peoples.
>
> As the United States asserted in the Shanghai Communique of 1972...we will continue to have an interest in the peaceful resolution of the Taiwan issue. I have paid special attention to ensuring that normalization of relations between our country and the People's Republic of China will not jeopardize the well-being of the people of Taiwan. The people of our country will maintain our current commercial, cultural, trade, and other relations with Taiwan through nongovernmental means.

The Taiwan question was also addressed in the official U.S. statement accompanying the joint communique of December 15, 1978. The statement noted that the United States would recognize the PRC on January 1, 1979, "as the sole legal government of China." It then confirmed that the United States would meet the conditions set forth by the Chinese since 1973 for the normalization of relations. The statement said that on January 1, 1979,

> the United States of America will notify Taiwan that it is terminating diplomatic relations and that the Mutual Defense Treaty between the United States and the Republic of China is being terminated in accordance with the provisions of the Treaty. The United States also states that it will be withdrawing its remaining military personnel from Taiwan within four months.

The U.S. statement explained: "In the future, the American people and the people of Taiwan will maintain commercial, cultural, and other relations without official government representation and without

---

[238] The text of President Carter's speech may be found in Public Papers of the Presidents of the United States: Jimmy Carter, 1978, Book II (Washington, D.C.: GPO, 1979), pp. 2264-2266.

diplomatic relations." To accomplish this, the statement announced that the Administration would seek necessary changes in existing law. The statement concluded:

> The United States is confident that the people of Taiwan face a peaceful and prosperous future. The United States continues to have an interest in the peaceful resolution of the Taiwan issue and expects that the Taiwan issue will be settled peacefully by the Chinese themselves.

For its part, the PRC expressed confidence that the Taiwan issue had been resolved in principle, but refused to rule out the use of force as a means of bringing Taiwan back to the control of the mainland. The official Chinese statement on the establishment of diplomatic relations with the United States said:

> As is known to all, the Government of the People's Republic of China is the sole legal government of China and Taiwan is a part of China. The question of Taiwan was the crucial issue obstructing the normalization of relations between China and the United States. It has now been resolved between the two countries in the spirit of the Shanghai Communique and through their joint efforts, thus enabling the normalization of relations so ardently desired by the people of the two countries. As for the way of bringing Taiwan to the embrace of the motherland and reunifying the country, it is entirely China's internal affair.[239]

PRC spokesmen noted that the arms sales issue remained as the major problem yet unresolved. In a press conference on December 16, 1978, Hua Guofeng was emphatic in denying that China had agreed that the United States could continue selling arms to Taiwan:

> In the course of negotiations, the U.S. side mentioned that it would continue to sell arms to Taiwan for defense purposes after normalization. We can absolutely not agree to this. During the discussion, we made our

---

[239] NCNA, December 16, 1978, in FBIS-China, December 18, 1978, p. A2.

position clear on many occasions. On this
question, continued sale of arms to Taiwan
after normalization does not conform to the
principles of normalization, is detrimental to
a peaceful settlement of the Taiwan question
and will exercise unfavorable influence on
peace and stability in the Asia-Pacific region
and the rest of the world.[240]

Shortly after Deng's return to China from his
highly successful trip to the United States, the PRC
invaded Vietnam to teach Hanoi a "lesson" for its
occupation of Cambodia. In retrospect it appears likely
the Chinese decided to step up normalization before
launching their punitive "defensive counterattack"
against Vietnam. Moscow's reaction to a Chinese
expedition against the Vietnamese was unknown, but
potentially dangerous. In June 1978 Vietnam had joined
the Soviet-dominated Council for Mutual Economic
Cooperation and in November Hanoi had signed a treaty of
friendship and cooperation with the USSR. The sudden
decision to normalize relations with the United States
probably was timed by Beijing to throw the Kremlin off
guard sufficiently to reduce the danger of a Soviet
military response when Chinese troops moved into
Vietnam.

8.3   THE TAIWAN RELATIONS ACT

The Chinese invasion of Vietnam reminded many in the
United States that Beijing was not adverse to using
military means to achieve political objectives. This
lesson was not lost to Congress when it reconvened to
consider the nature of the post-normalization
relationship between the United States and the people of
Taiwan. As promised in his announcement of December 15,
1978, President Carter submitted to the Congress draft
legislation designed to handle future relations with
Taiwan. Most members of Congress felt the President's
plan to be inadequate because it generally avoided the
question of Taiwan's security.[241]

---

[240] Ibid., p. A5.

[241] The President's draft legislation, along with
documentation on the reaction of members of
Congress, can be found in Robert L. Downen, The
Taiwan Pawn in the China Game: Congress to the
Rescue (Washington, D.C.: Georgetown University,
CSIS, 1979).

After holding extensive hearings on the question of future U.S. relations with Taipei, the Congress rewrote major sections of the President's bill and passed S. 245/H.R. 2479 by more than two-thirds of both houses in late March 1979.[242] President Carter signed the revised bill on April 10, 1979, and it became known as the Taiwan Relations Act (TRA).

In contrast to the bill proposed by the President, the TRA specifically addressed U.S. interests and policies as these related to the security of Taiwan. Section 2 of the Act stated: "the Congress finds that the enactment of this Act is necessary...to help maintain peace, security, and stability in the Western Pacific." Thus, the TRA linked the future of Taiwan with American security interests in Asia. Section 2(b) defined U.S. policy in the Western Pacific as:

> (1) to preserve and promote extensive, close, and friendly commercial, cultural, and other relations between the people of the United States and the people on Taiwan, as well as the people on the China mainland and all other peoples of the Western Pacific area;
>
> (2) to declare that peace and stability in the area are in the political, security, and economic interests of the United States, and are matters of international concern;
>
> (3) to make clear that the United States decision to establish diplomatic relations with the People's Republic of China rests upon the expectation that the future of Taiwan will be determined by peaceful means;
>
> (4) to consider any effort to determine the future of Taiwan by other than peaceful means, including by boycotts or embargoes, a threat to the peace and security of the Western Pacific area and of grave concern to the

---

[242] One of the most useful collections of information about Taiwan and related U.S. interests can be found in the Senate hearings on S. 245. See U.S. Senate, Committee on Foreign Relations, *Taiwan* (Washington, D.C.: GPO, 1979). An excellent account of the congressional handling of S. 245 and H.R. 2479 can be found in Lester L. Wolff and David L. Simon, *Legislative History of the Taiwan Relations Act* (New York: American Association for Chinese Studies, 1982).

United States;

(5) to provide Taiwan with arms of a defensive character; and

(6) to maintain the capacity of the United States to resist any resort to force or other forms of coercion that would jeopardize the security, or the social or economic system, of the people on Taiwan.

Section 3 of the Act gives specific instructions on the implementation of the above policy:

(a) In furtherance of the policy set forth in section 2 of this Act, the United States will make available to Taiwan such defense articles and defense services in such quantity as may be necessary to enable Taiwan to maintain a sufficient self-defense capability.

(b) The President and the Congress shall determine the nature and quantity of such defense articles and services based solely upon their judgment of the needs of Taiwan, in accordance with procedures established by law. Such determination of Taiwan's defense needs shall include review by United States military authorities in connection with recommendations to the President and the Congress.

(c) The President is directed to inform the Congress promptly of any threat to the security or the social or economic system of the people on Taiwan and any danger to the interests of the United States arising therefrom. The President and the Congress shall determine, in accordance with constitutional processes, appropriate action by the United States in response to any such danger.

The Chinese reaction to the TRA, which in some respects went further than the Mutual Defense Treaty in specifying the extent to which a threat to Taiwan would be against U.S. interests, was remarkably quiet. Just prior to the passage of the TRA, Huang Hua told U.S. Ambassador Woodcock:

On a number of points the bills due to be adopted by both houses of Congress contravene the principles agreed to by the two sides and

the undertaking of the U.S. side at the time
of the establishment of diplomatic relations;
they constitute, in essence, an attempt to
maintain to a certain extent the U.S.-Chiang
"Joint Defense Treaty," continue to intervene
in China's internal affairs and give official
status to future U.S.-Taiwan relations. This
is of course unacceptable to the Chinese
Government. If the bills are passed as they
are worded now, and are signed into law, great
harm will be done to the new relationship that
has just been established between China and
the United States.[243]

Despite this warning, it was more than a year before the issue of the Taiwan Relations Act became prominent in Sino-American relations. The reason the Chinese dropped the issue in 1979 was due to private and public assurances from the Carter Administration that the TRA would be interpreted in a way consistent with the U.S.-PRC normalization agreement. When signing the TRA into law on April 10, President Carter said:

The act is consistent with the
understandings we reached in normalizing
relations with the Government of the People's
Republic of China. It reflects our
recognition of that Government as the sole
legal government of China....In a number of
sections of this legislation the Congress has
wisely granted discretion to the President.
In all instances, I will exercise that
discretion in a manner consistent with our
interest in the well-being of the people on
Taiwan and with the understandings we reached
on the normalization of relations with the
People's Republic of China as expressed in our
Joint Communique of January 1, 1979.[244]

With the issue of the Taiwan Relations Act temporarily settled, Sino-American relations throughout the remainder of 1979 were generally harmonious. A one-year moratorium on arms sales to Taiwan was adopted by the United States to ease the transition to full

---

[243] Xinhua, March 23, 1979, in FBIS-China, March 26, 1979, p. K1.

[244] Office of the White House Press Secretary, "Statement by the President on Public Law 96-8 (H.R. 2479)," April 10, 1979.

diplomatic relations. Both governments focused on the strategic aspects of their relationship.

The most important event in 1979 contributing to the sense of urgency in Sino-American strategic cooperation was the Soviet invasion of Afghanistan in December. Soviet involvement had begun as early as 1973, but the successive failures of Daoud, Taraki, and Amin to move Afghanistan along the socialist path finally led Moscow to install Babrak Karmal as President with the help of regular Soviet forces.

Both the United States and China viewed the Soviet invasion of Afghanistan as a serious threat to their security. Washington's concern focused on the possibility that the move was a preliminary step toward intervention in Iran or Pakistan. In response to the Soviet invasion, President Carter announced that the United States would use any means necessary to prevent Soviet domination of the Middle East. He also reversed the downward trend of American defense spending and started to rebuild U.S. military forces. China saw the invasion of Afghanistan as part of the USSR's southern strategy to isolate and contain PRC influence in Asia. The fact that Soviet troops quickly occupied and virtually annexed the Wakhan Corridor, the 30-mile stretch connecting the heart of Afghanistan with China, tended to confirm Beijing's suspicions. In response to the invasion, China began supplying light weapons to the mujahedin. Discussions on possible American and Chinese strategic cooperation were held during January and May 1980 between U.S. Defense Secretary Harold Brown and Chinese Vice Premier Geng Biao.

8.4   THE MID-1980 TURNING POINT

The overall positive tone of Sino-American strategic relations throughout 1979 and the first half of 1980 was not disrupted by the Taiwan issue. The Chinese press contained few harsh statements about Taiwan's authorities or U.S. interference in Taiwan. In June 1980, however, Sino-American relations began to feel the strain of unresolved issues stemming from profound differences over the Taiwan issue.

The most frequently cited cause for the sudden worsening of relations was Ronald Reagan's campaign speeches in which he spoke of reestablishing official relations with Taipei. Xinhua responded to the presidential candidate's June 13 speech in Detroit, noting that "Reagan's position runs diametrically opposite to the principles governing the establishment of diplomatic relations between China and the United States." The authoritative commentary went on to say:

> Reagan's declaration for the reestablishment of "official relations" with Taiwan is obviously a great retrogression. It reflects an attempt among certain short-sighted people in the United States to revive their own dream of "two Chinas." Whatever the supporting arguments, his position, if carried into practice, would wreck the very foundation of Sino-U.S. relations.[245]

An even more strongly worded commentary appeared in Renmin Ribao the next day. The article said:

> If the United States reestablished "official relations" with Taiwan according to the policy announced by Reagan, it would imply that the very principle which constitutes the foundation of Sino-U.S. relations is thoroughly destroyed and that Sino-U.S. relations will retrogress against the will of the two peoples. As for the absurd calls for a return of the U.S. military presence on Taiwan and a revival of the U.S.-Taiwan "Mutual Defense Treaty," they constitute brazen interference in China's internal affairs.[246]

Despite hurried efforts by the Carter Administration to warn against the reestablishment of official relations with Taiwan and a subsequent reworking by the Reagan team of their China policy, the climate of Sino-American relations after mid-June 1980 changed. Reagan's speeches seem to have been the precipitating event, yet other developments also contributed to the chilling of Sino-American relations at this point. One factor was the State Department's decision in June 1980 to permit Northrop and General Dynamics to go to Taiwan to discuss the sale of their version of the FX fighter. In July Zhao Ziyang told visiting Senator Byrd: "The Chinese people feel strongly against the U.S. Government's handling of its relations with Taiwan and particularly its continued sales of weapons to Taiwan." These actions, Zhao said, "are incompatible with the principles as outlined in the communique on the establishment of diplomatic relations between China and the United States. They are likely to

---

[245] Xinhua, June 13, 1980, in FBIS-China, June 16, 1980, p. B3.

[246] Renmin Ribao, June 14, 1980, in FBIS-China, June 16, 1980, p. B4.

produce an unfavorable impact on the stability of the Asia-Pacific region."[247]

Another factor, which did not become visible until a few months later, was a reassessment of the Soviet threat by the Chinese. Policy circles in the Chinese capital were reevaluating strategic relations with the United States in view of the determination of Washington to stand firm against Soviet hegemonism. As previously noted, this change in PRC perceptions formed the foundation for China's "independent" foreign policy and enabled Beijing to assume a much harder line on the Taiwan issue.

In an effort to reassess his China policy, Reagan sent George Bush and Richard Allen in August 1980 to Japan and China for extensive consultations. Upon their return, Reagan clarified his policy toward the Far East in an important campaign statement on August 25, 1980, in Los Angeles. He set forth five principles which his administration later followed when in office:

> First, U.S.-Chinese relations are important to American as well as Chinese interests. Our partnership should be global and strategic. In seeking improved relations with the People's Republic of China, I would extend the hand of friendship to all Chinese. In continuing our relations...I would continue the process of expanding trade, scientific and cultural ties.
>
> Second, I pledge to work for peace, stability and the economic growth of the Western Pacific area in cooperation with Japan, the People's Republic of China, the Republic of Korea and Taiwan.
>
> Third, I will cooperate and consult with all countries of the area in a mutual effort to stand firm against aggression or a search for hegemony which threatens the peace and stability of the area.
>
> Fourth, I intend that United States relations with Taiwan will develop in accordance with the law of our land, the Taiwan Relations Act. This legislation is the product of our democratic process, and is designed to remedy the defects of the totally

---

[247] Xinhua, July 8, 1980, in FBIS-China, July 9, 1980, p. B2.

inadequate legislation proposed by Jimmy
Carter....

Fifth, as President I will not accept the
interference of any foreign power in the
process of protecting American interests and
carrying out the laws of our land....

It is my conclusion that the strict
observance of these five principles will be in
the best interests of the United States, the
People's Republic of China and the people of
Taiwan.[248]

In amplifying his fourth point, Reagan criticized
President Carter's decision to accept China's three
conditions for normalization. Reagan argued "that a
condition of normalization--by itself a sound policy
choice--should have been the retention of a liaison
office on Taiwan of equivalent status to the one which
we had earlier established in Beijing." Reagan went on
to say that the Congress, in correcting "the inadequate
bill which Mr. Carter proposed," provided in the TRA
"adequate safeguards for Taiwan's security and
well-being" and provided "the official basis for our
relations with our long-time friend and ally....And,
most important, it spells out our policy of providing
defensive weapons to Taiwan." Reagan then asked
rhetorically: "You might ask what I would do
differently. I would not pretend, as Carter does, that
the relationship we now have with Taiwan, enacted by our
Congress, is not official."

As moderate as Reagan's new position seemed to many
of his conservative supporters, the PRC strongly
objected to his remarks regarding the status of the
Taiwan Relations Act. Beijing's reaction set the tone
for subsequent Chinese statements on Sino-American
relations during most of the first two years of the
Reagan Administration. Renmin Ribao on August 28 noted:
"Reagan once again defended his erroneous stance on the
Taiwan question and continued to advocate establishment
of 'official relations' with Taiwan." The commentary
said of Reagan's interpretation of the TRA:

It is known to all that the "Taiwan Relations
Act" is nothing but a domestic act of the
United States. It can in no way serve as a
legal basis for handling U.S.-Chinese

---

[248] "Ronald Reagan on U.S. Policy Toward Asia and the
Pacific," Press Release, Los Angeles, California,
August 25, 1980.

> relations. It should be pointed out that many parts of the Act, including its claim to reserving the United States' right to continue interfering in the Taiwan problem, run counter to the fundamental principles of the communique on the establishment of diplomatic relations between China and the United States. Therefore, the Chinese Government has more than once made clear its solemn stance against the Act and demanded that the U.S. have the overall interests of Sino-U.S. relations in mind and strictly abide by the principles of the Sino-U.S. agreement and truly respect China's sovereignty and territorial integrity.[249]

The commentary pointed out that the correct approach to the TRA was the one adopted by President Carter, whereby the Act would be implemented in accordance with the normalization agreement. The authoritative statement emphasized: "It must be pointed out what is really intolerable is the attempt to make Sino-U.S. relations retrogress by imposing on China a U.S. domestic act which is harmful to the political foundations on which China and the United States established diplomatic relations."

Beijing turned this fundamental disagreement over the TRA into a strong bargaining ploy by linking Reagan's policy toward Taiwan with his overriding strategic concern to use Sino-American relations to counter the Soviet threat. The <u>Renmin Ribao</u> commentary said:

> Reagan has gone even further than the "Taiwan Relations Act." He insisted on restoring "official relations" between the United States and Taiwan....This is not a matter of "semantics" but an overt call for "two Chinas." Should Reagan's erroneous proposition be put into practice, it would inevitably lead to grave retrogression in Sino-U.S. relations.
>
> China takes Sino-U.S. friendly relations seriously and does not wish to see the relations impaired. This is actuated not only by her own interests, but more importantly by the overall interest of safeguarding world peace and opposing hegemonism. It has been

---

[249] <u>Renmin Ribao</u>, August 28, 1980, in <u>FBIS-China</u>, August 28, 1980, p. B1.

proved that the normalization of Sino-U.S. relations is not only in the interest of the Chinese and American peoples but is also conducive to stabilizing the world situation. Thus, when China evaluates the U.S. Government's strategic decisions and foreign policy, she regards its China policy as one of the most important criteria; for what is involved is global strategy, not a problem of a local nature.

Any action detrimental to Sino-U.S. relations will have serious adverse effect on the struggle against hegemonism and for safeguarding world peace....It would be impossible for any American statesman to possess a correct strategic viewpoint and pursue a wise foreign policy if he fails to handle Sino-U.S. relations from the viewpont of overall interest, or worse, if he causes harm to Sino-U.S. relations....Reagan's erroneous stand on the Taiwan question has a vital bearing on the strategic situation in the world....Whither goes Reagan, we shall wait and see.

Trying to determine the PRC's motives in linking U.S. relations with Taiwan with Sino-American strategic cooperation is at the heart of this study. Was the Taiwan issue suddenly so important to Beijing that strategic relations with the United States could be sacrificed? Were the Chinese merely using a clever bargaining strategy to gain U.S. concessions on Taiwan and other issues? Or did the Renmin Ribao article hint that China's security was not as dependent upon close American strategic support as Americans generally thought?

Clearly, the commentary stressed the importance Beijing placed on continued friendly U.S.-China relations. But there was also a veiled threat that if Reagan improved relations with Taiwan, then Sino-American strategic cooperation would suffer as a result. It will be recalled that in 1969-1972 and 1978-1979 Chinese leaders deliberately made the Taiwan issue secondary in order to initiate and complete the normalization process. The key difference between these earlier periods and mid-1980 was not the appearance of Reagan, but rather a shift in perceptions on the part of the PRC leadership. China felt confident in its ability to apply pressure on the United States over the Taiwan issue after mid-1980 because its leaders had downgraded the Soviet threat. As previously noted, two key factors contributed to this perception: the determination of the United States to resist further Soviet aggression in the wake of the invasion of Afghanistan, and the Soviet willingness to reduce Sino-Soviet tensions. Feeling more secure, the PRC could afford to be less flexible on the Taiwan issue.

A significant hint of this shift in strategic perceptions was given by Li Xiannian in an interview with an Italian journalist in September 1980. The journalist asked Li whether he saw the most likely point of Soviet aggression to be Europe or China. The Chinese official responded:

> We maintain that in its strategy the USSR is placing the emphasis on the West European countries. It is trying to penetrate the Persian Gulf, the Middle East and North Africa to encircle and gain control of the oil routes. We do not rule out a tense situation on the Sino-Soviet border, too. The USSR has concentrated over a million troops there. But its sights are not set on China alone. Its sights are on the United States and Japan, too. But three-fourths of its armed forces, including nuclear forces, are concentrated in Europe.[250]

In one of many ironies associated with U.S. policy toward China, it was the determination of the United States to stand up to the Soviet Union which convinced the Chinese that they no longer needed a highly visible strategic relationship with Washington to secure their safety. This highly important shift in thinking was confirmed in late 1983 by Huan Xiang, director of China's Institute for International Affairs, in his interview with Der Spiegel previously quoted.[251]

This accords with the findings of some American scholars who have concluded that one of Beijing's primary assumptions regarding its foreign policy is that China's interests are best served when superpower rivalry is intense. As John Garver noted:

> During the 1950s, Beijing broke with the Soviet Union largely because of Moscow's policy of peaceful coexistence with the United States. This reflected Beijing's belief that

---

[250] Turin La Stampa, September 12, 1980, in FBIS-China, September 25, 1980, p. 7.

[251] Der Spiegel, December 26, 1983, in FBIS-China, December 29, 1983, pp. A7-A8.

China's interests demanded that the two
superpowers remain in a state of acute
rivalry. A similar logic was at work in
1969-1971. Whereas Beijing had concluded in
1958-1959 that superpower contradictions would
best be exacerbated by breaking with the CPSU
and the Soviet Union, in the late 1960s it
concluded that rapprochement with the USA was
the proper strategy to achieve the same
objective.[252]

The PRC faced a similar juncture in its foreign
policy at the time of the 1980 presidential campaign in
the United States. The two superpowers viewed each
other with great hostility. Washington had determined
to confront Moscow and prevent further hegemonism. The
wrecking of Soviet-American detente gave Beijing great
flexibility in its relations with both superpowers. As
Hu Yaobang noted some years later, the period 1978-1980
was one of intense debate within China over the wisdom
of joining a "strategic partnership" with the United
States.[253]

China's leaders reached a consensus on PRC policy
toward the superpowers. Rather than depending so
heavily upon a strategic relationship with the United
States, Beijing concluded that a nonaligned policy
better served its purposes. This policy would permit
normalized relations with both countries, yet enable the
PRC to pursue bilateral issues from a position of
strength and flexibility. China's strong bargaining
posture was made possible because both superpowers
wanted stable relations with Beijing in order to free
resources to confront the other. It was an ideal
situation for China, and Beijing quickly seized the
opportunity. The PRC's "independent foreign policy"
thus had its origins in mid-1980.

Unfortunately, both the Carter and the Reagan
administrations failed to notice this important change
in China's strategic perceptions. After assuming a much
tougher stand against the Soviets, the United States
approached the PRC in response to Deng's earlier calls
for increased strategic cooperation. Contrary to U.S.
expectations, China retreated from its previous stance
and instead insisted that the United States reduce its
support of Taiwan.

---

[252] John W. Garver, *China's Decision for Rapprochement with the United States, 1968-1971* (Boulder, CO: Westview Press, 1982), p. 39.

[253] *Los Angeles Times*, January 25, 1984, Part I, p. 5.

The close correlation in time between Beijing's refusal to cooperate strategically with Washington and Reagan's campaign statements caused many Americans to blame Reagan's policy of supporting Taiwan for undermining U.S.-PRC relations. The bitter, but misdirected feelings held by some can be seen in the following statement of Richard Holbrooke, Carter's Assistant Secretary of State responsible for East Asian affairs. Holbrooke wrote in the <u>Asian Wall Street Journal</u> shortly after Reagan came to office:

> The strategic relationship with China, not Taiwan, is the main issue, with global and historic importance. That it has been submerged under the Taiwan issue only illustrates anew that trivia can command center stage while great issues wait in the wings.[254]

As part of its evolving independent foreign policy, Beijing assumed a firmer position on the Taiwan issue in its relations with the United States. A number of considerations entered into this decision. First, the elderly cadre on the mainland realized that the political, economic, social, and demographic trends on Taiwan might make reunification more difficult in the future. Wanting to complete the unification process before their passing, the aging communist leaders concluded that the next ten to fifteen years were crucial in resolving the issue. This stepped-up timetable permitted little flexibility on the Taiwan issue in negotiations with the United States.

Second, conservative opposition to Deng's reforms mounted as he sought to institutionalize his pragmatic brand of socialism. Changes in the party and state bureaucracy, coupled with political appointments of Deng's supporters, threatened those whose views differed from that of the reformists. China's 1979-1980 retreat from the initial goals of the Four Modernizations made Deng vulnerable to criticism over his handling of the Taiwan issue as well. To placate his conservative critics, Deng no doubt found it useful to toughen his stand on Taiwan.

Third, the Chinese believed that unless they voiced strong opposition to U.S. policy toward Taiwan, the Reagan Administration might approve the sale of an advanced fighter and other sophisticated weapons to

---

[254] Richard Holbrooke, "Reagan's Foreign Policy: Steady As She Goes," <u>Asian Wall Street Journal</u>, April 8, 1980, p. 4.

Taiwan. The President was considered friendly to Taiwan, and the sentiments of his conservative supporters were well known. U.S. sales might also precipitate a commitment by other western powers to sell advanced weapons to Taiwan. This would have the effect of strengthening the ROC and encouraging Taipei to reject PRC proposals for peaceful reunification.

Fourth, unless China assumed a hard line on the Taiwan issue, it would lose face in the world community. A great deal of noise had been made to warn the United States not to interfere in China's internal affairs. To appear moderate on the Taiwan issue in the face of Reagan's campaign statements would signal a certain weakness of the part of Beijing.

8.5   CHINA BECOMES INFLEXIBLE

From August 1980, following the uproar over Reagan's campaign statements, the PRC hardened its position on the Taiwan issue with the United States. The next incident arose in October 1980 when the American Institute in Taiwan (AIT) and its Taiwan counterpart, the Coordination Council for North American Affairs (CCNAA), signed an agreement giving each other's representatives diplomatic privileges and immunities. Although the United States viewed the agreement as a "minor thing" and in keeping with the spirit of the Taiwan Relations Act, the PRC complained that Washington was extending "official status to the two organizations." Once again, in an authoritative Renmin Ribao commentary, the Chinese pointed to the disruptive effects the TRA and U.S. ties with Taiwan were having on Sino-American strategic relations. The article warned: "Clearly a question of major importance for the leaders of the United States is whether to pursue relations further or to reverse them."[255]

During the final months of 1980, two developments occurred which were to have important impact on Sino-American relations and the Taiwan issue. One involved domestic political affairs in the three capitals. In the United States, Ronald Reagan, a conservative widely known for his sympathetic ties to Taiwan and strong anti-communist sentiments, was elected President. Throughout his administration, Reagan's conservative supporters, reminding him that his election was due largely to their backing, would push the President for greater support of Taiwan.

---

[255] Renmin Ribao, October 9, 1980, in FBIS-China, October 9, 1980, p. B1.

In China, the trial of the Gang of Four got under way, an event interpreted by most observers as indirect criticism of the radical policies of Mao Zedong. The trial had the effect of putting Deng Xiaoping's faction more firmly in control, but it also resulted in greater fractionalization between those who favored a pragmatic approach to China's modernization and those who felt the reforms betrayed the ideals of the communist revolution. Opposition to Deng's economic and social programs from conservative elements in the military, bureaucracy, and party removed much of Deng's flexibility on the Taiwan issue in dealing with the United States. The vocal pro-Taiwan supporters of the new American President made a hardline position on Taiwan a political necessity in Beijing.

In Taiwan, supplemental elections were held for the Legislative Yuan, demonstrating Taipei's determination to move closer to a representative democracy. The trend toward greater democracy on Taiwan had three important effects on the Taiwan issue in Sino-American relations: it made Taiwan more "indigestible" to the communist mainland; it further weakened the cultural and personal links between Taiwan and China; and it convinced Taiwan's supporters in the United States that the island should not fall into the hands of the communists.

As important as these political developments were to the Taiwan issue in Sino-American relations, of far greater immediate impact was the decision by the Dutch government in November 1980 to sell Taiwan two Zwaardvis submarines to be built by the Rijn-Schelde-Verolme Shipyards. The PRC strongly protested the sale, calling it "detrimental to the peaceful unification of Taiwan and the mainland and only (serving) to increase tension in the Taiwan Strait area. No country friendly to China should make such a decision which is absolutely unacceptable to the Chinese people."[256]

Throughout December 1980 and January 1981 the PRC warned that if the submarine sale were allowed to go through, relations between Beijing and The Hague would suffer seriously. The Netherlands reached a final decision to go ahead with the sale in mid-January, at which time the Chinese Foreign Ministry notified the Dutch government that their relations would have to be downgraded to the level of charge d'affaires. The actual downgrading did not occur until May 5, 1981, however, after months of highly publicized efforts by the PRC to get the Dutch to change their minds.

---

[256] Xinhua, December 3, 1980, in FBIS-China, December 4, 1980, p. G1.

The strong Chinese reaction to the sale was directed as much to the incoming Reagan Administration as to the Dutch. After pointing to the numerous Chinese warnings, a January 17, 1981 Xinhua commentary asked: "Why, then, is the Netherland's Government insisting on doing this stupid thing despite the opposition by both the Chinese and Netherlands people?" The commentary went on:

> The answer has to be found in U.S. backstage support....The United States...told the Netherlands that the U.S. Government itself was also planning to sell weapons to Taiwan....Some advisers of U.S. President-elect Reagan...said that the attitude of the new U.S. President toward Taiwan would be even more active that the present President, Carter. Obviously, the adverse current now emerging in a number of countries to create "two Chinas" and interfere in China's internal affairs originates from the pro-Taiwan forces in the United States. We sternly warn those attempting to create the adverse current of "two Chinas" in the international community that the Chinese people will not tolerate them, be they small countries, big powers or superpowers, or whether they choose to use "two Chinas" or "one China, one Taiwan" or other forms of "two Chinas."[257]

In the final Renmin Ribao commentary on the submarine sale and subsequent downgrading of relations with The Hague, China indirectly warned the Reagan Administration that it would suffer similar consequences if it persisted in selling arms to Taiwan:

> As is well known, the Chinese Government's stand on the Taiwan question is clear-cut and steadfast: Taiwan is a sacred, inalienable part of Chinese territory and the PRC Government is the sole, legitimate government of China. The Chinese Government and people will say no to any "two Chinas" scheme and any intention to establish official ties with and sell arms to the Taiwan authorities whatever the pretext. What attitude to take on the Taiwan question has always been one of the important bases for the establishment of

---

[257] Xinhua, January 17, 1981, in FBIS-China, January 19, 1981, p. G2.

> diplomatic relations between China and other
> countries....By clinging to a wrong course,
> the Dutch Government has not only damaged the
> interest of the Chinese people, but also that
> of the Dutch people, thus impairing the
> antihegemonist struggle of the world's people.
> Whoever started the trouble should be the one
> to end it. The friendly relations between the
> two countries could be restored if the Dutch
> Government changes its erroneous stand by
> calling off its submarine deal with Taiwan.[258]

At the same time that Beijing was warning of the serious consequences of selling arms to Taiwan, American supporters of the ROC were increasing their calls for significant arms sales to Taipei. Conservatives looked at arms sales as one sure indication of whether Reagan would live up to his campaign promises to improve relations with Taiwan. Many others, including a large number of Senators and Congressmen, felt that Carter had deliberately withheld the sale of advanced weapons to Taiwan in order to smooth Sino-American relations. One Senate Foreign Relations Committee report concluded: "the failure to approve or even address Taiwan's top priorities--an advanced fighter (the FX), the Harpoon (naval) missile and the Standard (air defense) missile--raised questions about the willingness of the United States to improve and modernize Taiwan's defensive military capabilities." According to the report, Taiwan's military felt these weapons were essential for the island's defense:

> Given that Taiwan is subject to assault
> "with very short early-warning time," the
> military believes that, "the success and
> failure of Taiwan and Penghu defense
> operations lie in whether or not Taiwan can
> maintain naval and air superiorities and
> effectively control the Taiwan Strait." To do
> so, "the enhancement of ROC's naval and air
> combat effectiveness cannot bear any delay."
> This requires, "higher performance defensive
> weapons, equipment, and spare parts on a
> long-term supply and updating basis" and,
> specifically, a high performance aircraft, the
> Harpoon anti-ship missile and the Standard
> missile as priority items.[259]

---

[258] *Renmin Ribao*, May 6, 1981, in *FBIS-China*, May 7, 1981, p. G2.

Thus, at the outset of the Reagan Administration, the arms sales issue had become the focal point for much of the debate raging in Washington and Beijing over how far the United States could go in its support of Taiwan without irreparably damaging Sino-American relations. The key weapon system around which the debate centered was a replacement fighter for Taiwan's aging inventory of interceptors, half of which would reach the end of their life expectancy around 1986.

Midway through the Carter Administration, Taipei requested permission from the United States to purchase a follow-on aircraft to the Northrop F-5E/F. The logical plane and the one approved in principle by the Department of State and Department of Defense was Northrop's F-5G.[259] A combination of factors--political pressure on Congress to give General Dynamics an opportunity to compete with Northrop's export fighter, the desire to avoid antagonizing Beijing during the sensitive normalization talks, and Taipei's own unwillingness to make a firm decision on which aircraft it wanted--caused repeated delays in what otherwise would have been a large, but fairly routine, arms sales transaction. By the time the Reagan Administration came to office, the replacement fighter issue had become a political time bomb which threatened to derail U.S.-China relations.

---

[259] U.S. Senate, Committee on Foreign Relations, Implementation of the Taiwan Relations Act; the First Year: A Staff Report (Washington, D.C.: GPO, June 1980), pp. 10, 23.

[260] For background on the fighter sale issue, see Robert G. Sutter and William deB. Mills, "Fighter Aircraft Sales to Taiwan: U.S. Policy," Issue Brief, IB81157 (October 28, 1981), Library of Congress, Congressional Research Service.

9
Period of Contention: 1981-1982

Despite the fact that Taiwan had reemerged as the key issue between the United States and China by the end of the Carter Administration, both Washington and Beijing sought to minimize their differences during the first few months of 1981 to give the new administration a chance to adjust to office. President Reagan, at some cost in political support from the conservatives, did not carry out his campaign pledge to recognize as "official" the U.S. relationship with Taiwan.

In April 1981 Deng Xiaoping acknowledged this shift in Reagan's view, telling a group of visiting Japanese parliamentarians that he was "happy with a policy shift by the administration of U.S. President Ronald Reagan towards China."[261] In June Reagan sent Secretary of State Alexander Haig to China in an attempt to bridge the differences between the two countries that had emerged during the campaign. Just prior to Haig's arrival, Zhao Ziyang laid out the fundamental Chinese position that U.S.-PRC relations had to be conducted according to the principles contained in the normalization agreement of January 1, 1979. Zhao said:

> In the final analysis, a possible improvement in Sino-American relations depends on whether the U.S. Government will abide by the principles of the joint communique on the establishment of diplomatic relations between China and the United States in handling the relations between the two countries. This is the most important and even the most fundamental point. Only when this point is reached can one speak of further improving the relations between the two countries.[262]

---

[261] Kyodo, April 14, 1981, in FBIS-China, April 14, 1981, p. D2.

During his trip, Haig emphasized the strategic importance of Sino-American relations. He said that "a fundamental strategic perspective" governed Reagan's Asian policy and that the key element was the Soviet threat. While Haig was in the Far East, it was disclosed in Washington that the United States and the PRC were jointly operating a secret monitoring station in Xinjiang to keep track of Soviet missile tests.[263] Despite early efforts by the Reagan Administration to maintain and expand Sino-American strategic cooperation, the Chinese indicated that their policy toward the Soviet Union had changed. Immediately following Haig's visit, Li Xiannian said: "We would like better relations with the Soviet Union. We want continued negotiations on normalization."[264]

Undaunted, Secretary Haig announced toward the end of his Asian tour that the United States would consider selling arms to China on a case-by-case basis.[265] Later, in testimony before the House Committee on Foreign Affairs, Assistant Secretary of State John Holdridge explained that Haig's announcement was "not a decision to sell any specific weapons systems or military technology; it will merely enable Beijing to make requests to purchase from U.S. commercial sources any items on the U.S. munitions list, including weapons."[266]

Speculation immediately arose that Haig had struck a deal with the Chinese: in return for China's acquiescence to American arms sales to Taiwan, Washington would permit Beijing to purchase U.S. weapons. To end such conjecture, the PRC Foreign Ministry said:

> We have time and again made it clear that we would rather receive no U.S. arms than accept continuing U.S. interference in our internal affairs by selling arms to Taiwan, to which we can never agree. Should the United

---

[262] *Xinhua*, June 7, 1981, in *FBIS-China*, June 8, 1981, p. F6.

[263] *International Herald Tribune*, June 22, 1981, p. 1.

[264] *China Post*, June 25, 1981, p. 1.

[265] *China News*, June 17, 1981, p. 1.

[266] See Holdridge's testimony in U.S. House of Representatives, Committee on Foreign Affairs, *The New Era in East Asia* (Washington, D.C.: GPO, 1981), pp. 342-345.

180

> States continue to sell arms to Taiwan in disregard of our repeated expressions of resolute objection, we certainly will give a strong response.[267]

The Reagan Administration took further steps to demonstrate its desire to improve relations with the PRC. Holdridge informed Congress that "our China relationship is global and strategic" and based on "the premise that China is not our adversary, but a friendly, developing country with which, without being allied, we share important strategic interests." Holdridge then announced that the Administration wanted to liberalize export controls over the sale of dual-use technology to China and also to make the PRC eligible for U.S. economic and security assistance. Regarding the problem of Taiwan, Holdridge said:

> We want to continue to improve the substance of our unofficial relations with the people of Taiwan. On his trip, the Secretary told the Chinese that we would continue to manage these relations--as we have since normalization--on the basis of the joint communique. As we have consistently stated, our own law establishes a basis for the continuation of these unofficial relations. It is clear that we have certain differences over Taiwan, which of course include the sale of defensive arms.[268]

By using the phrase "continue to manage these relations...on the basis of the joint communique," Holdridge gave public notification to Beijing of the Reagan Administration's intent to interpret the Taiwan Relations Act in accordance with the normalization agreement. This was, it will be recalled, the position of the Carter Administration and one with which the Chinese were comfortable--at least until June 1980. But a year later, the PRC reacted in a way to suggest it had somehow been slighted by the Reagan Administration. In an interview with the director of Hong Kong's *Ming Pao* newspaper in August 1981, Deng Xiaoping implied the United States had treated China with disrespect:

> China hopes that Sino-American relations will further develop rather than retrogress. However, this should not be one-sided. If the

---

[267] *Xinhua*, June 10, 1981, in *FBIS-China*, June 10, 1981, p. B1.

[268] Holdridge, *The New Era in East Asia*, pp. 343-344.

United States adopts a wrong view, it will formulate a wrong policy. It is nothing serious even if the United States causes a retrogression in Sino-American relations. If worst comes to worst and the relations retrogress to those prior to 1972, China will not collapse. It did not collapse before 1972, much less will it collapse now. In the 1950s, we got some help from the Soviet Union. Later, we did not get any. But, have we not survived? The Chinese people have high aspirations. They will never bow and scrape and beg for help....In the interest of the whole world and in the interest of the Chinese and the Americans, China and the United States should cooperate on an equal footing. If the United States does not play fair but forces China to act according to the will of the United States, China will not agree, nor is there any reason for China to agree.[269]

Once in office, therefore, the Reagan Administration attempted to smooth over differences with China over Taiwan and other issues. Beijing, however, seems to have interpreted the retreat from Reagan's campaign statements as evidence of need and weakness. When China pushed on the Taiwan issue, there was surprisingly little resistance from the Administration. Instead, there was an effort to accommodate the PRC and to reach an understanding in order to preserve what was viewed to be an essential strategic relationship. Although Beijing had already determined that its interests lie in a more independent foreign policy, its leaders recognized China's excellent bargaining position. Understandably, the PRC continued to push the Reagan Administration to gain concessions on Taiwan and on as many other issues as possible. The Administration did not seem to recognize the PRC bargaining strategy and to strengthen its own position until late in 1982. By that time, many of the critical decisions on Taiwan had already been made. The FX decision and the August 17, 1982 Joint Communique are two cases in point.

---

[269] Ming Pao, August 25, 1981, in FBIS-China, August 25, 1981, p. W6.

9.1 THE FX DECISION

While Chinese and American leaders were embroiled in internal debate and heated diplomacy over the FX, Taipei complicated Reagan's decision by refusing to choose between the F-5G and F-16/J79 variations of the FX. Instead, Taiwan notified Washington that it would accept any combination of the two planes.

Taipei was indecisive because many on Taiwan felt the Reagan Administration would eventually fulfill its promises to upgrade Taiwan's defenses. High-ranking officials within the Administration kept signalling that the approval of an advanced fighter was in the making. Edwin Meese, for example, said the Reagan Administration was "committed" to sell advanced weapons to Taiwan, a statement confirmed by the State Department as being "standard United States policy."[270]

As it turned out, proponents of the FX sale underestimated both the bureaucratic skill of the opposition and the persuasive power of the argument that the sale would jeopardize Sino-American strategic relations.

Throughout October and November 1981 serious negotiations were underway between China and the United States over future arms sales to Taiwan. In October President Reagan met Premier Zhao Ziyang at Cancun, Mexico, during the North-South economic congress. The two men talked amicably but with little meeting of the minds. Later that month, Foreign Minister Huang Hua spent two days in Washington discussing Sino-American relations. At a banquet given in his honor on October 29, Huang warned of "storms" and "reefs" ahead and emphasized the importance of handling Sino-American relations "with a strategic perspective."[271] Huang Hua told U.S. leaders that China would oppose the sale of any weapons to Taiwan unless the United States made a public commitment to reduce arms sales gradually over a fixed period, with a final cutoff date around 1986.[272]

Domestic political pressure, meanwhile, continued to build on President Reagan to reach a decision on the FX. Supporters of Taiwan pointed to successful elections on the island in November 1981 as proof of Taipei's commitment to democracy.[273] Conservatives also

---

[270] China Post, May 14, 1981, p. 12.

[271] Xinhua, October 30, 1981, in FBIS-China, October 30, 1981, p. B1.

[272] Robert G. Sutter, "China-U.S. Relations," Issue Brief, IB76053 (November 22, 1982), Library of Congress, Congressional Research Service, p. 18.

noted that the PRC journal <u>Research on International Problems</u> had stated in July 1981 that the TRA encouraged Taiwan to reject China's peaceful proposals. "As a result," the journal said, "China may be forced to resort to nonpeaceful methods to settle the Taiwan problem against its wish."[274]

Considerable congressional support for the FX sale was also found. In a poll conducted by the Washington-based American Council for Free Asia in mid-June 1981, U.S. Senators were asked: "Should President Reagan decide to approve the sale of the FX (F-16-79) fighter planes to Taiwan, would you vote to approve this sale when the issue comes before the Senate?" Only six Senators expressed opposition to the sale, while 59 expressed approval.[275] Beijing's harsh crackdown on Chinese dissidents added fuel to the arguments of those who favored the sale. Widespread coverage was given to Hu Yaobang's description of China's literary and political dissidents as "dark phenomena in our present socialist society" and pledge of "an unrelenting struggle against these evils."[276] Also strengthening the pro-sale position were reports that China was building the F-8, a new fighter which would increase the PRC threat to Taiwan.[277]

Opponents of the sale emphasized the negative effect it would have on Sino-American strategic relations, pointing to the postponement of the trip of PLA Deputy Chief of Staff Liu Huaqing as an example. Liu had been scheduled to come to Washington to discuss Chinese arms purchases and the transfer of military technology.[278] Jimmy Carter's trip to Beijing in late August and early September 1981 tended to strengthen the case of those arguing against the FX sale to Taiwan. Carter said that while his administration had never agreed to limit the duration of arms sales to Taiwan, he had told the Chinese that U.S. weapons sales would be "defensive in nature," "not advanced," and "no threat to the mainland."[279] There was strong feeling in some

---

[273] See <u>China Post</u>, November 14, 1981, p. 1; and <u>ibid</u>., November 16, 1981, p. 1.

[274] <u>New York Times</u>, July 4, 1981, p. 3.

[275] American Council for Free Asia, Press Release, June 21, 1981.

[276] <u>Washington Post</u>, September 26, 1981, p. A1.

[277] <u>American Relations</u>, 9, 9 (September 1981), p. 6.

[278] <u>News Digest</u>, November 12, 1981, p. 8.

circles that the FX would be perceived as an offensive weapon by China and that the plane had capabilities far beyond those required by Taiwan for its defense needs.[280]

The House Subcommittee on Asian and Pacific Affairs sent a letter to President Reagan on June 18, 1981, urging him not to approve the FX. Three principal arguments were presented: there was no PRC military threat to Taiwan; Beijing was pursuing a policy of peaceful reunification with Taipei; and the sale of an advanced fighter would jeopardize the delicate and mutually beneficial relations between the United States and China. Other members of the House Foreign Affairs Committee argued in favor of the sale. They sent a letter to President Reagan on November 17, 1981, urging him to approve the FX sale on the grounds that Beijing's refusal to renounce the use of force against Taiwan constituted a sufficient threat to justify modern replacement aircraft for the island's outdated inventory.

In addition to the public debate over the FX, there were numerous bureaucratic power plays between those favoring and opposing the sale. The stakes were high. Many bureaucrats had spent years painstakingly trying to build a constructive relationship with China. Those convinced that short-sighted, conservative backers of Reagan were about to undermine that effort by forcing the Chinese to downgrade relations used every available means--including leaks and rumors--to prevent the sale.[281] Someone, for example, leaked a CIA and Pentagon report concluding that Taiwan did not need an advanced fighter.[282]

As of early December, a decision still had not been reached. On December 7, the State Department wrote to one Republican congressman that the FX decision "is a most sensitive issue, as I am sure you appreciate, and as of now no decision, not even in principle, has been made."

---

[279] Washington Post, August 28, 1981, p. A14; and ibid., September 4, 1981, p. A4.

[280] See A. Doak Barnett, The FX Decision: "Another Crucial Moment" in U.S.-China-Taiwan Relations (Washington, D.C.: Brookings Institution, 1981).

[281] See Rowland Evans and Robert Novak in Washington Post, November 30, 1981, p. A11.

[282] Newsweek, November 2, 1981, p. 29.

The Chinese apparently got wind of a pending arms transaction to Taiwan in mid-December, because several harsh statements were made by PRC leaders at that time. Li Xiannian in a December 13 interview in Japan's <u>Mainichi</u> <u>Shimbun</u> said that Taiwan is "China's domestic question and China will resolve it on its own. Should the United States push ahead with its plan to sell arms to Taiwan, it will make Chiang Ching-kuo happy but will bring harsh criticisms from the one billion Chinese people." On the same day Deng Xiaoping told a reporter from Yugoslavia's <u>Zagreb</u> <u>Vjesnik</u> that should the United States go ahead and sell arms to Taiwan, "We will react sharply. China will not swallow this."

Huang Hua said in Tokyo on December 15 that if the United States continued arming Taiwan, "This would prove an obstacle to the island's return to the People's Republic."[283] In an interview with <u>Sankei</u> <u>Shimbun</u> on December 23, Liao Chengzhi voiced similar sentiments. He said that contacts had been made between the two Chinese sides and that "we would like to attain unification while Mr. Chiang Ching-kuo is alive." Liao then elaborated on China's reunification proposal and noted that U.S. arms sales interfered:

> We will not send even a single man of the Chinese PLA into Taiwan. Since Taiwan needs armed forces for defense, it will be all right if their armed forces are charged with that mission. Taiwan can maintain its armed forces, police and even secret service organization....What we oppose is the U.S. attempt to sell arms to Taiwan and to keep two Chinas intact. The United States says that it set forth a law pertaining to Taiwan and Mr. Reagan says that they are going to sell arms in accordance with this law. This is a two-China policy to its bitter end. This is why we oppose it. The arms sale issue has nothing to do with Taiwan's maintenance of armed forces.

On December 25 Li Xiannian told <u>Yomiuri</u> <u>Shimbun</u>: "The Taiwan issue is now posing a barrier to the development of China-U.S. relations, but China will never make concessions on the Taiwan question....If concessions should be made, the present leadership, including Premier Zhao Ziyang, would have to resign en masse."

---

[283] <u>Xinhua</u>, December 15, 1981, in <u>FBIS-China</u>, December 16, 1981, p. D4.

On December 29, in a possible trial balloon to test the Chinese reaction, the United States announced that it was going ahead with a sale of $97 million in spare parts to Taiwan. The Chinese response to this "routine transaction" was exceptionally strong. The PRC Foreign Ministry urged "the U.S. Government to clarify its decision to sell arms parts to Taiwan," and reaffirmed once again that "the Chinese Government resolutely opposes the U.S. sale of weapons to Taiwan."[284]

In an important Renmin Ribao commentary, the Chinese made it clear that the arms sales issue had reached a point of crisis. The article, quoted at length below because of its impact on the FX decision, said:

> It is now three years since China and the United States established diplomatic relations. During these three years, Sino-American relations have developed very well in the political, economic, scientific and technological and cultural fields, as a result of the common efforts of the governments and peoples of the two countries....However, to put it bluntly, there has always existed an obstacle on the road of the development of Sino-American relations, and that obstacle is the question of U.S. arms sales to Taiwan.

The article accused the Reagan Administration of intending to continue to sell arms to Taiwan and even to increase the level of sales. The commentary claimed the U.S. side had declared that China had no right to interfere in the matter. "In this way the gravity of the problem is increased and, as a result, the problem has now reached a point where it absolutely must be solved."

Regarding U.S. arms sales to Taiwan, the commentary made the Chinese position very clear:

> We have consistently been opposed to other countries selling arms to the Taiwan authorities. Since any country establishing diplomatic relations with China acknowledges that there is only one China, that the PRC is the sole legal government of China, and that Taiwan is part of China, it should obviously not sell arms to the Taiwan authorities, who

---

[284] Xinhua, December 29, 1981, in FBIS-China, December 29, 1981, p. B1.

constitute a local force in China. Anyone who
acts in this way is violating China's
sovereignty and interfering in China's
internal affairs. Naturally, the United
States is no exception in this respect.

After China and the United States
established diplomatic relations, the U.S.
Government should not have engaged in any more
activities in violation of China's sovereignty
and of interference in China's internal
affairs, such as by selling arms to Taiwan.
On the one hand, the United States has
recognized that Taiwan is part of China, and,
on the other, it has regarded Taiwan as an
'independent political entity,' and has also
supplied arms to support this local regime in
opposing the legitimate Chinese Central
Government which the United States has
recognized. This behavior obviously violates
the principles of the communique on the
establishment of Sino-American diplomatic
relations, and is also prohibited by the
principles of international law.

The article stated that the Chinese Government has
consistently expressed "its solemn and just stand
regarding this erroneous attitude of the U.S.
Government." The commentary then gave the essential
bargaining position of the PRC:

> What China requires from the United States on
> the Taiwan issue is that it should properly
> respect China's sovereignty and territorial
> integrity and not interfere in China's
> internal affairs. This is the most elementary
> requirement of a sovereign state....The
> Chinese people...resolutely will not tolerate
> any foreign country's intentions to violate
> China's sovereignty, carve up its territory
> and interfere in its internal affairs. This
> is a major question that involves the national
> emotions of one billion Chinese people. The
> Chinese Government, as the representative of
> the Chinese people's will, absolutely will not
> take an unprincipled, forebearing and
> conciliatory attitude on issues involving its
> own territory and sovereignty. On the issue
> of how to solve the problem of U.S. arms sales
> to Taiwan, China both sticks to its principles
> and is also reasonable.

The article continued: "Here, a fundamental principle must first be affirmed. This means that in accordance with the principles of international relations and the communique on the establishment of Sino-American relations, the United States should properly respect China's sovereignty and should not interfere in its internal affairs and should not sell arms to Taiwan. Under the premise of recognizing this principle, both sides can hold consultations on ways to solve the problem."

In the view of Beijing, the Reagan Administration had "tried by every means to deny facts in an attempt to avoid being constrained" on arms sales. The article said: "If you want to preserve and develop Sino-American relations, then the problem of U.S. arms sales to Taiwan must be solved on the basis of properly respecting China's sovereignty. There is no way this problem can be solved by ignoring China's sovereignty."

The commentary then went on to reaffirm the Chinese government's "endeavor to solve the Taiwan issue by peaceful means." *Renmin Ribao* said:

> It is precisely because the Chinese Government has made a series of major efforts that a new situation has emerged in the solution of the Taiwan issue. This has also objectively created the most favorable conditions for the United States to halt its arms sales to Taiwan, to refrain from interfering again in China's internal affairs, and to eliminate the obstacle that threatens relations between the two countries.

The commentary said that under these conditions of peaceful reunification, if the United States continues to sell arms to Taiwan, then U.S. intentions must be called into question and the United States considered a hegemonist power. In its conclusion the commentary tied Sino-American strategic cooperation to the arms sales issue:

> The Chinese Government has always viewed and handled Sino-American relations from the angle of global strategy. On the issue of how to solve the problem of U.S. arms sales to Taiwan, the Chinese Government both safeguards China's sovereignty and considers the overall strategic situation. At present, the Chinese people and the people of the whole world who love peace and uphold justice are watching with concern whether or not the U.S. Government can correctly solve the issue of arms sales to Taiwan. This will be a severe

test of whether or not the United States truly
treasures its relations with China and has a
concept of global strategy.[285]

The Renmin Ribao article clearly linked continued
U.S. support to Taiwan with continued Sino-American
strategic cooperation. Caught in the pressure of the
moment, the Reagan Administration missed the important
point that if the Chinese were willing to downgrade
strategic cooperation with the United States over the
Taiwan issue, then the value of strategic cooperation to
the Chinese must have declined. Instead, the
Administration decided to compromise on the Taiwan issue
in order to preserve the strategic relationship.

A few days after the commentary, while Congress was
out of session and therefore unable to react, the
Administration turned down Taiwan's request for an
advanced fighter. On January 11, 1982, the State
Department announced:

> Concerned agencies of the U.S. Government,
> including the Departments of State and Defense
> and other national security elements, have
> been addressing the question of Taiwan's
> defense needs over a period of many months and
> have taken into consideration the many factors
> which bear on the judgments which must be made
> in implementing this policy....
>
> A judgment has...been reached by the
> concerned agencies on the question of
> replacement aircraft for Taiwan. The
> conclusion is that no sale of advanced fighter
> aircraft to Taiwan is required because no
> military need for such aircraft exists.
> Taiwan's defense needs can be met as they
> arise, and for the foreseeable future, by
> replacing aging aircraft now in the Taiwan
> inventory with comparable aircraft and by
> extension of the F-5E coproduction line in
> Taiwan.[286]

---

[285] This important commentary can be found in Renmin Ribao, December 31. 1981, in FBIS-China, December 31, 1981, pp. B1 ff.

[286] "No Sale of Advanced Aircraft to Taiwan," Department of State Bulletin, 82, 2059 (February 1982), p. 39.

Several months later, Secretary of State Alexander Haig, who was widely given credit for convincing the President to turn down the FX, was questioned in congressional hearings as to why the Congress had not been consulted prior to the FX decision. The Secretary responded:

> There was certainly no intention to avoid Congressional consultation in reaching the F-X decision, but events in mid-late December in Poland and China's extreme reaction to our notification of a Taiwan spare parts transaction to the Congress forced a decision earlier than we expected, before Congress returned from recess.[287]

The Secretary's statement is interesting, because it illustrates China's effectiveness in linking Sino-American strategic cooperation with the Taiwan issue. The United States in December 1981 had urged Beijing to oppose the imposition of martial law in Poland and to condemn the role of the Soviet Union in the crackdown on Solidarity. China rebuffed U.S. efforts, however, signing instead an agreement with Poland increasing trade by 30%. The PRC position was reasonable enough, given the CPC's own concern about a Solidarity-type movement among its labor force. But the fact that the Administration was willing to time its announcement of the FX decision in order to convince Beijing to support Washington on Poland suggests that the United States had not yet detected the shift in China's strategic perceptions.[288]

Having made a decision favorable to Beijing and confident that Sino-American relations were once again back on track, the Administration dispatched John Holdridge to China to explain the FX decision. Holdridge also was to tell the Chinese that the United States would not be selling Taiwan the Harpoon missile.

---

[287] U.S. House of Representatives, Committee on Appropriations, Subcommittee on Foreign Operations, Foreign Assistance and Related Programs, Appropriations for 1983, Part I, 97th Cong., 2d sess. (1982), p. 131.

[288] The best description of events surrounding the FX decision can be found in Tad Szulc, "The Reagan Administration's Push Toward China Came from Warsaw," Los Angeles Times, January 17, 1982, Part IV, p. 1; and Rowland Evans and Robert Novak, "Taiwan Turnabout," Washington Post, January 16, 1982, p. A11.

Contrary to U.S. expectations, Holdridge received harsh criticism. The PRC Foreign Ministry lodged "a strong protest" against the extension of the F-5E coproduction line, saying "The Chinese Government will never accept any unilateral decision made by the U.S. Government."[289]

The focus of the Chinese protest centered not on the sale itself, but on the fact that the United States unilaterally announced the sale the day Holdridge arrived in Beijing.[290] The Chinese were saying that, henceforth, they wanted to be included in decisions regarding arms sales to Taiwan--a significant expansion of their previously held position on the issue.

9.2 THE ARMS SALES CONTROVERSY

On January 31 Xinhua commented that while the PRC considered U.S. arms sales to Taiwan an "infringement" of China's sovereignty, Beijing was willing "to negotiate with the United States for an end to the sales within a time limit." The article implied that China was being reasonable on this issue because of the larger security concerns of both countries.[291] Sources within the United States confirmed that Washington had entered into negotiations with Beijing to try to resolve the arms sales issue.[292]

On the tenth anniversary of the Shanghai Communique, Xinhua again linked the Taiwan issue to continued Sino-American strategic cooperation. The article said:

> Sino-U.S. relations have truly come to a critical point that will determine if relations improve or deteriorate. China has consistently held that because of the interests of global strategy, it is necessary for Sino-U.S. ties to develop. This is what China has strived to achieve. However, the

---

[289] Xinhua, January 12, 1982, in FBIS-China, January 12, 1982, p. B1.

[290] "Commentary: Going Too Far," Embassy of the People's Republic of China, Press Release No. 82/002, January 15, 1982, pp. 1-2.

[291] New York Times, February 1, 1982, p. A3.

[292] See Wall Street Journal, January 20, 1982, p. 27; and Washington Post, January 26, 1982, p. A14.

United States must observe the sovereignty of China as a prerequisite for a better relationship. Unfortunately, some people in the United States always try to interfere in the internal affairs of China, flouting China's sovereignty. They seek to create "two-Chinas" by one means or another, and even regard Taiwan as an "unsinkable aircraft carrier" in the Far East for the United States....

In view of the fact that the Taiwan issue is inherited from history, the Chinese Government, while sticking to its principled position, has been very patient and realistic in its negotiations with Washington and has put forward many reasonable and just proposals. However, the matter has developed to such a point that China is forced into a corner without any options. If the United States insists on a long-term policy of selling arms to Taiwan, Sino-U.S. relations will retrogress....It must be made clear that in the wake of retrogression, China will not only be able to survive and fare better, but will continue with the policies it has pursued in recent years. Chinese views on international affairs, especially its opposition to hegemony, will not change. Neither will its open-door and other policies.[293]

The PRC in March and April punctuated their emphatic stand on Taiwan by taking issue over what seemed to be minor incidents. The first, and the one which received the most coverage in Beijing's press, was Taiwan's plan to fly its national flag and to play its national anthem at the opening and closing ceremonies of the Fifth World Women's Softball Championships scheduled for July 1982 in Taipei. Beijing's protests over the proposed display of ROC nationalism created an international incident. In the end, several teams, including those from China and Japan, withdrew from the games.

The second incident occurred when President Reagan signed legislation giving Taiwan its own immigration quota separate from that of the mainland. The PRC on March 30 protested the Act as "another U.S. move to create 'two Chinas' by treating Taiwan as a 'separate

---

[293] Xinhua, March 1, 1982, in FBIS-China, March 2, 1982, p. B1.

foreign state' on the issue of immigration."[294]

The third incident involved the $97 million spare parts package to be sold to Taiwan announced in December 1981. Beijing's earlier strong protest over the sale led to the postponement of the formal announcement and influenced the Administration's decision not to sell the FX to Taiwan. In late March, despite concerns that the PRC might downgrade relations, the Administration decided to go ahead with the sale. Those wanting to proceed with the congressional notification argued that the transaction had been postponed for several months, that Taipei needed the spares to keep vital elements of its armed forces functioning, and that the sale was far lower that the $600 million in equipment sold to Taiwan by Carter with little protest from Beijing.[295]

Upon hearing of the pending notification, the PRC loudly threatened to downgrade relations with the United States if the spare parts package was submitted to Congress.[296] When the Administration indicated that it would proceed with the notification in any case, the Chinese backed down slightly, announcing that they would protest the transaction but not downgrade relations.[297] At the same time, however, the PRC released the outlines of a recent American proposal to resolve the arms sales issue. The plan, which eventually formed the basis of the August 17, 1982 Joint Communique, called for a pledge by Washington not to provide Taiwan with military equipment beyond the quantity and quality of its current arsenal, and a promise to eventually terminate military sales if Taiwan and the mainland reconciled their differences peacefully.[298]

The Administration notified the Congress of its intention to sell $60 million in spare parts to Taiwan on April 13. The remaining $37 million provided for services associated with stockpiling the supplies and did not require congressional notification. As expected, the Chinese government lodged "a strong protest with the U.S. government against this act of infringing upon China's sovereignty"; but the PRC also went out of its way to point out that the transaction was for spare parts, not arms. The Foreign Ministry

---

[294] Xinhua, March 30, 1982, in FBIS-China, March 30, 1982, p. B1.

[295] New York Times, April 1, 1982, p. A11.

[296] Ibid., April 6, 1982, p. A1.

[297] Wall Street Journal, April 7, 1982, p. 3.

[298] New York Times, April 6, 1982, p. A1.

statement noted: "At present, the Sino-U.S. bilateral discussions on the question of U.S. arms sales to Taiwan are still underway."[299]

In short order, the Chinese again began to apply pressure on the United States. On April 21 Liao Chengzhi told a Japanese guest: "no optimism can be warranted about the continued smooth relations between Beijing and Washington."[300] The next day in talks with former Japanese Premier Masayoshi Ohira, Zhao Ziyang said there was "little space" on the Chinese side for a compromise over Taiwan. Zhao told his guest that the Chinese had waited for three years for a resolution of the arms sales issue, but "we cannot allow such a situation to go on for any longer."[301] On May 2, a few days before the arrival of Vice President George Bush, the Chinese called the U.S. policy of selling arms to Taiwan "a time bomb" in Sino-American relations. The People's Daily said, "The problem of U.S. arms sales to Taiwan has reached a stage where it must be solved."[302]

On May 7, the day of Bush's arrival, Ji Pengfei gave an interview with Thai journalists in which the question of U.S.-PRC-USSR relations was raised in the context of the Taiwan issue. Ji's response confirmed that China was now pursuing an independent foreign policy and that strategic cooperation with the United States no longer justified China's patience on the Taiwan issue:

> U.S.-PRC relations are progressing well on the one hand, but on the other hand, the United States is selling weapons to Taiwan. Such conduct is unacceptable. PRC-U.S. relations have been established for three years now. The issue of weapons sales to Taiwan should be ended now. It is the biggest issue....If, after negotiations, the United States agrees to suspend the sale of weapons to Taiwan, the fine relations between the two countries will

---

[299] "Spokesman of Chinese Foreign Ministry Issues Statement on U.S. Sale of Military-Related Spare Parts to Taiwan," Embassy of the People's Republic of China, Press Release No. 82/006, April 14, 1982, pp. 1-2.

[300] Kyodo, April 21, 1982, in FBIS-China, April 21, 1982, p. K2.

[301] AFP, April 22, 1982, in FBIS-China, April 22, 1982, p. B1.

[302] New York Times, May 3, 1982, p. A5.

continue. Relations will be affected if the
United States persists in selling weapons.
Certainly we do not want to see U.S.-PRC
relations regress, but if the United States is
persistent, we have a policy of
antihegemonism. Some say that China will turn
toward the Soviet Union if its relations with
the United States worsen. This opinion is
wrong. China is an independent country. We
are not dependent on the Soviet Union or the
United States; we depend on ourselves.
China's policy is to oppose the two
superpowers, win over the Second World and
unite with the Third World.[303]

It was against this backdrop that Vice President
Bush returned to China, the highest ranking official
from the Reagan Administration then to visit Beijing.
Bush described his trip as one "to discuss all
issues--bilateral, international--with all frankness and
candor." He called China "an equal partner in world
affairs," and said he would "reaffirm to the Chinese
leadership the fundamental principles upon which we have
established normal relations, including the United
States' position recognizing only one China."[304] Quite
clearly, the Vice President's mission was to put the
arms talks back on track and to try to restore PRC
confidence in the intentions of President Reagan to live
up to the normalization agreement.

The PRC received Bush as an old friend. Deng told
the Vice President: "You know China well. We sincerely
welcome you as an old friend of China....Through your
visit, we hope we will be able to dispel the shadows and
dark clouds overhanging our relations."[305]

Underlying Deng's friendly remarks were harsh
realities. Despite the greater flexibility in foreign
policy enjoyed by the PRC, China's leaders understood
their country's position was fraught with risks. PRC
security rested not on its own military strength but on
the status of the confrontation between the two
superpowers and the willingness of both governments to
pursue friendly relations with Beijing. Despite its
harsh rhetoric over the Taiwan issue, China could not
base its security upon the generosity of Moscow's

---

[303] Bangkok Matuphum, May 20, 1982, in FBIS-China, May 21, 1982, p. E1.

[304] New York Times, May 6, 1982, p. A3.

[305] Xinhua, May 8, 1982, in FBIS-China, May 10, 1982, p. B2.

leaders or risk a serious rupture of Sino-American relations.

It is to the credit of the Reagan Administration and close allies such as Japan that they repeatedly warned Beijing that a downgrading of relations with Washington could not be limited to diplomatic ties. Adverse effects would be felt across the entire spectrum of relations with the West: economic, cultural, scientific, technological, and political. The pragmatic leadership in Beijing was not willing to pay this high cost.

Vice President Bush is credited with bringing the Chinese back to the negotiating table to discuss the arms sales issue. Bush also delivered a letter from President Reagan to Chairman Hu Yaobang discussing Sino-American relations. Previously, the President had sent personal letters to Vice Chairman Deng Xiaoping and Premier Zhao Ziyang. In his letters, the President stated his intention to live up the normalization agreement and his desire to resolve the difficulties standing in the way of friendly U.S.-PRC relations. Reagan wrote Deng Xiaoping:

> The United States firmly adheres to the positions agreed upon in the Joint Communique on the establishment of diplomatic relations between the United States and China. There is only one China. We will not permit the unofficial relations between the American people and the people of Taiwan to weaken our commitment to this principle....
>
> We fully recognize the significance of the nine-point proposal of September 30, 1981 and the policy set forth by your government as early as January 1, 1979. The decisions and the principles conveyed on my instructions to your government on January 11, 1982, reflect our appreciation of the new situation created by these developments.
>
> In this spirit, we wish to continue our efforts to resolve our differences and to create a cooperative and enduring bilateral and strategic relationship. China and America are two great nations destined to grow stronger through cooperation, not weaker through division.

In his letter to Premier Zhao, President Reagan said in regard to Taiwan:

> The differences between us are rooted in the long-standing friendship between the American people and the Chinese people who live on Taiwan. We will welcome and support any peaceful resolution of the Taiwan question. In this connection, we appreciate the policies which your government has followed to provide a peaceful settlement....
>
> We expect that in the context of progress toward a peaceful solution, there would naturally be a decrease in the need for arms by Taiwan. Our positions over the past two months have reflected this view....

The President's letter to Hu Yaobang stressed the strategic importance of Sino-American relations: "As sovereign nations, our two countries share a common responsibility to promote world peace. We face a grave challenge from the Soviet Union which directly threatens our peoples and complicates the resolution of problems throughout the globe. It is vital that our relations advance and our cooperation be strengthened."

Following closely on the heels of Vice President Bush was Senate Majority Leader Howard H. Baker, who visited the PRC from May 30 to June 10. Senator Baker encountered an important difference in emphasis on the Chinese position regarding Taiwan. The Senator noted in his report:

> As with Vice President Bush three weeks before, the focus for the Chinese of each and every conversation were the impediments to building a strong relationship: the Taiwan Relations Act and, pursuant to it, arms sales....There was, however, a noticeable and perhaps significant shift in direction between the approach taken by Chinese officials in their discussions with Vice President Bush and with me. With the Vice President, the clear focus was arms sales and the insistence that they be terminated. In my case, the focus had shifted from arms sales, pursuant to the Taiwan Relations Act, to the Act itself.

Senator Baker said the Chinese felt "the very existence of the Act was inconsistent with a one-China policy." On several occasions his hosts inquired as to whether the Act could be amended. The Senate Majority Leader then speculated on what this new emphasis on the TRA could mean:

There would seem to me to be several
possible alternative reasons for the apparent
escalation of the Act itself as an issue of
contention in the relationship. One
possibility, of course, is that the Chinese
took the opportunity of raising the Act as
legislation with the Senate leadership.
Alternatively, they may be optimistic that the
arms sale issue is moving toward resolution
that would be satisfactory to both parties and
they were simply laying down a marker for
future negotiations. Finally, and most
pessimistically, the Chinese may escalate the
TRA as an issue of contention regardless of
the outcome of the discussion on the arms sale
issue and intend to force the issue into
active contention in the relationship.[306]

Future developments proved that all three of the
Senate Majority Leader's speculations were correct. The
Chinese had in fact set their sights not only on
limiting arms sales to Taiwan, but also on eliminating
or changing the Taiwan Relations Act. To achieve the
latter objective, the PRC would have to deal with the
U.S. Congress.

As a legislative body, Congress was much less
susceptible to Chinese pressure than the Administration.
Rather than being concerned about the intricacies of
foreign policy, most members of Congress reflected the
more subjective side of Sino-American relations. A
great many were disturbed, for example, when, during
Baker's visit, China announced it had arrested an
American citizen, Ms. Lisa Wichser, on charges that she
"collected information and stole many of China's
confidential documents."[307] It was obvious that Wichser
was not a spy and that she was the unfortunate victim of
a general crackdown by Chinese security police on
foreign scholars and other visitors.

Members of Congress were also aware that no clear
consensus existed among the American public on the
Taiwan issue. A number of public opinion polls taken
during this period reflected the ambivalence with which
most Americans viewed U.S. relations toward China and

---

[306] U.S. Senate, The United States and China: A Report
to the United States Senate by the Senate Majority
Leader (Washington, D.C.: GPO, June 1982), pp. 3-4.

[307] "U.S. Teacher Ordered to Leave China After Being
Detained for Stealing China's Secrets," Embassy of
the People's Republic of China, Press Release No.
82/011, June 8, 1982.

Taiwan. Louis Harris told a meeting in Washington on July 27, 1982: "By 70 to 25 percent, the vast majority of Americans now believe the People's Republic of China is a friendly nation toward the United States, a complete turnabout from the 74 to 17 percent majority who felt China was a hostile power back in 1974."[308]

A poll conducted in July by Sindlinger and Company revealed another side of American feelings. To the question "Should the United States continue to sell advanced fighter aircraft to Taiwan?" 51% said "yes" and 42% said "no." To the question "Do you favor selling military arms to the People's Republic of China?" 22% responded "yes" while 71% replied "no." And then in the most far-reaching question, "Do you believe that Taiwan should be considered a province of the People's Republic of China or a separate country?" 8% said "province" and 84% said "a separate country."[309]

The lack of public consensus on U.S. China policy tended to reenforce Congress' inclination not to reinterpret, revoke, or to in any way alter the Taiwan Relations Act. There were other considerations as well. No member felt he could muster enough votes to change the Act. Most members felt the hearings on the TRA were adequate, and believed reopening the debate over Taiwan would be counterproductive because of the uncertainty of the outcome. Few members could see any political gain in trying to spearhead a change in the TRA. Also, most were too busy to take up an issue as complicated as U.S. China policy. Congress considered President Reagan a friend of Taiwan. The desire not to go over the head of the President on this issue dampened the enthusiasm of many Republicans who felt Taipei should receive more advanced weapons. The Republicans were also concerned that if Sino-American relations did blow up in the Administration's face, it would be Republicans, not Democrats, who would be blamed.

Many members of Congress saw the Taiwan Relations Act as being useful to the Administration in bargaining with the Chinese. The TRA gave a legal commitment to Taiwan, and no administration could change that commitment without going through Congress. Although some conservative members felt that pro-PRC elements in

---

[308] Presentation of Louis Harris to the Nuclear Weapons Freeze Campaign, Washington, D.C., July 27, 1982.

[309] Poll conducted July 15 through August 4, 1982, by nationwide telephone interviews of 2,717 voting-age Americans. The poll was commissioned by the Heritage Foundation of Washington, D.C., which distributed the results in a letter addressed to members of Congress on August 19, 1982.

the State Department and other foreign policy bureaucracies were encouraging the Chinese to attack the TRA, there was little concern on the Hill that the Chinese lobbying efforts would be effective.

Given the economic recession at home and general reluctance to become involved in such a potentially dangerous political issue, most members of Congress were satisfied to let the TRA protect Taiwan's security and to allow the Administration to work out the details. Several forceful speeches were given on the floors of the Senate and the House advocating the need to sell arms to Taiwan or to pursue Sino-American strategic relations, but the issue never crystalized to the point where it became a matter of general congressional concern. Therefore, despite the fact that the TRA gave the Congress a substantial role in U.S. policy toward Taiwan, that policy remained almost exclusively in the hands of the Executive Branch.

The Administration, however, was convinced that China really wanted strategic cooperation and that only the Taiwan issue prevented the relationship from developing. On June 1 Deputy Secretary of State Walter Stoessel told the National Council on U.S.-China Trade: a "strong U.S.-China relationship is one of the highest goals of President Reagan's foreign policy." He defined China "as a friendly country with which we are not allied, but with which we share many common interests. Strategically, we have no fundamental conflicts of interests, and we face a common challenge from the Soviet Union."

Stoessel reconfirmed the Reagan Administration's acceptance of the principles underlying the normalization agreement and peaceful coexistence as the basis of Sino-American relations. The Deputy Secretary pointed out that Reagan had taken four important initiatives to demonstrate his desire to improve relations with China: the expansion of technology transfers, the provision for arms transfers, the removal of legislative restrictions on trade and other relations with China as a member of the communist bloc, and the expansion of consular relations. Stoessel said: "We recognize that a secure, modernizing China is important to the United States from a global and strategic perspective." He mentioned that arms sales to Taiwan were "the one serious issue that threatened good relations," and expressed hope that "this complex, historical issue" can be resolved by "statesmanship, vision, and good will" on the part of both the United States and China.[310]

---

[310] Walter J. Stoessel, "Developing Lasting U.S.-China Relations," U.S. Department of State, Current

Once again demonstrating that friendly U.S. gestures would not alter China's fundamental strategic perceptions, Foreign Minister Huang Hua called the United States a hegemonistic power before the United Nations on June 11. Huang said: "One superpower has been pressing forward to expand its sphere of influence. Not wishing to be outdone, the other superpower has exerted its utmost to build up its strength and to try to regain its former position of world supremacy. The two superpowers have been contending for world hegemony."[311]

Policy, No. 398 (June 1, 1982).

[311] "Huang Hua Speaks at U.N. Special Session on Disarmament," Embassy of the People's Republic of China, Press Release No. 82/012, June 15, 1982.

10
The August 17, 1982
Joint Communique

Just as the January 1982 FX decision had been preceded by intense bureaucratic and political jockeying, so the August 17 Communique was accompanied by heated policy debates in the United States. From press leaks, it seems there were at least two versions of the communique prepared by Secretary of State Alexander Haig. The first version renounced "any long-term agreement" for the sale of arms to Taiwan. In the second version the United States pledged "to reduce gradually such sales and to eventually terminate them."[312] Senator Barry Goldwater asked the State Department about the drafts and was told no such communiques had been prepared. The Senator then called President Reagan and was informed the White House had no knowledge of the drafts.

As evidence unfolded, it became apparent that Haig's subordinates responsible for Chinese and East Asian affairs had secretly prepared the drafts with Haig's knowledge. Yet both Haig and the Department denied the drafts existed, even when inquiries were made from the White House. As Goldwater commented when all of this became public: "It was clear to me and to the White House that President Reagan, Vice President Bush, and national security advisor William Clark had been lied to by the State Department about what they were planning."[313] When key members of Congress were told on June 23 of the actions of Haig and his associates, they became quite angry and demanded that some action be taken. The next day, President Reagan informed Haig that he would accept his resignation.

As Congress became aware of the drafts and possible duplicity by elements of the State Department, members began to ask the President to move ahead as soon as

---

[312] Washington Times, July 2, 1982, p. 1.

[313] Washington Post, July 2, 1982, p. A26; and Washington Times, July 2, 1982, p. 1.

possible on the F-5E coproduction sale to Taiwan, announced on January 11. In the June 23 meeting, national security advisor William Clark told the congressmen that there would be "no backing away" from Taiwan and "no time limit on the sale of arms" to Taipei.[314]

Conservatives outside the government expressed outrage at the State Department's machinations and also began to apply pressure on the President to approve the F-5E sale. On July 9 representatives from 28 conservative groups met in Washington and warned the President that he would receive an "extremely acrimonious" political backlash from his supporters if he agreed to any cutoff of arms to the ROC.[315]

Beijing reacted with contempt for the conservatives, saying that with "their minds crammed with the prejudices of the 1950s, they are devoid of an elementary knowledge about international affairs." People's Daily editorialized:

> It is easily seen that the long-term and fundamental goal of these conservative die-hards is to create "two Chinas" and keep Taiwan under the control and aegis of the United States in a vain attempt to continue the division of China indefinitely....We advise these old-liners to take a dose of sobriety to sober up and return to reality.[316]

During the confirmation hearings of George Shultz, who succeeded Haig as Secretary of State, he was asked about U.S. policy toward China and Taiwan. Shultz said he approved of the continued supply of "defensive arms" to Taiwan and pledged to carry out the provisions of the Taiwan Relations Act. Shultz also described the development of Sino-American relations as being of "great importance." He indicated that he would recommend to the President an early decision on the F-5E.[317] China responded with a warning to Shultz not to bow to pressure from Washington's Taiwan lobby. The People's Daily observed: "Sino-U.S. relations would be

---

[314] Washington Post, July 3, 1982, p. A13.

[315] Ibid., July 9, 1982, p. A5.

[316] "'People's Daily' Refutes 'Two Chinas' Statement by U.S. Conservative Organizations," Embassy of the People's Republic of China, Press Release No. 82/014, July 19, 1982.

[317] Washington Post, July 14, 1982, p. A15.

sabotaged if the views held by Goldwater and his ilk prevail."[318]

With Shultz in place at State, the President determined in mid-July to proceed with official notification to the Congress of his intention to sell Taiwan the F-5Es promised in the January 1982 announcement on the FX. At the same time, in an effort to break the deadlocked talks with Beijing over arms sales, the Administration offered China a proposal drafted by the National Security Council (NSC). The proposal included a new U.S. assurance that in the future it would not sell Taiwan weapons of higher quantity or quality than those sold in the past. On July 30 in a closed briefing with key congressional supporters, the President and his aides explained that this was their final offer to the Chinese and that the F-5E sale would proceed within two weeks. Presidential aides said the assurances given to Beijing were left deliberately vague in order to give the United States the freedom to determine whether the flow of arms at current levels would be sufficient in the future. Implicit in the Administration's explanation was the right of the United States to adjust its mix of arms to Taiwan to account for inflation, technological advances, and increased threats from the mainland.[319]

Beijing twice rejected the new proposal; but, when it became apparent that the President intended to go ahead with the F-5E sale regardless of whether the communique had been signed, China agreed to the NSC formula. Those close to the negotiations reported that, until the last moment, the PRC took an extremely tough position, warning of serious consequences if the F-5E sale went forward. By this point, however, the President had become personally involved in the negotiations and the Administration had become accustomed to the Chinese bargaining tactic of pushing until the last concession had been wrung from the opponent before agreeing to any proposal.[320]

There were reasons behind the President's firmness. Having given more to the Chinese than any of his predecessors, Reagan felt as a matter of principle that he could make no further concessions. The President realized that the F-5E coproduction line in Taiwan would

---

[318] Ibid., July 19, 1982, p. A9.

[319] New York Times, July 31, 1982, p. A2.

[320] This and other Chinese bargaining strategies are discussed in Lucian W. Pye, Chinese Commercial Negotiating Style (Santa Monica, CA: Rand Corporation, 1982).

have to be shut down in September 1982 unless an extension was announced. Moreover, since he was convinced that Taiwan needed more F-5Es to replace its obsolete aircraft, the defense provisions of the Taiwan Relations Act required that the sale be made. Based upon these and other considerations, the Administration apparently gave Beijing an August 18-19 deadline by which to sign the NSC proposal.

10.1 PROVISIONS

The August 17, 1982 U.S.-PRC Joint Communique wove together many of the elements of Sino-American relations. In the first paragraph, the United States reaffirmed its acceptance of the principles of the 1979 normalization agreement: the government of the PRC is the sole legal government of China; an acknowledgment of the Chinese view that there is but one China and Taiwan is part of China; but "within that context," the United States will maintain "unofficial relations with the people of Taiwan."
    The second paragraph pointed out that the arms sales issue had never been resolved but set aside in order to bring about the normalization of Sino-American relations. Paragraph three went on to reconfirm both sides' recognition that "respect for each other's sovereignty and territorial integrity and non-interference in each other's internal affairs constitute the fundamental principles guiding United States-China relations."
    Paragraph four contained an important reference to China's "fundamental policy of striving for peaceful reunification of the Motherland." Both the Message to Compatriots in Taiwan issued on January 1, 1979, and the Nine-Point Proposal of Ye Jianying issued on September 30, 1981, were specifically mentioned as major efforts on the part of China to promulgate this "fundamental policy."
    In paragraph five the United States, after emphasizing the importance it places on Sino-American relations, reiterated that "it has no intention of infringing on Chinese sovereignty and territorial integrity, or interfering in China's internal affairs, or pursuing a policy of 'two Chinas' or 'one China, one Taiwan.'" The United States said that it "understands and appreciates" China's fundamental policy of "striving for a peaceful resolution of the Taiwan question." Because of China's new reunification policy, the United States noted that "the new situation which has emerged with regard to the Taiwan question" had created an environment in which the arms sales issue might be solved.

Paragraph six contained substantive and controversial commitments by the United States. It stated:

> Having in mind the foregoing statements of both sides, the United States Government states that it does not seek to carry out a long-term policy of arms sales to Taiwan, that its arms sales to Taiwan will not exceed, either in qualitative or in quantitative terms, the level of those supplied in recent years since the establishment of diplomatic relations between the United States and China, and that it intends to reduce gradually its sales of arms to Taiwan, leading over a period of time to a final resolution. In so doing, the United States acknowledges China's consistent position regarding the thorough settlement of this issue.

In paragraph seven both sides promised to make every effort over time to resolve the arms sales issue, which is referred to as being "rooted in history." Paragraph eight stated that Sino-American relations were in the interests of both countries, as well as conducive to world peace and stability. Both governments promised, "on the principle of equality and mutual benefit," to "strengthen their ties in the economic, cultural, educational, scientific, technological and other fields."

In the final paragraph, in order to "bring about the healthy development" of Sino-American relations, the two countries reaffirmed "the principles agreed on by the two sides in the Shanghai Communique and the Joint Communique on the Establishment of Diplomatic Relations." No mention of strategic cooperation or hegemony was made, but reference was given to the fact that the two sides would seek, on the basis of the above principles, to "maintain world peace and oppose aggression and expansion."

Predictably, reaction to the August 17 Communique varied. Many breathed a sigh of relief that Sino-American relations had overcome yet another hurtle. Some of the more optimistic even felt that the issue of Taiwan arms sales had been removed permanently as an obstacle in relations between the two countries. Others criticized the President for sacrificing the interests of Taiwan. Some were concerned that a dangerous corner in Sino-American relations had been turned. Charles Cross, the first director of the American Institute in Taiwan, wrote in the New York Times:

> The Administration...has now taken a step which preceding administrations carefully avoided.
>
> By welcoming Peking's nine-point proposal on Taiwan and establishing a negotiable connection between U.S. arms sales to Taiwan and the latter's responses to the P.R.C.'s gestures toward reunification, the President has moved us into a dangerous area....
>
> Our interest has heretofore been confined to keeping the process peaceful, without other involvement. The Chinese were never in doubt, from the beginning of normalization on Jan. 1, 1979, that the carefully selected weapons sold to Taiwan were only for that purpose. If we slide off this simple principle in an effort to accommodate Peking, neither we nor the Chinese will be able to finesse the Taiwan issue in the future, particularly since there is no disposition in Taiwan to change the status quo.[321]

Most felt that the communique was sufficiently vague to satisfy everyone. Senator S. I. Hayakawa wrote:

> The communique means either what you want it to mean or what you fear it means. There is enough ambiguity in the document, it seems, that no one need take offense. The wonderful thing about language is its ability to mean whatever you want it to mean. What we have in the communique is a situation not uncommon in human affairs: total ambiguity.[322]

The ambiguity of the communique proved a mixed blessing. Both sides interpreted the agreement to suit their own purposes. Subsequent U.S. qualifications removed many of the roadblocks to military sales to Taiwan, while Beijing claimed a major victory in its efforts to limit arms sales in the future.

---

[321] New York Times, June 3, 1982, p. A22.

[322] S.I. Hayakawa, "Ambiguity: The China Syndrome," New York Times, August 30, 1982, p. A17.

10.2 U.S. INTERPRETATIONS

The presidential statement accompanying the August 17 Communique provided important insight into the official U.S. interpretation of the document. The President stressed the importance of Sino-American strategic cooperation, noting:

> Building a strong and lasting relationship with China has been an important foreign policy goal of four consecutive American administrations. Such a relationship is vital to our long-term national security interests and contributes to stability in East Asia. It is in the national interest of the United States that this important strategic relationship be advanced. This communique will make that possible, consistent with our obligations to the people of Taiwan.

The President went on to say: "Regarding future U.S. arms sales to Taiwan, our policy, set forth clearly in the communique, is fully consistent with the Taiwan Relations Act. Arms sales will continue in accordance with the Act and with the full expectation that the approach of the Chinese government to the resolution of the Taiwan issue will continue to be peaceful."

Recognizing the importance of economic stability and positive business psychology to the future of Taiwan, Reagan concluded his statement by saying:

> I am proud, as an American, at the great progress that has been made by the people on Taiwan, over the past three decades, and of the American contribution to that process. I have full faith in the continuation of that process. My Administration, acting through appropriate channels, will continue strongly to foster that development and to contribute to a strong and healthy investment climate, thereby enhancing the well-being of the people of Taiwan.

President Reagan's determination to continue to sell Taiwan necessary defensive arms was confirmed in a telephone call by the President to Dan Rather of CBS Evening News on the day of the communique's release. Rather had commented earlier on the air: "Taken together, Mr. Reagan has now reversed policy and infuriated conservative members of his own party on two scores: first the tax increase, now China." The

President heard Rather's remarks and called him to correct the CBS interpretation of the communique. The President said: "There has been no retreat by me, no change whatsoever. We will continue to arm Taiwan."[323]

President Reagan also set forth his understanding of the communique in a Human Events interview in February 1983. In answer to conservative criticism that he had reneged on his campaign promises to live up to the defense provisions of the Taiwan Relations Act, the President said:

> Now, our communique is a very carefully worked out deal, and we did not give an inch. In that communique, the People's Republic has agreed that they are going to try and peacefully resolve the Taiwanese issue. We, in turn, linked our statement about weaponry to that and said that if they make progress and do, indeed, peacefully work out a solution agreeable to both sides, then, obviously, there would no longer be any need for arms. And all the reference to reducing arms is tied to progress in that. We will abide by the Taiwan Relations Act, the law of this country, which says that we will help maintain Taiwan's defensive posture and capability....If the day ever comes that those two find that they can get together and become one China, in a peaceful manner, then there wouldn't be any need for arms sales to Taiwan. And that's all that was meant in the communique. Nothing was meant beyond that.[324]

The Administration's interpretation of the communique was also given privately to Republican congressmen on August 17. During the meeting, top Administration officials said the TRA would remain the guide for U.S. policy toward Taiwan. The communique was described as a victory for the Administration because it permitted the sale of the F-5E without downgrading Sino-American relations. The congressmen were assured that if one day the PRC stepped up hostilities, the United States would increase arms sales to counter the threat. An important interpretation of the qualitative and quantitative limitations referred to in paragraph six of the communique was also given. These limitations were not intended to fix the level of arms sold to

---

[323] Time, August 30, 1982, p. 21.

[324] Human Events, February 26, 1983, p. 19.

Taiwan, but rather to tie weapons transfers to the level of threat existing in the Taiwan Strait.

Further clarification of the U.S. position came indirectly through ROC channels. In its statement on the August 17 Communique, Taiwan reiterated "its solemn position that it will consider null and void any agreement, involving the rights and interests of the government and people of the Republic of China, reached between the United States government and the Chinese communist regime." The ROC revealed:

> During the process of discussions on the so-called Joint Communique, the U.S. side has kept the government of the Republic of China informed of its developments, and at the same time the government of the Republic of China has presented to the United States its consistent position of firmly opposing the issuance of such a document. On July 14, 1982, the U.S. side, through appropriate channels, made the following points known to the Republic of China that the U.S. side:
>
> 1. has not agreed to set a date for ending arms sales to the Republic of China,
>
> 2. has not agreed to hold prior consultations with the Chinese communists on arms sales to the Republic of China,
>
> 3. will not play any mediation role between Taipei and Peiping,
>
> 4. has not agreed to revise the Taiwan Relations Act,
>
> 5. has not altered its position regarding sovereignty over Taiwan,
>
> 6. will not exert pressure on the Republic of China to enter into negotiations with the Chinese communists.

Assistant Secretary of State John Holdridge appeared before the House Committee on Foreign Affairs on August 18 to explain the August 17 Communique and to clarify some of its language.[325] In his prepared

---

[325] Holdridge's testimony and answers to questions from the Committee can be found in U.S. House of Representatives, Committee on Foreign Affairs,

statement Holdridge said two considerations guided U.S. negotiations: the "fundamental national interest of the United States to preserve and advance its strategic relations with China" and "our historic obligations to the people of Taiwan."

The Assistant Secretary noted that because of improved relations between China and the United States, "Taiwan has never been more secure." Holdridge argued that whereas the TRA commits "the U.S. to sell to Taiwan arms necessary to maintain a sufficient self-defense capability," friendly Sino-American relations and Beijing's own fundamental peaceful policy toward Taiwan enabled the United States to conclude: "so long as that policy continued, the threat to Taiwan would be greatly diminished." On the basis of this reasoning, Holdridge explained, "We were thus able to consider a policy under which we would limit our arms sales to the levels reached in recent years and would anticipate a gradual reduction of the level of arms sales."

Holdridge specifically linked the qualitative and quantitative limitations in paragraph six with the continuation of China's peaceful approach to reunification. He said:

> Let me summarize the essence of our understanding on this point: China has announced a fundamental policy of pursuing peaceful means to resolve the long-standing dispute between Taiwan and the Mainland. Having in mind this policy and the consequent reduction in the military threat to Taiwan, we have stated our intention to reduce arms sales to Taiwan gradually, and said that in quantity and quality we would not go beyond levels established since normalization....While we have no reason to believe that China's policy will change, an inescapable corollary to these mutually interdependent policies is that should that happen, we will reassess ours. Our guiding principle is now and will continue to be that embodied in the Taiwan Relations Act: the maintenance of a self-defense capability sufficient to meet the military needs of Taiwan, but with the understanding that China's maintenance of a peaceful approach to the Taiwan question will permit gradual reductions in arms sales.

China-Taiwan: United States Policy (Washington, D.C.: GPO, 1982).

The Assistant Secretary defined the "new situation" referred to in paragraph five as meaning that "for the first time, China has described its peaceful policy toward Taiwan" in terms of being fundamental. In response to questions from the Committee, Holdridge said that the term "final resolution" in paragraph six did not have an exact meaning, but rather "a variety of different formulae that one might consider in reaching a final solution." Two possible interpretations offered by Congressman Stephen Solarz and not rejected by Holdridge were a final resolution of the arms sales issue and the peaceful resolution of differences between Taiwan and the mainland. The Assistant Secretary also noted that the United States was not operating under any specific time frame in its promise to reduce arms sales "over a period of time."

A further interpretation of the role of the communique in U.S. policy toward Taiwan was given by State Department Legal Advisor Davis Robinson on September 27, 1982, in testimony before the Senate Committee on the Judiciary. In answer to criticism that the communique bypassed the role of Congress in determining the defensive needs of Taiwan, Robinson emphasized that the communique

> is not an international agreement and thus imposes no obligations on either party under international law. Its status under domestic law is that of a statement by the President of a policy which he intends to pursue....The Taiwan Relations Act is and will remain the law of the land unless amended by Congress. Nothing in the Joint Communique obligates the President to act in a manner contrary to the Act or, conversely, disables him from fulfilling his responsibilities under it.[326]

Subsequent arms transactions by the Reagan Administration indicated that, to a certain extent at least, indexing would be applied to the quantitative and qualitative limitations placed on future arms sales to Taiwan. Such indexing, tied to the actual threat faced by Taiwan from the PRC, was found to be the most convenient way to reconcile the communique with the TRA, which made no reference to qualitative or quantitative limits on arms sales to Taipei. Moreover, no

---

[326] Prepared statement of Davis R. Robinson, Legal Advisor, Department of State, given before U.S. Senate, Committee on the Judiciary, Subcommittee on Separation of Powers, September 27, 1982, pp. 1-2, ms.

prohibitions on the transfer of advanced military
technology or weapons components were found in either
the communique or the TRA. A resourceful U.S.
Administration, and a government in Taipei willing to
work quietly with appropriate American
instrumentalities, would be able to find ways to
maintain Taiwan's defense needs.

10.3 PRC INTERPRETATIONS

Not surprisingly, the PRC chose to adopt an entirely
different set of interpretations to the August 17
Communique. In its official statement on the
communique, the Chinese Foreign Ministry said:

> In compliance with the...principles
> governing the relations between the two
> countries, the U.S. arms sales to Taiwan
> should have been terminated altogether long
> ago. But considering that this is an issue
> left over by history, the Chinese Government,
> while upholding the principles, has agreed to
> settle it step by step. The U.S. side has
> committed that, as the first step, its arms
> sales to Taiwan will not exceed, either in
> qualitative or in quantitative terms, the
> level of those supplied in recent years since
> the establishment of diplomatic relations
> between the two countries, and that they will
> be gradually reduced, leading to a final
> resolution of this issue over a period of
> time. The final resolution referred to here
> certainly implies that the U.S. arms sales to
> Taiwan must be completely terminated over a
> period of time. And only a thorough
> settlement of this issue can remove the
> obstacles in the way of developing relations
> between the two countries.

The Foreign Ministry went on to say: "The Chinese
side refers in the Joint Communique to its fundamental
policy of striving for peaceful reunification of the
motherland for the purpose of further demonstrating the
sincere desire of the Chinese Government and people to
strive for a peaceful solution to the Taiwan question.
On this issue, which is purely China's internal affair,
no misinterpretation or foreign interference is
permissible."[327]
The Chinese logic was inevitable: any connection
between limitations on future U.S. arms sales to Taiwan

and China's policy of peaceful unification was invalid. A <u>Renmin Ribao</u> editorial of August 17 made this point explicit:

> Taiwan is China's territory and the method we choose to solve the Taiwan problem is entirely a problem of China's internal affairs. The United States has no right to demand that China undertake any obligations as to the methods it chooses in solving the Taiwan problem, nor should the United States put forth as a prerequisite condition for the cessation of arms sales to Taiwan that China commit itself to not solving the Taiwan problem by any means other than peaceful ones.[328]

Yet another important difference in interpretation arose over the role of the Taiwan Relations Act in deciding the level of arms sales to Taiwan in the wake of the August 17 Communique. Whereas the Administration affirmed the legal precedence of the TRA, the Chinese strongly disagreed. The Foreign Ministry said in its official statement:

> It must be pointed out that the present Joint Communique is based on the principles embodied in the Joint Communique on the establishment of diplomatic relations between China and the United States and the basic norms guiding international relations and has nothing to do with the "Taiwan Relations Act" formulated unilaterally by the United States. The "Taiwan Relations Act" seriously contravenes the principles embodied in the Joint Communique on the establishment of diplomatic relations between the two countries, and the Chinese Government has consistently been opposed to it. All interpretations designed to link the present Joint Communique to the "Taiwan Relations Act" are in violation of the spirit and substance of this communique and are thus unacceptable.

---

[327] "Chinese Foreign Ministry Spokesman on China-U.S. Joint Communique," Embassy of the People's Republic of China, <u>Press Release No. 82/017</u>, August 17, 1982.

[328] <u>Renmin Ribao</u>, August 17, 1982, in <u>FBIS-China</u>, August 17, 1982, p. B4.

The August 17 <u>Renmin Ribao</u> editorial was again more explicit, targeting the TRA as the principal obstacle now standing in the way of progressive Sino-American relations.

> The dark cloud that has blurred the prospects of Sino-U.S. relations has not been completely swept away. The United States has given some promises, but we have to wait and see whether or not it will prove its sincerity by its actions....It is still necessary to point out that the fundamental obstacle to the development of Sino-U.S. relations is the U.S. "Taiwan Relations Act." The so-called "Taiwan Relations Act" completely violates the principles of the Sino-U.S. Joint Communique on establishing diplomatic relations. If the decision-makers in Washington insist on handling the relations between the two countries in accordance with this U.S. domestic act, Sino-U.S. relations will not only come to a standstill, but will definitely face another crisis.

10.4 RELATIONS IN THE POST-COMMUNIQUE PERIOD

Despite the differing interpretations placed on the August 17 Communique, a major political hurtle had been cleared. Both sides felt able to pursue policies on a business-as-usual basis which earlier might have seriously damaged Sino-American relations because of the public stands taken by the two governments.

Two days after the Communique's release, the Reagan Administration officially notified Congress of its intent to permit Taiwan to coproduce with Northrop an additional 30 F-5Es and 30 F-5Fs over the next two and a half years. The total package was valued at $622 million, of which $382 million were earmarked for the planes and $240 million approved for government-furnished equipment for the aircraft.[329] Beijing had been told of the pending sale and did not strongly protest. There were two further arms transfers to Taiwan in late 1982. The first was the delivery of 500 air-to-ground Maverick missiles approved by President Carter in 1978. The second transaction occurred on November 30, when the Administration announced that it was selling Taiwan $97 million in

---

[329] <u>Washington Post</u>, August 20, 1982, p. A16.

various armored vehicles. The PRC reported both sales but without strong protest.

China chose the post-communique period to announce publicly its decision to pursue a more independent foreign policy, one open to the normalization of relations with both superpowers yet closely allied to neither. In his address to the Twelfth National Congress of the CPC, Hu Yaobang described China's foreign policy as being "independent" and as following "an overall long-term strategy." Regarding relations with the Soviet Union, Hu indicated that improved relations were possible "if the Soviet authorities really have a sincere desire to improve relations with China and take practical steps to lift their threat to the security of our country." As far as Sino-American relations were concerned, Hu noted that "a cloud has all along hung over the relations between the two countries. This is because the United States...has passed the Taiwan Relations Act...and it has continued to sell arms to Taiwan, treating Taiwan as an independent political entity." Hu said the August 17 Communique provided "a step-by-step solution to the question of U.S. arms sales to Taiwan, leading to a final thorough settlement. We hope that these provisions will be strictly observed."

Hu Yaobang strongly criticized both superpowers for their hegemonism and rivalry, which threatened world peace. The head of the CPC reaffirmed China's identification with the Third World, saying: "Socialist China belongs to the third world....China regards it as her sacred international duty to struggle resolutely against imperialism, hegemonism and colonialism together with the other third world countries."[330]

Thus, within a few weeks of the August 17 Communique, largely justified by the Administration on the grounds that Sino-American strategic cooperation had to be preserved, the PRC publicly announced it was pursuing an "independent" foreign policy of marginal strategic value to the United States. China's shift in foreign policy direction from close cooperation with the West against the Soviet threat to a policy seeking normalized relations with both superpowers and alignment with neither was based on a fundamental change in Chinese threat perceptions. This shift in strategic thinking had been developing since at least mid-1980.

The key factors in China's reevaluation of its strategic links with the West had very little to do with U.S. unofficial ties with Taiwan, or even the arms sales

---

[330] Hu Yaobang, "Create a New Situation in All Fields of Socialist Modernization," *The Twelfth National Congress of the CPC* (Beijing: Foreign Languages Press, 1982), p. 55ff.

issue. Rather, China's strategic decision revolved around the critical questions of whether Moscow was serious in seeking to improve relations with China and whether the renewed determination of the United States to counter Soviet hegemonism would be adequate to secure peace in East Asia. The Chinese answered both of these questions in the affirmative.

By signing the August 17 Communique, the United States did little to alter Chinese strategic perceptions or the direction of PRC foreign policy. But it did greatly complicate the question of Taiwan's future security. As one American analyst noted, observers on Taiwan felt that the long-term trend of American policy was moving "in the direction of meeting PRC demands and conditions while gradually cutting back contacts and accommodating U.S. ties with Taiwan for the sake of improved relations with the PRC."[331]

Those relations remained strained, however. In October 1982 Foreign Minister Huang Hua spoke before the U.S. Council on Foreign Relations in New York and pointed to "the question of Taiwan" as being the key issue obstructing Sino-American relations. The principles agreed to in the normalization agreement, Huang said, should have solved the issue, but instead

> the United States passed the "Taiwan Relations Act," which in essence continues to treat Taiwan as an independent political entity....This Act has been a dark cloud hanging over the relations between our two countries and a serious obstacle to the development of Sino-U.S. relations.

Huang went on to say: "I once said that the U.S. authorities had made many nice remarks about developing our bilateral relations. Yet what has happened can be described by a Chinese saying: 'Loud thunder, but little rain.'" The Foreign Minister then listed several areas, besides Taiwan, in which the PRC felt the United States had slighted China. These included "discrimination against China...in the trade relations and in scientific and educational exchanges between the two countries" and "discriminatory restrictions on the export of high technology and sophisticated equipment to China." Huang Hua concluded:

---

[331] Robert G. Sutter, "Trip Report on Visit to Taiwan, August 13-19, 1982," Library of Congress, Congressional Research Service, August 25, 1982, p. 2.

> In view of the recent developments, one cannot help asking: Does the U.S. government regard China as a friend or an adversary? If Sino-U.S. relations are to develop, it is imperative to proceed from the over-all interests of these relations and stop making insincere statements and taking embarrassing actions.[332]

Thus, as the crucial period 1981-1982 drew to a close, Sino-American relations were still plagued by the Taiwan issue. China, having gained a major psychological and political victory over Taiwan through the August 17 Communique, was determined to continue to apply pressure on Washington over arms sales and the TRA. Moreover, other aspects of Sino-American relations, most notably economic and technological, were also pinpointed by Beijing as issues over which they were dissatisfied with the U.S. performance.

---

[332] Xinhua, October 7, 1982, in FBIS-China, October 8, 1982, p. B1.

11
Epilogue

11.1 A MORE REALISTIC CHINA POLICY

The bitter negotiations and internal debate over the August 17 Communique changed the Administration's attitude toward China somewhat. New policy players were in place in the State Department and NSC. Reagan and his advisors had learned not to give in to harsh PRC rhetoric. As a result, the Reagan Administration in 1983 moved to place its relationship with China on a more realistic footing. According to Paul Wolfowitz, who replaced Holdridge as Assistant Secretary of State for Asian and Pacific Affairs, the Administration wanted "to put U.S.-China relations back on a stable, realistic footing, to resume the process of building the essential elements of confidence and trust, to continue our dialogue on important international issues, and to address openly and honestly the various bilateral issues that were commanding attention on both sides."[333]

One important step in that direction was the reaffirmation by the Administration that Japan, not China, was the centerpiece of U.S. strategy in the Western Pacific. This shift in emphasis was stressed by President Reagan on February 23, 1983, in a speech before the American Legion in Boston. The President said: "the U.S.-Japanese relationship remains the centerpiece of our Asian policy."[334] China was seen as a major regional, as opposed to a global, power.

---

[333] Prepared statement of Paul Wolfowitz, "Sino-American Relations Eleven Years After the Shanghai Communique," given before U.S. House of Representatives, Committee on Foreign Affairs, Subcommittee on Asian and Pacific Affairs, February 28, 1983, p. 5, ms.

[334] The text of the President's speech can be found in Washington Post, February 23, 1983, p. A12.

One major result of the deemphasis on China in U.S. policy was to accentuate the perception that differences between the two countries were unavoidable. Rather than attempting to "solve" the various issues, a "problem management" approach was adopted which permitted the Administration to handle Sino-American relations on several different levels concurrently. China had effectively used this approach for some time in its relations with the United States. A number of statements made by U.S. officials during this period indicated a willingness to continue to disagree with Beijing, particularly over Taiwan, while at the same time to seek expanded areas of cooperation.

On February 18 Secretary Shultz told participants in the Conservative Political Action Conference: "We're not going to turn our backs" on Taiwan, mentioning that "they fought on our side" in the Korean and Vietnam wars.[335] In his address to the American Legion Convention on February 23, the President said: "We are committed to maintaining our relationship with the people of Taiwan, with whom we have a long and honorable relationship."[336]

In remarks on February 28 before the House Committee on Foreign Affairs, Wolfowitz stated: "We continue to have some differences over Taiwan. However, the relationship with China is important enough to us--and it seems also to the Chinese--that we will work hard to manage those differences in a way that preserves our focus on our strong interests in bilateral and international cooperation."[337] Similar sentiments were voiced by Secretary Shultz in a March 5 speech in San Francisco:

> China's new, more constructive, though guarded, role is welcome, and a closer relationship with China will benefit the people of both our countries. However, frustrations and problems in our relationship are inevitable. They will arise not only out of differences concerning Taiwan but out of the differences between our two systems. We believe that these problems can be managed and that the community of interests that promises further progress is real. Our relationship

---

[335] *Washington Post*, February 19, 1983, p. A5.

[336] *Ibid.*, February 23, 1983, p. A12.

[337] Paul Wolfowitz, "Sino-American Relations Eleven Years After the Shanghai Communique," p. 8.

with China has brought tangible results and can be a potent force for stability in the future of the region....

Progress in U.S.-China relations need not come at the expense of relations with our other friends in the region, including our close unofficial relationship with the people of Taiwan. To the contrary, it can contribute to the peace and economic progress of the entire region. The key to managing our differences over Taiwan lies in observing the commitments made in our three joint communiques and allowing the parties themselves to resolve their differences peacefully with the passage of time. To improve our relations we must both work to reduce impediments to expanding trade in technology, as well as other economic relations, consistent with our long-term security needs. We must also seek to resolve any misunderstanding or dispute through consultations and negotiations rather than by unilateral action.

In so doing, we work to build a long-term, enduring, and constructive relationship on a basis of mutual confidence. As I made clear in Beijing, Chinese leaders will find the United States ready to join with them on that basis in pursuing our common interests in peace and modernization. We value Sino-American relations and want them to advance.[338]

During his trip to Beijing in February 1983, Shultz found the Chinese to be low-key and businesslike. The American press optimistically projected future Sino-American military cooperation because of friendly talks between the Secretary of State and Chinese Defense Minister Zhang Aiping.[339] The Chinese quickly dispelled this idea. Zhao Ziyang told a group of journalists shortly after the Shultz-Zhang meeting: "No military ties exist between China and the United States."[340] An

---

[338] George Shultz, "The U.S. and East Asia: A Partnership for the Future," U.S. Department of State, Current Policy, No. 459, March 5, 1983, p. 3.

[339] See Washington Post, February 5, 1983, p. A22; New York Times, February 5, 1983, p. 1; and Wall Street Journal, February 22, 1983, p. 34.

even more pointed rejection of Sino-American military cooperation was announced in March, following the disclosure of a secret Pentagon document recommending arms sales to China "if it is possible and appropriate" to allow the PRC to counter Soviet forces in the Far East. The Chinese Foreign Ministry annnounced: "At present, the question of the U.S. providing arms to China or China asking the U.S. for arms supplies simply does not exist."[341]

Immediately after Shultz's departure, a Xinhua commentary reviewed his trip and highlighted the many differences existing between the two sides. Particularly irksome to the Chinese were continued U.S. arms sales to Taiwan. The commentary said: "Unless this problem is resolved, mutual trust between China and the United States is out of the question and bilateral relations cannot possibly develop on a sound basis." The United States was criticized, because (1) "U.S. officials made distortions in interpreting the (August 17) communique," (2) "senior U.S. officials attended the 'national day's' reception given by a Taiwan organization in the United States," (3) "the U.S. Government allowed Taiwan's 'Coordination Council for North American Affairs' to open a new office in Boston," and (4) "the ceiling set by the United States for its arms sales to Taiwan far exceeded the maximum annual figures published by the U.S. Government departments."

According to Xinhua, Chinese officials told Shultz that the Taiwan Relations Act is "a serious stumbling block in the way of Sino-U.S. relations and, therefore, should be annulled." Other bilateral disagreements raised with the Secretary of State were "the discriminatory and restrictive policies followed by the United States in economic, trade, cultural and technical exchanges." Despite these and other differences, the newspaper concluded, "the establishment of a stable and enduring relationship between China and the United States is in the interests of both peoples and conducive to world peace and security."[342]

---

[340] Xinhua, February 4, 1983, in FBIS-China, February 4, 1983, p. B2.

[341] AFP, March 25, 1983, in FBIS-China, March 25, 1983, p. B1.

[342] Xinhua, February 6, 1983, in FBIS-China, February 7, 1983, pp. B7-B9.

11.2 RELATIONS SOUR ONCE AGAIN

In a series of far-reaching decisions in early 1983, the Administration decided to clear the backlog of arms requested by Taipei but held in abeyance during the delicate negotiations leading up to the August 17 Joint Communique. In February the United States announced that it was selling Taiwan 66 F-104Gs, previously owned by West Germany, for a total of $31 million. The PRC did not strongly protest the sale in public, but applied considerable pressure on Bonn in private to warn against similar transactions in the future.

In March the State Department released figures setting ceilings for arms sales to Taiwan at $800 million for FY 1983 and $760 million for FY 1984. These figures were highly important, because they were the first indication that the United States had applied a quantitative index to the level of its arms sales to Taiwan in the post-communique period. The figures for 1979, 1980, and 1981--the base years referred to in the communique--were $598 million, $601 million, and $295 million, respectively. To reconcile the 1983 and 1984 figures with the base years, the State Department explained that an "inflationary index" had been applied. Thus, the $598 million of 1979 would be equivalent to $830 million in current, inflated dollars.[343] (Applying the same logic, the State Department a year later set the FY 1985 level of arms sales to Taiwan at $760 million.) The PRC was outraged at this "double-dealing" by the Reagan Administration and lodged a strong note of protest with the U.S. Ambassador in Beijing.[344]

Another important arms transaction occurred in July 1983. The Administration sold Taiwan $530 million in military equipment, including land- and sea-based Chaparral missiles for air defense, SM-1 Standard missiles for shipborne air defense, AIM-7F Sparrow radar-homing air-to-air missiles, conversion kits for M-4 tanks, tank-recovery vehicles, and aircraft spare parts and supplies. The Standard and Sparrow missiles had been sought by Taiwan for several years. The sophisticated nature of these missiles indicated that the United States had applied at least a minimal qualitative indexing to its arms sales.

---

[343] *Washington Post*, March 22, 1983, p. A12.

[344] See AFP, March 18, 1983, in *FBIS-China*, March 18, 1983, pp. B1-B2; AFP, March 21, 1983, in *FBIS-China*, March 21, 1983, p. B1; and *Washington Post*, March 31, 1983, p. A26.

According to U.S. defense experts close to the situation, a degree of quantitative and qualitative indexing was required--on technical grounds alone--for Taiwan to maintain a minimum adequate defense in the Taiwan Strait. It was the recognition of this fact, coupled with the legal requirements of the Taiwan Relations Act, which necessitated indexing. Two other weapons systems urgently requested by Taiwan--an advanced fighter and the Harpoon ship-to-ship missile--have thus far remained above the qualitative ceiling established by the Administration.

During 1983 there were numerous other issues which arose between the United States and the PRC. Trade difficulties were among the most substantive. One area of concern to China was its textile trade with the United States. More than a quarter of all PRC exports to the United States were textiles. Although China ranked fourth in textile exports to the United States (behind Hong Kong, Taiwan, and South Korea), the growth of its textile exports had been so rapid--41% in 1980, 73% in 1981, 30% in 1982--that American manufacturers viewed Chinese products as their most serious competitor.[345] The United States limited the growth of textile imports to less than 1% annually from the other major international producers. Beijing, however, demanded a 6% increase. After months of unsuccessful negotiations, Washington unilaterally decided to hold Chinese textile imports to the 1982 level. Beijing called the U.S. action "blackmail" and retaliated by halting further purchases of U.S. cotton, synthetic fibers, and soybeans and by lowering imports of other American agricultural products.[346] The matter was resolved a few months later, when Washington agreed to give China a 3% annual increase in its textile quota.

Another bitter issue between the two sides involved Chinese tennis star Hu Na, who defected to the United States in 1982 during a tournament in California. Accusing KMT agents of causing Hu Na to seek political asylum, the PRC warned that unless the tennis player were returned the incident would be "sure to adversely affect the cultural exchanges between the two countries."[347] The question of whether to grant Hu Na political asylum became a hotly debated issue within the Administration, with different agencies assuming conflicting positions. After the President indicated that he would adopt Hu Na himself rather than have her

---

[345] *Washington Post*, January 7, 1983, p. A24,

[346] *New York Times*, January 20, 1983, p. A1.

[347] *New York Times*, August 4, 1982, p. A1.

returned against her will to China, the Immigration and Naturalization Service announced that she would be granted permission to remain in the United States. Beijing termed the April 4, 1983 decision "a grave incident" and one that "will certainly affect bilateral exchanges."[348] On April 7 China's Ministry of Culture declared that all remaining items of cultural exchange with the United States for 1982 and 1983 would be canceled. The U.S. Embassy in Beijing tersely replied: "We deeply regret the over-reaction of the Chinese to the Hu Na case."[349] Cultural relations between the two countries were restricted until President Reagan's trip to China in April 1984, when the exchange programs were reinstituted.

In January 1983 the PRC announced that it wanted to join the Asian Development Bank (ADB), but on the condition that Taiwan first be expelled. Previously, Beijing had replace Taipei in both the International Monetary Fund (IMF) and the World Bank. Contrary to the IMF and World Bank, where the ROC claimed to represent all of China, in the ADB Taipei only represented Taiwan. Moreover, Taiwan was a contributing member no longer drawing upon ADB assets.

The U.S. position was to back China's admission but to oppose Taiwan's removal--a policy viewed in Beijing as another attempt by the Reagan Administration to create "one China, one Taiwan."[350] In November 1983 the Senate and the House of Representatives passed an appropriations bill upholding the membership of "Taiwan--Republic of China" in the Asian Development Bank and warning that U.S. funding for ADB might be curtailed if Taiwan were expelled.

Beijing relaxed its view of Taiwan's explusion and indicated that it might be willing to acquiesce in some form of continued participation by Taiwan, but under a name other than "the Republic of China." In mid-1984 the U.S. position on the ADB issue was:

---

[348] Washington Post, April 5, 1983, p. A3.

[349] Washington Post, April 8, 1983, p. A1.

[350] For background information see China Post, January 14, 1983, p. 2; Xinhua, March 8, 1983, in FBIS-China, March 8, 1983, p. A1; New York Times, March 22, 1983, p. D14; Xinhua, May 2, 1983, in FBIS-China, May 3, 1983, pp. U1-U3; and Renmin Ribao, May 3, 1983, in FBIS-China, May 4, 1983, pp. U1-U2.

--The United States, consistent with its recognition policy, believes China is eligible for membership in the Bank.

--However, Taiwan has played a constructive role in the Bank and has an important economic role in the region. We believe that role should be acknowledged through continued Taiwan participation.

--As the expressed sentiment of Congress clearly indicates, the explusion of Taiwan would have serious implications for continued U.S. participation in and funding for the Bank.

--The Bank has the matter under review, and we hope that with the cooperation of all parties a satisfactory solution can eventually emerge.[351]

In late March and early April 1983 a large delegation of House members led by Speaker Tip O'Neill visited China. Vice Chairman Peng Zhen called Taiwan a "wart" as well as the crux of the matter in developing Sino-American relations. O'Neill used the occasion to criticize the Reagan Administration, saying that U.S. policy toward China had "always been mistaken" and promising that Congress would work to promote closer ties between the two governments.[352]

Other actions by the Congress, however, prompted PRC protests. In early 1983 resolutions were introduced into the Senate and House of Representatives stating: "Taiwan's future should be settled peacefully, free of coercion and in a manner acceptable to the people on Taiwan and consistent with the laws enacted by Congress and communiques entered into between the United States and the People's Republic of China." Beijing condemned the resolutions for having "openly violated China's sovereignty and interfered in China's internal affairs."[353]

---

[351] U.S. Department of State, "Briefing Paper," n.d., pp. 2-3.

[352] For PRC coverage of the visit, see FBIS-China, March 29, March 30, and April 4, 1983. Also, Washington Post, March 30, 1093, p. A20.

[353] Xinhua, March 12, 1983, in FBIS-China, March 14, 1983, p. B1.

Toward the end of the year the Senate Foreign Relations Committee passed the Pell Resolution, which stated that the people of Taiwan should enjoy the right of self-determination and that a settlement of the reunification issue should be in accord with the Taiwan Relations Act. Hu Yaobang complained that the congressional action "in essence is abetting and supporting Taiwan and obstructing China's peaceful reunification." He accused the Congress of "crude interference in China's internal affairs."[354] To avoid another incident, the Reagan Administration disassociated itself from the Pell Resolution, indicating that its passage by the Senate would go beyond what had been worked out with the Chinese and therefore would be unhelpful.[355]

Other issues which arose between the United States and China during the first half of 1983 included a federal court ruling against China on 1911 Imperial Chinese Railway bonds, Pan Am's decision to open service to Taipei as well as to the Chinese mainland, controversies surrounding the research and writing activities of American scholars in China, additional political asylum cases, and delays in approving the sale of computers and other advanced equipment and high technology to China.

As a result of these incidents, Sino-American relations for the first half of 1983 were rather sour. Deng Xiaoping told Japanese Foreign Minister Yoshio Sakurauchi on April 28: "There is no prospect of improvement in China-U.S. relations unless the U.S. Government changes its thinking." Deng said the basic problem lay with the U.S. pursuit of a policy of "two Chinas" or "one China and another half China." The Chinese statesman said the Reagan Administration was wrong in thinking that China had more to gain from the relationship than the United States. Deng emphasized that China would not "swallow" this kind of American treatment.[356]

---

[354] Xinhua, November 29, 1983, in FBIS-China, November 29, 1983, p. B1.

[355] U.S. Department of State, "Briefing Paper," n.d., p. 2.

[356] Kyodo, April 28, 1983, in FBIS-China, April 28, 1983, p. D1.

11.3 SALE OF HIGH TECHNOLOGY TO THE PRC

Concerned over the steady deterioration of Sino-American relations during the previous months, the United States in May and June 1983 took several steps to improve its ties with the PRC. The most important action was the decision to approve the export of high technology to China. Although given relatively low visibility as an issue compared to Taiwan, access to advanced American technology was critical to the success of the Four Modernizations and therefore a substantive improvement in Sino-American relations from the perspective of Beijing. The Chinese Foreign Ministry immediately signalled its approval, saying: "We welcome this step taken by the U.S. Government."[357]

Commerce Secretary Malcolm Baldrige, who announced the new policy during his trip to China in spring 1983, explained to the House Special Subcommittee on U.S.-China Trade in September that the new guidelines would enable his department to clear almost three-quarters of all high technology sales to China. Baldrige said the decision "represents a major change in our policy," one that had been agreed to by the Departments of Defense, State and Commerce, the Joint Chiefs of Staff, the National Security Council, and President Reagan. The new policy placed China in the same category for export licensing as other friendly nations, but added three zones. In the first of these, representing most of the shipments, the Commerce Department was given the authority for approval. In the second, very high technology zone the Defense Department and other agencies would review approvals. In the third zone relating to advanced military systems there would exist "a strong presumption for denial."[358]

Secretary of Defense Caspar Weinberger's trip to China in September 1983 reinforced the Administration's signal that it was serious in wanting to move forward in the crucial area of high-tech transfers and to improve Sino-American relations in general. During the Secretary's visit, the Chinese announced that the long-awaited exchange trips of Premier Zhao Ziyang and President Reagan would occur the following spring. Despite the friendly welcome, the Chinese were noncommital to Weinberger's suggestions for greater strategic cooperation and persistent in their criticism of U.S. policy toward Taiwan. Zhao told American

---

[357] *Xinhua*, June 28, 1983, in *FBIS-China*, June 28, 1983, p. B1.

[358] See *Xinhua*, September 28, 1983, in *FBIS-China*, September 28, 1983, p. B7.

reporters just prior to meeting with Secretary Weinberger: "You all know, naturally, the main obstacle in the development of Sino-American relations is the Taiwan issue. These relations will be able to grow only when this obstacle is removed."[359]

While Weinberger was in China, PRC Foreign Minister Wu Xueqian toured the United States. In a speech before the National Assembly on United States-China Relations on September 28, Wu pointed out: "The development of Sino-U.S. relations over the past few years has not been plain-sailing; there have been twists and turns. The root cause lies in the attitude of the United States toward the question of Taiwan." Wu said the Taiwan Relations Act "treated China's Taiwan province as an independent political entity." He noted that the U.S. policy of "selling large amounts of arms to Taiwan" had infringed on China's sovereignty and for a time brought "the hard-won good relations between the two countries to the verge of rupture." The Foreign Minister stressed:

> If the United States truly desires to see a peaceful settlement of the Taiwan question, it should strictly abide by the relevant principles and provisions set forth in the joint communique on the establishment of diplomatic relations between China and the United States and the joint communique of 17 August last year; it should refrain from doing anything detrimental to the peaceful reunification of China, refrain from having any official or semi-official relations with Taiwan and gradually reduce, both qualitatively and quantitatively, its arms sales to Taiwan, leading to a final termination. Otherwise, it will only make a peaceful settlement more difficult and thus result in blocking the road toward a peaceful settlement.[360]

At a year-end meeting of the Sixth NPC Standing Committee in December 1983, Wu Xueqian gave a generally upbeat report on Sino-American relations. He noted that "the U.S. secretary of state, secretary of commerce and secretary of defense visited China one after another this year", expressing "the wish to establish a steady

---

[359] *Renmin Ribao*, September 28, 1983, in *FBIS-China*, September 28, 1983, p. B2.

[360] *Renmin Ribao*, September 28, 1983, in *FBIS-China*, September 28, 1983, p. B6.

and long-term relationship with China. The United States has relaxed its restrictions on technology transfer to China." Wu stressed that the Taiwan issue remained unresolved, however. The Foreign Minister said: "some Americans consistently regard Taiwan as a 'political entity' and an 'unsinkable aircraft carrier,' advocating 'two China's' or 'one China, one Taiwan.' The Taiwan issue is still the main obstacle in Sino-U.S. relations."[361]

11.4 EXCHANGE VISITS OF PREMIER ZHAO ZIYANG AND PRESIDENT REAGAN

The visit of Chinese Premier Zhao Ziyang to the United States in January 1984 resulted in the further relaxation of U.S. high technology export controls to China. A new accord on industrial cooperation was signed, along with a renewed pact on science and technology. Progress was also made on an agreement on nuclear-power cooperation, whereby China would receive U.S. assistance in its nuclear energy program.[362] Previously, the U.S. government had refused to allow American firms to participate in China's nuclear program because the PRC's views on nuclear proliferation were not satisfactorily spelled out. Premier Zhao specifically addressed this concern in an after dinner toast on January 10: "We do not advocate or encourage nuclear proliferation. We do not engage in nuclear proliferation ourselves, nor do we help other countries development nuclear weapons."[363]

Although Zhao reiterated China's stand on Taiwan in private conversations with American officials, his trip was characterized by a low-key approach to this controversial subject and by concentration on the economic, commercial, and technological aspects of Sino-American relations. This theme was also pursued with success during President Reagan's exchange visit to China in April 1984.

While in the PRC, the President signed accords on the reestablishment of cultural exchanges (held in abeyance for a year because of the Hu Na incident), the avoidance of double taxation, and technical cooperation. The President also witnessed the initialing of an

---

[361] Xinhua, December 7, 1983, in FBIS-China, December 8, 1983, pp. K14-K15.

[362] Wall Street Journal, January 13, 1984, p. 24.

[363] New York Times, January 13, 1984, p. A6.

agreement on cooperation in peaceful uses of nuclear energy.

The Chinese reminded the President that Taiwan remained the chief obstacle to progressive relations between the United States and the PRC. According to Beijing's summary of the visit, Zhao Ziyang told the President:

> The Taiwan issue remains the major obstacle blocking the steady and lasting growth of Sino-U.S. relations. He said relations between the two countries are still in a sprouting stage and need careful nurturing by the two sides. The Premier said the U.S. Government has time and again promised to carry out a one-China policy, but there are still people advocating escalation of U.S.-Taiwan relations and they even encourage the so-called independence of Taiwan. The Premier said he hopes that when Sino-U.S. relations are developing in a good direction, nothing that harms the feelings of the Chinese people would happen again, especially after Reagan's visit to China.
>
> On U.S. arms sales to Taiwan, Premier Zhao Ziyang said: China hopes to see a drastic reduction in such sales leading to a final solution. He said if marked progress can be made in this regard, it will have positive effects on promoting mutual trust between the two sides.[364]

Foreign Minister Wu Xueqian was more explicit in his remarks to Secretary Shultz on the arms sales issue. Xinhua reported that Wu called U.S. arms sales to Taiwan an issue that needs "the most urgent solution" and that the Taiwan question remains the "main obstacle" in the way of Sino-U.S. relations. Wu said: "We have noticed the reduction of U.S. arms sales to Taiwan in the fiscal year 1985, but the amount of reduction is extremely limited." The Foreign Minister reminded Shultz that the United States "should not upgrade" the arms sold to Taiwan. He urged Washington to adopt "positive measures to effectively settle the question of U.S. arms sales to Taiwan quantitatively and qualitatively in line with the principles laid down in the Sino-U.S. joint communiques."[365]

---

[364] Beijing Radio, April 28, 1984, in FBIS-China, May 1, 1984, pp. B9-B10.

Relations between the United States and the PRC in the wake of President Reagan's trip to China, while generally positive, continued to vacillate. From the point of view of increased military cooperation, Defense Minister Zhang Aiping's visit to the United States in June was successful. In addition to reaching agreement on undisclosed military matters, Zhang and Weinberger discussed the sale of American weapons and defense technology, particularly those of use to the PRC in countering the Soviet armor and air threat along the Sino-Soviet border. Reportedly, the United States agreed in principle to sell China Hawk anti-aircraft missiles, Improved TOW anti-tank weapons, and artillery technology and ammunition. Zhang was also taken on tours of U.S. military bases and major defense plants, including Boeing, Rockwell International, and General Dynamics.[365] The level of weapons actually purchased by the Chinese remained problematical, however. As one official told the U.S. Congress: "they want the technology with which to manufacture their own weapons."[367]

Politically, Sino-American strategic relations were given a boost in June and July, because of increased strains in Sino-Soviet relations caused in part by tensions along the Sino-Vietnamese border. In a series of articles appearing in the Chinese press in mid-July, the PRC accused the Soviet Union of becoming more stubborn and hostile under the leadership of Konstantin Chernenko. Strategic cooperation with Washington, however, was specifically ruled out. In Outlook magazine the PRC said: "China does not intend to be a card in the hands of Americans in dealing with their rival or adversary."[368]

On the other hand, the nuclear power agreement initialed in China during Reagan's trip hit a snag. Alarmed over persistent intelligence reports that the PRC had given Pakistan design assistance for nuclear weapons in the late 1970s, congressional leaders told the Administration that they would oppose the U.S.-China nuclear agreement unless more specific assurances were given by the Chinese on their nonproliferation policies. In an effort to push the agreement through during Reagan's China visit, the Administration accepted

---

[365] Xinhua, April 28, 1984, in FBIS-China, May 1, 1984, p. B11.

[366] Washington Post, June 15, 1984, p. A1.

[367] New York Times, June 12, 1984, p. A3.

[368] Washington Post, July 16, 1984, p. A13.

Premier Zhao Ziyang's after dinner toast remarks on January 10 in place of a written pledge that China would not assist other nations develop nuclear weapons. Zhao reiterated China's commitment to nonproliferation in his speech to the National People's Congress in May 1984. After consulting with Congress, the Administration asked the PRC for additional pledges. Chinese officials reportedly became very upset and accused the United States of once again backsliding in their agreements with the PRC.[369]

Also on the negative side, the PRC continued to blame the United States along with the Soviet Union for world tensions. In his speech before the National People's Congress on May 15, 1984, Zhao Ziyang stated: "The rivalry between the two superpowers for global hegemony is the root cause of international tensions."[370] Chinese perceptions on this issue were explained in an article appearing in Renmin Ribao later that month:

> For quite a long time after the war, the United States was the creator of tension in Asia. After the United States was defeated in the Vietnam war in the early 1970s and withdrew from the Asia mainland, the Soviet Union dramatically increased its military strength in the Soviet Far East and the Pacific. By the end of the 1970s it was supporting Vietnam's invasion of Kampuchea, while itself invading Afghanistan. This caused the United States to react. Since last year, the Soviet Union has deployed 135 SS-20 medium-range missiles in the Asian region; it has reinforced its troops in Afghanistan and launched new offensives there; it has continued to support Vietnam's invasion of Kampuchea, and has also held a landing exercise on the Vietnamese coast. In order to counter these Soviet military moves, the United States is also greatly reinforcing its military deployment in the Asia-Pacific region. The intensification of Soviet-U.S. military confrontation in this region has posed a severe threat to Asian security and

---

[369] See Washington Post, May 18, 1984, p. A15; ibid., June 21, 1984, pp. A1, A17; and ibid., June 22, 1984, p. A6.

[370] Zhao's speech may be found in Xinhua, May 31, 1984, in FBIS-China, June 1, 1984, pp. K1-K20.

caused grave concern among the countries of the Asia-Pacific region. Who, if not the Soviet Union and the United States together, should bear the responsibility for causing deterioration of the situation in Asia?[371]

This view of world affairs was markedly different from that expressed in 1978-1980, when China sought to create a united front with the United States to counter the Soviet threat. By equating the United States with the Soviet Union as the "root cause of international tension," Beijing further distanced itself from strategic cooperation with Washington. The PRC perception was consistent with China's "independent foreign policy," but it also limited China's value to the United States in its global confrontation with the Soviet Union. U.S. efforts to get the Chinese to restrain from accusing Washington of hegemony were not successful.

The Taiwan issue continued to be the major irritant in Sino-American relations. <u>Ban Yue Tan</u> identified the Taiwan Relations Act and arms sales as the most important matters to be resolved. In a May editorial the magazine said:

> The key for the steady and prolonged development of Sino-U.S. relations lies in the settlement of the Taiwan issue. The U.S. "Taiwan Relations Act" constitutes a basic obstacle to Sino-U.S. relations, which are laid on the foundation of three communiques....Only when the principles prescribed in these communiques are strictly implemented can Sino-U.S. relations develop steadily. As far as the issue of U.S. arms sales to Taiwan is concerned, the United States should take concrete action to faithfully carry out the relevant provisions in the "17 August communique." Our state will strive to settle the Taiwan issue in a peaceful way. However, how China settles the Taiwan issue is completely a matter of China's internal affairs. Our state cannot make any commitment on this matter to any foreign country. We do not require the U.S. Government to do any special thing, but we only hope that it will not place obstacles in the way of China's peaceful reunification.[372]

---

[371] <u>Renmin Ribao</u>, June 9, 1984, in <u>FBIS-China</u>, June 12, 1984, p. A1.

The announcement by the United States on June 20 of its decision to sell Taiwan twelve C-130H military transport aircraft for $325 million was troubling to Beijing on two counts. First, it reinforced China's conviction that U.S. arms sales delayed national reunification; and second, the transaction expanded further the U.S. interpretation of the August 17 Communique. In its protest against the sale, the PRC Foreign Ministry said:

> So far, the United States has never supplied any C-130 advanced military transport aircraft to Taiwan, and its function far exceeds that of the military transport aircraft the United States has supplied to Taiwan in the past.
>
> This action of the United States obviously violates the relevant provisions of the Sino-U.S. communique of August 17, 1982.[373]

According to U.S. sources, the sale had been made because Taiwan's existing transport aircraft (C-119G) badly needed replacement. Supplying Taipei with the same aircraft would not be practical because of the difficulty in keeping the aircraft flying and in securing spare parts. The August 17 Communique did not prevent the United States from replacing obsolescent equipment in Taiwan's inventory when similar equipment could not be found or maintained.

According to the Department of State, U.S. policy on arms sales to Taiwan at the end of July 1984 included the following principles:

> --We have consistently refused to be bound by either a termination date or an amount by which we will reduce arms sales each year.
>
> --We consider the sale of defensive arms to Taiwan to be a routine matter consistent with U.S. policy since U.S.-PRC normalization and with the August 17 communique.

---

[372] *Ban Yue Tan*, May 10, 1984, in *FBIS-China*, June 11, 1984, p. A1.

[373] *Xinhua*, June 20, 1984, in *FBIS-China*, June 21, 1984, p. B4.

--Under the Taiwan Relations Act we sell Taiwan "defense articles and services" to meet Taiwan's defense needs. At the same time, in the August 17 communique with China we stated that it was our policy to reduce gradually our arms sales to Taiwan and to limit the quality of those arms to levels of recent years. Our policy is predicated on China's pursuit of a peaceful approach to the Taiwan question.

--Recent arms sales notified to the Congress have included missiles, aircraft spare parts, and equipment for tanks already in Taiwan's inventory.

--Arms sales for FY 1983 totalled approximately $784 million. FY 1984 sales are estimated at $780 million. A level of $760 million is proposed for FY 1985.

--The Chinese have publicly expressed their view that some of the arms in the July 1983 package exceeded the quality limits implied in the August 17 communique. We consider the items in the package are consistent with items already in Taiwan's inventory.[374]

---

[374] U.S. Department of State, "Briefing Paper," n.d., pp. 1-2.

Part III

Conclusion

12
Summary and Policy Recommendations

12.1   LIMITS OF SINO-AMERICAN STRATEGIC COOPERATION

Successive U.S. administrations have determined that friendly Sino-American relations are in the national security interests of the United States. Although the Reagan Administration has broadened the base of U.S.-PRC relations to include a wide range of commercial, scientific, technological, cultural, and other ties, the strategic dimensions of the relationship remain paramount.

The value of strategic relations with China depends upon several interrelated factors. Among the most important are the strength of the PRC, its political direction, and the state of Sino-Soviet and Soviet-American relations.

In terms of China's national power, the PRC is one of the major countries of the world. Its strength is rapidly increasing under the socialist modernization program of Deng Xiaoping and his reformist faction. China's potential should not be overestimated, however. Major weaknesses exist within its armed forces, economy, and political and social institutions which seriously challenge the survival of the current leadership, the nation's ability to defend itself against a Soviet attack, and the success of China's economic development.

U.S. interests are served by a moderately strong, stable China, pursuing a policy of broad contact with the West and friendly relations with the United States. Some American assistance to China's Four Modernizations is in the U.S. interest. The amount and type of assistance, however, must be compatible with other U.S. interests, such as the promotion of democratic institutions, the free enterprise system, and freedom of the individual. The United States should not help to create a more totalitarian China, nor a China capable of directly threatening U.S. military, political, or commercial interests. Since the course of China's political development is uncertain, a degree of caution in U.S. policy toward China is essential.

The Sino-Soviet split plays a vital role in Sino-American strategic cooperation. Both Moscow and Beijing have sought since mid-1980 to move gradually toward normalized relations, but divisive elements of the Sino-Soviet conflict remain unresolved. The various historical, geographical, ideological, personality, and other factors which led to the breakup of the Sino-Soviet alliance and military confrontation throughout most of the 1960s and 1970s have created deep schisms between the two countries.

Profound differences over border issues, economic direction, and national security objectives ensure that both Moscow and Beijing will continue to deploy large numbers of troops along the Sino-Soviet border. China and the Soviet Union are two major continental powers competing for influence over the same Asian rim nations. A mutual acceptance of individual spheres of influence will be exceedingly difficult.

Despite their differences, it is in the national interests of both China and the Soviet Union that tensions be reduced and relations become more stable. Efforts by the two governments since 1980 to reach rapprochement have been partially successful. Serious obstacles remain, however. The Soviet Union is unlikely to make concessions on the three principal security concerns of China: Soviet support for Vietnam during its occupation of Kampuchea; USSR troops occupying Afghanistan; and Soviet forces deployed in Mongolia and along the Sino-Soviet border. Concessions on these points would require a significant shift in USSR strategy vis-a-vis both China and the United States. This Moscow appears unwilling to do.

Greatly complicating Sino-Soviet relations are Kremlin perceptions of the U.S. threat. Soviet deployments around the periphery of Asia--particularly in Vietnam, Afghanistan, and in the Soviet Far Eastern provinces--are aimed at countering the U.S. threat as well as that of China. As long as the Soviet Union views the United States as its principal threat and the major obstacle to the expansion of its political influence in Asia, USSR deployments will remain.

Signs of strain once again surfaced in Sino-Soviet relations following President Reagan's April 1984 trip to China. Moscow especially objected to the President's anti-Soviet remarks while in the PRC and closer consultations between the United States and China on military cooperation. In mid-1984 Soviet and Chinese interests clashed over Vietnam. Evidence strongly suggests that Sino-Soviet normalization will be arduous, tensions between the two countries will remain fairly high, and both will continue to view each other as major threats.

Under these circumstances, the United States need not fear that China will play "the Soviet card" in such as way as to damage seriously U.S. interests. Soviet forces will continue to be diverted along the Sino-Soviet border and a substantial percentage of Soviet military forces will remain targeted on the PRC.

Given the global extent of the Soviet threat to U.S. interests, it is appropriate for Washington to seek expanded strategic cooperation with China. The military component of that cooperation is especially appealing--but also misleading. There are definite limiting factors to Sino-American military relations. These include:

1. Domestic opposition to close military ties in both China and the United States.

2. The size of PLA modernization requirements, which dwarf any possible U.S. military assistance programs.

3. The limited ability of the PLA to absorb U.S. weapons technology.

4. Opposition from American allies in the Western Pacific to U.S. efforts to strengthen the PRC.

5. China's own sense of self-reliance, which restricts the amount of western assistance accepted into the country.

6. Beijing's limited foreign exchange reserves and the many competing needs for these assets.

7. The realization in both the United States and the PRC that the likely Soviet response to increased Sino-American strategic cooperation will be an increase in the USSR's own military forces in the region.

Beijing recognizes that U.S. efforts to counter the Soviet military presence in East Asia provide China with some degree of deterrence against a Soviet attack. Limited military cooperation with the United States is useful to China to the extent that it increases Beijing's flexibility in dealing with the Soviet Union and complicates Soviet planning. Moreover, some low-level conventional and clandestine cooperation between China and the United States is useful in areas such as Indochina and Afghanistan.

Politically, Sino-American strategic cooperation can be used by both countries to advance their individual interests. A U.S.-PRC united front on specific issues is effective in countering Soviet political objectives in Southeast Asia and elsewhere. However, there are limits to political strategic cooperation as well. These include:

1. The desire of the PRC to pursue an independent foreign policy and its condemnation of the United States as a hegemonistic power.

2. Beijing's opposition to many U.S. foreign policies.

3. The fundamental ideological differences between the United States and the People's Republic of China.

4. The potential conflict of interest in Asia as China grows stronger and demands a greater voice in regional affairs.

5. Beijing's continuing efforts to normalize Sino-Soviet relations.

6. China's self-identification as a member of the Third World, which by definition must struggle against the two superpowers.

Given the limitations on both military and political strategic cooperation, it is highly unlikely that China will become an ally of the United States. Its intervention on the side of the United States in a war against Moscow is doubtful. Some military cooperation is useful and valuable psychologically up to the point where the Soviet Union counters with increased military preparations of its own. Politically, there is much the two sides can do to cooperate, but these areas will have to be defined individually as they arise. China's cooperation can never be assumed by the United States, because the PRC is pursuing its own international agenda and national objectives.

The United States should continue to cooperate strategically with the PRC when it serves U.S. interests and when China demonstrates a willingness to do so. But the tenuous nature of such cooperation means that is should not be permitted to undermine other, more permanent U.S. interests and objectives. Sino-American strategic cooperation is not a firm foundation on which to build U.S. policy in East Asia. Rather, U.S. policy

must be based on American strength in the Western
Pacific and on cooperation with those governments which
identify with the basic principles underlying the
American political, economic, and social systems.
Cooperation with countries not sharing these
ideals--such as the PRC--may be cautiously pursued, but
not at the expense of true friends and allies.

12.2 THE TAIWAN QUESTION

Taiwan is one of the most dynamic societies in the
Pacific Basin. Politically, its government is evolving
into a representative democracy. Economically, Taiwan
is becoming a fully industrialized society based on
capitalism and free enterprise. Socially, the people of
Taiwan enjoy a living standard parallel to that of the
West and possess similiar levels of personal freedom.
These advances have been made possible because of the
hard work of the people of Taiwan, sound government
policies, and continued U.S. support. Should Washington
end its support, there is high probability that the
democratic and free economic institutions built on the
island would be significantly eroded.
    U.S. interests in Taiwan are recognized in the
Taiwan Relations Act of 1979. To protect these
interests, the TRA specifies that the United States
should provide Taiwan with defense articles and services
necessary to enable Taiwan to maintain a sufficient
self-defense capability. There is honest disagreement
over how to define Taiwan's legitimate defense needs.
But since the arms sale issue is so sensitive to
Beijing, successive U.S. administrations have been
sorely tempted to downgrade the PRC threat to Taiwan to
avoid selling Taipei advanced weapons such as the FX
fighter and Harpoon missile. The United States has
justified its refusal to sell these weapons on the
grounds that Beijing does not <u>intend</u> to attack Taiwan,
although the PRC does possess the <u>military</u> <u>capabilities</u>
to mount several varieties of successful attacks against
Taiwan.
    In terms of military capabilities, the PRC is
overwhelming superior to Taiwan in several categories
such as surface-to-surface missiles, bombers, fighters,
infantry divisions, submarines, fast attack craft, and
surface missile craft. Although the PRC is unlikely to
launch an amphibious invasion of Taiwan, there are a
number of other military threats which the PRC could
successfully employ on fairly short notice. These
include the blockade or invasion of the offshore islands
of Kinmen and Matsu, a submarine enforced blockade of
the island of Taiwan, and a phased overwhelming of ROC
air and naval defenses.

To neutralize these threats, Taiwan attempts to purchase advanced weapons from abroad and to produce weapons domestically. Problems are being experienced in both efforts. Few countries are willing to risk political rupture of relations with Beijing to sell Taiwan the advanced weapons it needs. The United States, which is the most important source of arms for Taiwan, has consistently refused to sell Taipei an advanced replacement fighter or an effective ship-to-ship missile. Domestic production of weapons is very expensive on a per unit basis, and significant technological difficulties have been encountered.

As it stands, Taiwan's current deterrent capabilities against a PRC attack are marginal. What is troubling to Taipei is that Beijing's offensive military capabilities are likely to improve much more rapidly than Taiwan's defenses because of the PRC's greater defense budget, larger industrial base, and ability to acquire advanced weapons and technology from abroad.

Washington is in a dilemma of its own making. On the one hand, the TRA requires the United States to sell Taiwan the defense weapons and services it needs to maintain an adequate defense. On the other hand, Washington will soon be providing weapons technology and arms to Beijing, thus improving the PLA's military capabilities. Keeping these two aspects of U.S. China policy in balance necessitates qualitative and quantitative indexing on weapons sold to Taiwan. Otherwise, within the next few years, Taiwan will be unable to field an effective deterrence against possible PRC uses of force.

In terms of PRC intentions toward Taiwan, it must be kept in mind that one of Beijing's three major national priorities is to bring Taiwan under its control by the end of the 1980s. Alternate periods of forceful and peaceful approaches to reunification have been tried by the PRC since 1950.

Over the past ten years, China has pursued two distinct approaches to reunification. The first called for the "liberation of Taiwan" in terms often militaristic. Since normalization of Sino-American relations in 1979, the PRC has advocated "peaceful" reunification. Proposals have included Ye Jianying's nine-point plan of September 1981, the creation of "special administrative regions" under Article 31 of the 1982 PRC constitution, informal plans discussed with visiting Overseas Chinese scholars in 1983, and in 1984 various Hong Kong models, such as the "two systems in one country" proposal.

Taipei has rejected each of the PRC reunification plans. Taiwan's principal objections are: (1) the PRC cannot be trusted to keep its promises; (2) Taiwan already enjoys the "high degree" of autonomy promised by the PRC, as well as more freedom and prosperity than Chinese on the mainland; (3) Taipei believes Beijing is using negotiations to achieve what it cannot gain through the use of force; and (4) no one on Taiwan wants to be united with the communist-dominated mainland.

Taipei also rejects the various proposals offered by Beijing because each assumes that the PRC is the national government of China. The ROC cannot easily accept this, because its claims for legitimacy would be undermined. Even if no other government recognizes the ROC, the claim of legitimacy has to be upheld domestically on Taiwan to ensure social stability and political cohesion.

Some sort of accommodation between Beijing and Taipei may occur in the future. But it must evolve in a Chinese context. U.S. interests have been, and should remain, that the issue be settled peacefully. That interest implies that Taiwan be able to decide its future without undue military, political, economic, or psychological pressure from Beijing.

ROC authorities insist they are not against China's reunification. They emphasize, however, that the Chinese people should have a choice as to whether China should be democratic or communist. If Taiwan rejoins the communist mainland at this time, China will have little incentive to become more democratic in the future.

Beijing will probably adhere to its peaceful approach if Taipei elects to negotiate. Even if Taipei does not talk, the PRC's peaceful approach will likely remain in effect as long as Beijing values relations with the United States and the West. But a different leadership, a shift in priorities, or even a demonstration of nationalism might lead the PRC to adopt a harder, more militant policy toward Taiwan. It is important for Washington to remember that Chinese intentions can shift considerably faster than Taiwan's abilities to counter an increased threat.

Beijing is aware that the people of Taiwan oppose any attempt by the ROC to negotiate reunification at this time. But CPC leaders themselves face limited options. They must demonstrate to their domestic critics that steps are being taken to bring Taiwan under PRC control. The concessions offered Taiwan must not compromise the basic principles of communism. Expediently, capitalism and socialism could coexist in China for a time. But, from the perspective of the CPC, the two systems must not compete for the loyalty of the people. Eventually, communism must emerge as the dominate social system. Attempting to find adequate assurances to guarantee the lifestyle and wellbeing of the people of Taiwan, while at the same time not to compromise the basic principles and objectives of communism is difficult. It must also be kept in mind that China's leaders are individuals whose decisions are not always based upon humane considerations. Virtually all of China's top leadership participated in events causing the death of scores of millions of Chinese--some 27 million people died during the Great Leap Forward alone.[375] The loss of the entire population of Taiwan could be replaced by China's growth in population in one year.

The one overlapping interest shared by both Beijing and Taipei is China's modernization. But is Chinese nationalism and cultural affinity stronger than the principles which hold the CPC and KMT apart? Will one side or the other surrender its political legitimacy in order to accomplish the unification of the motherland?

Although surrender of one political system to another is a possibility which cannot be ruled out, its occurrence would be remarkable in any political culture and almost unprecedented in the Chinese context. Yet, if reunification cannot be achieved by peaceful means, then the probability of force being used is quite high. It would appear, therefore, that as long as Taiwan resists communization, there is a profound and long-term threat to its security from the PRC.

The United States has tended to downplay this ultimate threat to Taiwan in the interests of improving relations with China. Whereas it is true that friendly U.S.-PRC relations have reduced the level of immediate tensions in the Taiwan Strait region, an imminent invasion is unlikely in any case because of the difficulty of mounting an amphibious attack and the strong likelihood of American intervention under present conditions. The long-term threat to Taiwan, however, has not been reduced. Indeed, it may be increasing with U.S. help.

Beijing, in pursuing a peaceful resolution of the Taiwan issue, has accepted current realities and used improved relations with the United States to strengthen itself. Unless the United States provides more advanced weapons to Taipei, in time the PRC will be strong enough to attack Taiwan. Will the United States intervene at that time? Or will the United States, because of the PRC's increased military capabilities, be deterred from acting decisively in the Taiwan Strait?

The United States may be able to avoid this potential problem by fulfilling the TRA's arms sales provisions. Given the basic historical, moral, and legal interests involved in the U.S. commitment to

---

[375] Washington Post, July 11, 1984, p. A14, citing Ansley J. Coale, a Princeton University demographer who has worked extensively with PRC population data.

Taiwan, it is appropriate for Washington to assist Taipei to maintain its own minimal deterrence.

A policy of maintaining essential parity in the Taiwan Strait region is consistent with past U.S. policy. It requires some qualitative and quantitative adjustments in the level of arms sold to Taiwan, but these precedents have already been established. If done quietly and justified on the grounds of indexing, the gradual improvement of Taiwan's armed forces can be accomplished without jeopardizing Sino-American relations or essential levels of U.S.-PRC strategic cooperation.

12.3 TAIWAN AS A VARIABLE IN SINO-AMERICAN STRATEGIC RELATIONS

Taiwan has been an issue in Sino-American relations since the founding of the People's Republic of China in 1949. The ebb and flow of tensions over Taiwan indicate that the PRC attaches different values to the issue. The controversy surrounding the FX decision and the August 17 Communique demonstrates that, under certain conditions, problems over Taiwan could lead to a deterioration of the atmosphere of Sino-American relations. On the other hand, the fact that Sino-American relations improved in 1969-1972, 1978-1980, and mid-1983 to mid-1984 implies that the Taiwan issue will not hinder relations when Beijing feels more important issues are at stake.

An analysis of 272 PRC statements on Sino-American relations made during 1981-1982 shows little or no correlation between the Taiwan issue and other major bilateral issues. During this two-year period, over 45% of all PRC statements on Sino-American relations included references to the Taiwan issue. How the United States handled its ties with Taiwan did influence the general atmosphere of Sino-American relations, but there was no connection between the Taiwan issue and strategic cooperation or economic/technological exchanges.[376]

This finding, coupled with earlier observations that in 1969-1972 the Taiwan issue did not prevent initial contact between the United States and China nor in 1978-1980 did it interfere in the normalization process, strongly suggests that the Taiwan issue is somewhat like a floating variable in Sino-American relations. In other words, while the Taiwan question remains a genuine and serious concern to Beijing, its

---

[376] Martin L. Lasater, "PRC Perceptions of Sino-American Relations, 1981-1982," unpublished manuscript.

importance varies considerably depending upon the status of China's more pressing international and domestic concerns. Since 1969 these concerns have centered on the PRC's perception of the Soviet threat and progress in China's modernization. If both of these fundamental interests are being managed, Beijing places greater emphasis on the resolution of the Taiwan issue.

Under the Reagan Administration, the PRC felt confident that the United States would deter Soviet hegemony in Asia. Moreover, Washington repeatedly demonstrated its desire to enter into closer military cooperation with China. Beijing thus had a wide range of options in its relations with the Soviet Union. If Moscow appeared too aggressive, China could expand its security relationship with the United States. If Moscow reduced its threat, Beijing could back away from the United States in a nonaligned policy.

PRC flexibility increased between mid-1980 and mid-1984 because of the Soviet Union's desire to reduce Sino-Soviet tensions. The combination of confidence in the U.S. deterrent posture in East Asia, plus the USSR's willingness to move toward normalized relations with the PRC, permitted Beijing to pursue its independent foreign policy. This policy ideally suits China's national interests, but it rests upon the peaceful intentions of both superpowers. A change in the threat of either superpower would force the PRC to alter its foreign policy.

Second only to security interests in importance to China is the nation's economic development. The economic and political reforms currently underway in the PRC are so far-reaching that the continuation in power of Deng's faction rests in large measure upon the success of the Four Modernizations. Any significant failure might well lead to the collapse of the reformists' coalition. Access to western credit and technology is fundamental to the Four Modernizations. The United States plays an important role in this because of the scope of its own trade with and investment in China, and because Washington's attitude toward the PRC's modernization greatly influences the participation of other western countries in China's development.

Therefore, it is in Beijing's fundamental security and economic interests that friendly relations be maintained with the United States, despite the continuing irritation caused by the Taiwan issue.

Friendly Sino-American relations gave China a greater sense of security and more confidence in the success of the Four Modernizations. Ironically, this enabled the PRC to place greater emphasis on a solution to the Taiwan question. As China gets stronger, the United States can expect pressure on the Taiwan issue to increase, unless (1) Taipei indicates a willingness to negotiate; (2) the Soviet threat dramatically increases; (3) the Four Modernizations run into serious difficulties; or (4) Washington threatens to cut off its security, commercial, or technological support to China.

The United States has little influence over Sino-Soviet relations or domestic conditions within the PRC. Washington has some influence over the success of the Four Modernizations. The greatest influence the United States exercises is over Taiwan because of the island's heavy dependence on U.S. trade, investment, political support, and security assistance.

The question of whether the United States should "nudge" Taiwan into negotiations with the PRC is important to address. The various communiques signed by the United States and China have attempted to manage the Taiwan issue in such a way as to establish, preserve, and expand Sino-American relations. These communiques, while advancing U.S.-PRC ties, have added burdens to the people of Taiwan. It is more difficult for Taipei to survive today than in 1969. Any further concessions by the United States on the question of arms sales, the sovereignty issue, or the right of Taiwan to participate in international affairs will dangerously undermine Taiwan's stability and security.

The military and political advantages to the United States in its strategic relationship with the PRC are important, but limited. When appropriate, these should be taken advantage of and expanded. But a realistic sense of their potential should be kept in mind. Further U.S. concessions on Taiwan will not result in increased strategic cooperation with China. Even a total resolution of the Taiwan issue would not alter China's strategic perceptions or change its independent foreign policy. The strategic aspects of U.S.-PRC relations are largely determined by both countries' relations with the Soviet Union. Taiwan is a separate bilateral issue between China and the United States. Although Beijing may at times attempt to link the two issues as a bargaining ploy, they are not related.

12.4   POLICY IMPLICATIONS

The fundamental conclusion drawn from this study is that the Taiwan issue is a floating variable in Sino-American relations. Its value during any given period is heavily influenced by China's perception of the Soviet threat, the strength of the U.S. position vis-a-vis Moscow, and the status of China's economic development. Secondary influences include: domestic pressure on the PRC leadership to resolve the Taiwan issue; the public stance of American officials on the Taiwan issue; actions pursued by Taipei itself; and the attitude of other countries toward China and Taiwan.

The Taiwan question will remain sensitive because fundamental Chinese and American interests are involved. China does not intend to give up its claim to the island. Taiwan does not want to be reunited with a communist mainland. U.S. interests are tied to a peaceful resolution of the Taiwan question. Although the current PRC approach is peaceful, it is a tactical approach that could be changed in the future.

The United States must insist that the Taiwan question not be linked to other aspects of Sino-American relations. If the PRC "punishes" the United States for its policy toward Taiwan by actions in other areas of Sino-American relations, Washington should counter in areas of security and economic importance to China.

The United States can assume that if China feels secure from the Soviet threat and makes significant progress in its economic development, the Taiwan question will receive greater emphasis in Sino-American relations. On the other hand, the Soviet threat and China's modernization are long-term concerns which will not be resolved during this century. Therefore, the Taiwan issue will continue to vary in importance in the future. The United States should accept this and devise a long-term policy to serve American interests. This policy should not be based on old friendships with Taiwan, but rather anchored on fundamental American principles and values.

From the analysis presented in this study, it is apparent that fundamental U.S. interests are involved in unofficial relations with Taiwan. In addition to the political, economic, and security aspects of the relationship expressed in the Taiwan Relations Act, there are more basic historical, moral, and ideological principles involved. These are not as easily expressed or quantified as the balance of power equations underlying U.S. relations with the PRC. Nonetheless, they are at the heart of America's national strength and purpose. To compromise U.S. principles in the case of Taiwan would weaken moral fabric at home and send a negative signal abroad. It is only recently that the malaise of the Vietnam war legacy has been dispersed and replaced with a new sense of national confidence and self-worth. The United States is once again being perceived as the primary advocate and supporter of freedom, democracy, and capitalism. The short-term gains in improved Sino-American relations resulting from further concessions on Taiwan would not justify the long-term loss resulting from the compromise of basic American values. A policy based on the support of freedom, democracy, and capitalism on Taiwan will increase U.S. moral strength at home and improve the U.S. image abroad.

If in the future Beijing offers conditions of reunification which the people of Taiwan can accept, so be it. U.S. interests are best served by a peaceful resolution of the Taiwan question. In the meantime, the current dual-track policy of the United States should be maintained. Efforts should be made to improve and expand Sino-American strategic cooperation in the military and political spheres. At the same time, the United States should continue its support of the people of Taiwan through the implementation of the Taiwan Relations Act.

Sino-American relations in the future will not be altogether stable. That is to be expected given the major differences between the two countries and their conflicting national objectives in many areas. Nonetheless, the fundamental interests of both China and the United States are served by their relationship. Despite disagreement over Taiwan, leaders in both countries should work to improve relations.

Appendixes

A. MUTUAL DEFENSE TREATY BETWEEN THE UNITED STATES AND THE REPUBLIC OF CHINA, December 2, 1954

The Parties to this Treaty,
Reaffirming their faith in the purposes and principles of the Charter of the United Nations and their desire to live in peace with all peoples and all Governments, and desiring to strengthen the fabric of peace in the West Pacific Area,
Recalling with mutual pride the relationship which brought their two peoples together in a common bond of sympathy and mutual ideas to fight side by side against imperialist aggression during the last war,
Desiring to declare publicly and formally their sense of unity and their common determination to defend themselves against external armed attack, so that no potential aggressor could be under the illusion that either of them stands alone in the West Pacific Area, and
Desiring further to strengthen their present efforts for collective defense for the preservation of peace and security pending the development of a more comprehensive system of regional security in the West Pacific Area,
Have agreed as follows:

Article I

The Parties undertake, as set forth in the Charter of the United Nations, to settle any international dispute in which they may be involved by peaceful means in such a manner that international peace, security and justice are not endangered and to refrain in their international relations from the threat or use of force in any manner inconsistent with the purposes of the United Nations.

Article II

In order more effectively to achieve the objective of this Treaty, the Parties separately and jointly by self-help and mutual aid will maintain and develop their individual and collective capacity to resist armed attack and communist

subversive activities directed from without against their
territorial integrity and political stability.

Article III

The Parties undertake to strengthen their free institutions
and to cooperate with each other in the development of economic
progress and social well-being and to further their individual
and collective efforts toward these ends.

Article IV

The Parties, through their Foreign Ministers or their
deputies, will consult together from time to time regarding
the implementation of this Treaty.

Article V

Each Party recognizes that an armed attack in the West
Pacific Area directed against the territories of either of the
Parties would be dangerous to its own peace and safety and declares
that it would act to meet the common danger in accordance with
its constitutional processes.

Any such armed attack and all measures taken as a result
thereof shall be immediately reported to the Security Council
of the United Nations. Such measures shall be terminated when
the Security Council has taken the measures necessary to restore
and maintain international peace and security.

Article VI

For the purposes of Articles II and V, the terms
"territorial" and "territories" shall mean in respect of the
Republic of China, Taiwan and the Pescadores; and in respect
of the United States of America, the island territories in the
West Pacific under its jurisdiction. The provisions of Articles II
and V will be applicable to such other territories as may be
determined by mutual agreement.

Article VII

The Government of the Republic of China grants, and the
Government of the United States of America accepts, the right
to dispose such United States land, air and sea forces in and
about Taiwan and the Pescadores as may be required for their
defense, as determined by mutual agreement.

Article VIII

This Treaty does not affect and shall not be interpreted
as affecting in any way the rights and obligations of the Parties
under the Charter of the United Nations or the responsibility
of the United Nations for the maintenance of international peace
and security.

Article IX

This Treaty shall be ratified by the Republic of China and the United States of America in accordance with their respective constitutional processes and will come into force when instruments of ratification thereof have been exchanged by them at Taipei.

Article X

This Treaty shall remain in force indefinitely. Either Party may terminate it one year after notice has been given to the other party.

B. SHANGHAI COMMUNIQUE, February 28, 1972

President Richard Nixon of the United States of America visited the People's Republic of China at the invitation of Premier Chou En-lai of the People's Republic of China from February 21 to February 28, 1972. Accompanying the President were Mrs. Nixon, U.S. Secretary of State William Rogers, Assistant to the President Dr. Henry Kissinger, and other American officials.

President Nixon met with Chairman Mao Tse-tung of the Communist Party of China on February 21. The two leaders had a serious and frank exchange of views on Sino-U.S. relations and world affairs.

During the visit, extensive, earnest and frank discussions were held between President Nixon and Premier Chou En-lai on the normalization of relations between the United States of America and the People's Republic of China, as well as on other matters of interest to both sides. In addition, Secretary of State William Rogers and Foreign Minister Chi Peng-fei held talks in the same spirit.

President Nixon and his party visited Peking and viewed cultural, industrial and agricultural sites, and they also toured Hangchow and Shanghai where, continuing discussions with Chinese leaders, they viewed similar places of interest.

The leaders of the People's Republic of China and the United States of America found it beneficial to have this opportunity, after so many years without contact, to present candidly to one another their views on a variety of issues. They reviewed the international situation in which important changes and great upheavals are taking place and expounded their respective positions and attitudes.

The U.S. side stated: Peace in Asia and peace in the world require efforts both to reduce immediate tensions and to eliminate the basic causes of conflict. The United States will work for a just and secure peace: just, because it fulfills the aspirations of peoples and nations for freedom and progress; secure, because it removes the danger of foreign aggression. The United States supports individual freedom and social progress for all the peoples of the world, free of outside pressure or intervention.

The United States believes that the effort to reduce tensions is served by improving communication between countries that have different ideologies so as to lessen the risks of confrontation through accident, miscalculation or misunderstanding. Countries should treat each other with mutual respect and be willing to compete peacefully, letting performance be the ultimate judge. No country should claim infallibility and each country should be prepared to re-examine its own attitudes for the common good. The United States stressed that the peoples of Indochina should be allowed to determine their destiny without outside intervention; its constant primary objective has been a negotiated solution; the eight-point proposal put forward by the Republic of Vietnam and the United States on January 27, 1972 represents a basis for the attainment of that objective; in the absence of a negotiated settlement the United States envisages the ultimate withdrawal of all U.S. forces from the region consistent with the aim of self-determination for each country of Indochina. The United States will maintain its close ties with and support for the Republic of Korea; the United States will support efforts of the Republic of Korea to seek a relaxation of tension and increased communication in the Korean peninsula. The United States places the highest value on its friendly relations with Japan; it will continue to develop the existing close bonds. Consistent with the United Nations Security Council Resolution of December 21, 1971, the United States favors the continuation of the ceasefire between India and Pakistan and the withdrawal of all military forces to within their own territories and to their own sides of the ceasefire line in Jammu and Kashmir; the United States supports the right of the peoples of South Asia to shape their own future in peace, free of military threat, and without having the area become the subject of great power rivalry.

The Chinese side stated: Wherever there is oppression, there is resistance. Countries want independence, nations want liberation and the people want revolution--this has become the irresistible trend of history. All nations, big or small, should be equal; big nations should not bully the small and strong nations should not bully the weak. China will never be a superpower and it opposes hegemony and power politics of any kind. The Chinese side stated that it firmly supports the struggles of all the oppressed people and nations for freedom and liberation and that the people of all countries have the right to choose their social systems according to their own wishes and the right to safeguard the independence, sovereignty and territorial integrity of their own countries and oppose foreign aggression, interference, control and subversion. All foreign troops should be withdrawn to their own countries.

The Chinese side expressed its firm support to the peoples of Vietnam, Laos and Cambodia in their efforts for the attainment of their goal and its firm support to the seven-point proposal of the Provisional Revolutionary Government of the Republic of South Vietnam and the elaboration of February this year on the two key problems in the proposal, and to the Joint Declaration of the Summit Conference of the Indochinese Peoples. It firmly

supports the eight-point program for the peaceful unification
of Korea put forward by the Government of the Democratic People's
Republic of Korea on April 12, 1971, and the stand for the
abolition of the "U.N. Commission for the Unification and
Rehabilitation of Korea." It firmly opposes the revival and
outward expansion of Japanese militarism and firmly supports
the Japanese people's desire to build an independent, democratic,
peaceful and neutral Japan. It firmly maintains that India
and Pakistan should, in accordance with the United Nations
resolutions on the India-Pakistan question, immediately withdraw
all their forces to their respective territories and to their
own sides of the ceasefire line in Jammu and Kashmir and firmly
supports the Pakistan Government and people in their struggle
to preserve their independence and sovereignty and the people
of Jammu and Kashmir in their struggle for the right of
self-determination.

There are essential differences between China and the United
States in their social systems and foreign policies. However,
the two sides agreed that countries, regardless of their social
systems, should conduct their relations on the principles of
respect for the sovereignty and territorial integrity of all
states, non-aggression against other states, non-interference
in the internal affairs of other states, equality and mutual
benefit, and peaceful coexistence. International disputes should
be settled on this basis, without resorting to the use or threat
of force. The United States and the People's Republic of China
are prepared to apply these principles to their mutual relations.

With these principles of international relations in mind
the two sides stated that:

- progress toward the normalization of relations between
  China and the United States is in the interest of all
  countries;
- both wish to reduce the danger of international military
  conflict;
- neither should seek hegemony in the Asia-Pacific region
  and each is opposed to efforts by any other country or
  group of countries to establish such hegemony; and
- neither is prepared to negotiate on behalf of any third
  party or to enter into agreements or understandings with
  the other directed at other states.

Both sides are of the view that it would be against the
interests of the peoples of the world for any major country
to collude with another against other countries, or for major
countries to divide up the world into spheres of interest.

The two sides reviewed the long-standing serious disputes
between China and the United States. The Chinese side reaffirmed
its position: The Taiwan question is the crucial question
obstructing the normalization of relations between China and
the United States; the Government of the People's Republic of
China is the sole legal government of China; Taiwan is a province
of China which has long been returned to the motherland; the
liberation of Taiwan is China's internal affair in which no

other country has the right to interfere; and all U.S. forces
and military installations must be withdrawn from Taiwan. The
Chinese Government firmly opposes any activities which aim at
the creation of "one China, one Taiwan," "one China, two
governments," "two Chinas," and "independent Taiwan" or advocate
that "the status of Taiwan remains to be determined."

The U.S. side declared: The United States acknowledges
that all Chinese on either side of the Taiwan Strait maintain
there is but one China and that Taiwan is a part of China.
The United States Government does not challenge that position.
It reaffirms its interest in a peaceful settlement of the Taiwan
question by the Chinese themselves. With this prospect in mind,
it affirms the ultimate objective of the withdrawal of all U.S.
forces and military installations from Taiwan. In the meantime,
it will progressively reduce its forces and military installations
on Taiwan as the tension in the area diminishes.

The two sides agreed that it is desirable to broaden the
understanding between the two peoples. To this end, they
discussed specific areas in such fields as science, technology,
culture, sports and journalism, in which people-to-people contacts
and exchanges would be mutually beneficial. Each side undertakes
to facilitate the further development of such contacts and
exchanges.

Both sides view bilateral trade as another area from which
mutual benefit can be derived, and agreed that economic relations
based on equality and mutual benefit are in the interest of
the peoples of the two countries. They agree to facilitate
the progressive development of trade between their two countries.

The two sides agreed that they will stay in contact through
various channels, including the sending of a senior U.S.
representative to Peking from time to time for concrete
consultations to further the normalization of relations between
the two countries and continue to exchange views on issues of
common interest.

The two sides expressed the hope that the gains achieved
during this visit would open up new prospects for the relations
between the two countries. They believe that the normalization
of relations between the two countries is not only in the interest
of the Chinese and American peoples but also contributes to
the relaxation of tension in Asia and the world.

President Nixon, Mrs. Nixon and the American party expressed
their appreciation for the gracious hospitality shown them by
the Government and people of the People's Republic of China.

C. **JOINT COMMUNIQUE ON ESTABLISHMENT OF U.S.-PRC DIPLOMATIC RELATIONS, January 1, 1979**

The United States of America and the People's Republic
of China have agreed to recognize each other and to establish
diplomatic relations as of January 1, 1979.

The United States of America recognizes the Government
of the People's Republic of China as the sole legal Government
of China. Within this context, the people of the United States

will maintain cultural, commercial, and other unofficial relations with the people of Taiwan.

The United States of America and the People's Republic of China reaffirm the principles agreed on by the two sides in the Shanghai Communique and emphasize once again that:

- o Both wish to reduce the danger of international military conflict.
- o Neither should seek hegemony in the Asia-Pacific region or in any other region of the world and each is opposed to efforts by any other country or group of countries to establish such hegemony.
- o Neither is prepared to negotiate on behalf of any third party or to enter into agreements or understandings with the other directed at other states.
- o The Government of the United States of America acknowledges the Chinese position that there is but one China and Taiwan is part of China.
- o Both believe that normalization of Sino-American relations is not only in the interest of the Chinese and American peoples but also contributes to the cause of peace in Asia and the world.

The United States of America and the People's Republic of China will exchange Ambassadors and establish Embassies on March 1, 1979.

D. U.S. STATEMENT ON ESTABLISHMENT OF U.S.-PRC DIPLOMATIC RELATIONS, January 1, 1979

As of January 1, 1979, the United States of America recognizes the People's Republic of China as the sole legal government of China. On the same date, the People's Republic of China accords similar recognition to the United States of America. The United States thereby establishes diplomatic relations with the People's Republic of China.

On that same date, January 1, 1979, the United States of America will notify Taiwan that it is terminating diplomatic relations and that the Mutual Defense Treaty between the U.S. and the Republic of China is being terminated in accordance with the provisions of the Treaty. The United States also states that it will be withdrawing its remaining military personnel from Taiwan within four months.

In the future, the American people and the people of Taiwan will maintain commercial, cultural and other relations without official government representation and without diplomatic relations.

The Administration will seek adjustments to our laws and regulations to permit the maintenance of commercial, cultural, and other non-governmental relationships in the new circumstances that will exist after normalization.

The United States is confident that the people of Taiwan face a peaceful and prosperous future. The United States

continues to have an interest in the peaceful resolution of
the Taiwan issue and expects that the Taiwan issue will be settled
peacefully by the Chinese themselves.

The United States believes that the establishment of
diplomatic relations with the People's Republic will contribute
to the welfare of the American people, to the stability of Asia
where the United States has major security and economic interest,
and to the peace of the entire world.

E. PRC STATEMENT ON ESTABLISHMENT OF U.S.-PRC DIPLOMATIC RELATIONS, January 1, 1979

As of January 1, 1979, the People's Republic of China and
the United States of America recognize each other and establish
diplomatic relations, thereby ending the prolonged abnormal
relationship between them. This is a historic event in Sino-U.S.
relations.

As is known to all, the Government of the People's Republic
of China is the sole legal government of China and Taiwan is
a part of China. The question of Taiwan was the crucial issue
obstructing the normalization of relations between China and
the United States. It has now been resolved between the two
countries in the spirit of the Shanghai Communique and through
their joint efforts, thus enabling the normalization of relations
so ardently desired by the people of the two countries. As
for the way of bringing Taiwan back to the embrace of the
motherland and reunifying the country, it is entirely China's
internal affair.

At the invitation of the U.S. Government, Teng Hsiao-p'ing,
Vice Premier of the State Council of the People's Republic of
China, will pay an official visit to the United States in January
1979, with a view to further promoting the friendship between
the two peoples and good relations between the two countries.

F. PRESIDENT CHIANG CHING-KUO'S FIVE PRINCIPLES ON U.S.-ROC RELATIONS IN THE POSTNORMALIZATION PERIOD, December 29, 1978

[President Chiang Ching-kuo informed Deputy Secretary of
State Christopher that future ties between the Republic of China
and the United States must rest on five underlying principles--
reality, continuity, security, legality, and governmentality.
The President's statement is summarized by Dr. James Soong,
Deputy-Director of the Government Information Office, as follows:]

The Republic of China is an independent sovereign state
with a legitimately established government based on the
Constitution of the Republic of China. It is an effective
government, which has the wholehearted support of her people.
The international status and personality of the Republic of
China cannot be changed merely because of the recognition of
the Chinese Communist regime by any country of the world. The
legal status and international personality of the Republic of

China is a simple reality which the United States must recognize and respect.

The United States has expressed its intention that it will continue to maintain cultural, economic, trade, scientific, technological, and travel relations with the Republic of China. The ties that bound our two countries and people together in the past, however, include much more than these. The Republic of China is ready and willing to continue these traditional ties. The United States, on the other hand, must also realize the importance of the continuity of these ties, not only in their present scope, but also on an expanded scale to meet future needs.

The security of the Asian-Pacific region is also of utmost importance to the well-being and livelihood of the 17 million people on Taiwan, as well as American interests in the area.

The Sino-U.S. Mutual Defense Treaty signed in 1954 was designed to be a vital link in the chain of the collective defense system of free countries in the West Pacific. The situation in this region has not changed. It is still unstable and insecure. The threat of invasion and subversion by Communist forces to the free nations of Asia, particularly after the fall of Vietnam, is even more serious than before.

Hence, the U.S. unilateral action to terminate the Sino-U.S. Mutual Defense Treaty will further destabilize this region and might create a new crisis of war. Thus, in order to ensure the peace and security of the West Pacific, which includes that of the Republic of China, it is imperative that the United States take concrete and effective measures to renew its assurances to countries in this region.

We are ready and determined to continue to do our share in securing stability and peace in the West Pacific. But in order to do this, we must have sufficient capabilities to defend ourselves, and thereby protect our neighbors. President Carter has indicated that he is still concerned about the peace, security, and prosperity of this region after the termination of the Sino-U.S. Mutual Defense Treaty, and will continue to supply the Republic of China with defense weapons. The U.S. must give us assurances of a legal nature which would ensure the fulfillment of this commitment.

We are at present faced with the pragmatic problems involved in continuing and maintaining 59 treaties and agreements, as well as other arrangements, between our two countries. Since both the Republic of China and the United States are governed by law, the private interests of both Chinese and American citizens require the protection of definite legal provisions. Appropriate legislative measures in both countries must therefore be taken to provide legal basis on which these security, commercial, and cultural treaties and agreements can continue to remain in full force and effect.

The complex nature of the activities of mutual interest to our two countries makes it impossible for them to be carried out by any private organization or individual. To facilitate the continuation and expansion of all relations between our two countries, it is necessary that government-to-government level mechanisms be set up in Taipei and Washington. This model alone can serve as the framework on which the future relationship of our two countries can be constructed.

G. TAIWAN RELATIONS ACT, April 10, 1979 (U.S. Public Law 96-8)

"An Act to help maintain peace, security, and stability in the Western Pacific and to promote the foreign policy of the United States by authorizing the continuation of commercial, cultural, and other relations between the people of the United States and the people on Taiwan, and for other purposes."

Short Title

SECTION 1. This Act may be cited as the "Taiwan Relations Act."

Findings and Declaration of Policy

SEC. 2. (a) The President having terminated governmental relations between the United States and the governing authorities on Taiwan recognized by the United States as the Republic of China prior to January 1, 1979, the Congress finds that the enactment of this Act is necessary—
(1) to help maintain peace, security, and stability in the Western Pacific; and
(2) to promote the foreign policy of the United States by authorizing the continuation of commercial, cultural, and other relations between the people of the United States and the people on Taiwan.
(b) It is the policy of the United States—
(1) to preserve and promote extensive, close, and friendly commercial, cultural, and other relations between the people of the United States and the people on Taiwan, as well as the people on the China mainland and all other peoples of the Western Pacific area;
(2) to declare that peace and stability in the area are in the political, security, and economic interests of the United States, and are matters of international concern;
(3) to make clear that the United States decision to establish diplomatic relations with the People's Republic of China rests upon the expectation that the future of Taiwan will be determined by peaceful means;
(4) to consider any effort to determine the future of Taiwan by other than peaceful means, including by boycotts or embargoes, a threat to the peace and security of the Western Pacific area and of grave concern to the United States;
(5) to provide Taiwan with arms of a defensive character; and
(6) to maintain the capacity of the United States to resist any resort to force or other forms of coercion that would

jeopardize the security, or the social or economic system, of the people on Taiwan.

(c) Nothing contained in this Act shall contravene the interest of the United States in human rights especially with respect to the human rights of all the approximately 18 million inhabitants of Taiwan. The preservation and enhancement of the human rights of all the people on Taiwan are hereby reaffirmed as objectives of the United States.

Implementation of United States Policy with Regard to Taiwan

SEC. 3. (a) In furtherance of the policy set forth in section 2 of this Act, the United States will make available to Taiwan such defense articles and defense services in such quantity as may be necessary to enable Taiwan to maintain a sufficient self-defense capability.

(b) The President and the Congress shall determine the nature and quantity of such defense articles and services based solely upon their judgment of the needs of Taiwan, in accordance with procedures established by law. Such determination of Taiwan's defense needs shall include review by United States military authorities in connection with recommendations to the President and the Congress.

(c) The President is directed to inform the Congress promptly of any threat to the security or the social or economic system of the people on Taiwan and any danger to the interests of the United States arising therefrom. The President and the Congress shall determine, in accordance with constitutional processes, appropriate action by the United States in response to any such danger.

Application of Laws; International Agreements

SEC. 4. (a) The absence of diplomatic relations or recognition shall not affect the application of the laws of the United States with respect to Taiwan and the laws of the United States shall apply with respect to Taiwan in the manner that the laws of the United States applied with respect to Taiwan prior to January 1, 1979.

(b) The application of subsection (a) of this section shall include, but shall not be limited to, the following:

(1) Whenever the laws of the United States refer or relate to foreign countries, nations, states, governments, or similar entities, such terms shall include and such laws shall apply with respect to Taiwan.

(2) Whenever authorized by or pursuant to the laws of the United States to conduct or carry out programs, transactions, or other relations with respect to foreign countries, nations, states, governments, or similar entities, the President or any agency of the United States Government is authorized to conduct and carry out, in accordance with section 6 of this Act, such programs, transactions, and other relations with respect to Taiwan (including, but not limited to, the performance of services

for the United States through contracts with commercial entities on Taiwan), in accordance with the applicable laws of the United States.

(3)(A) The absence of diplomatic relations and recognition with respect to Taiwan shall not abrogate, infringe, modify, deny, or otherwise affect in any way any rights or obligations (including but not limited to those involving contracts, debts, or property interests of any kind) under the laws of the United States heretofore or hereafter required by or with respect to Taiwan.

(B) For all purposes under the laws of the United States, including actions in any court in the United States, recognition of the People's Republic of China shall not affect in any way the ownership of or other rights or interest in properties, tangible and intangible, and other things of value, owned or held on or prior to December 31, 1978, or thereafter acquired or earned by the governing authorities on Taiwan.

(4) Whenever the application of the laws of the United States depends upon the law that is or was applicable on Taiwan or compliance therewith, the law applied by the people on Taiwan shall be considered the applicable law for that purpose.

(5) Nothing in this Act, nor the facts of the President's action in extending diplomatic recognition to the People's Republic of China, the absence of diplomatic relations between the people on Taiwan and the United States, or the lack of recognition by the United States, and attendant circumstances thereto, shall be construed in any administrative or judicial proceeding as a basis for any United States Government agency, commission, or departments to make a finding of fact or determination of law, under the Atomic Energy Act of 1954 and the Nuclear Non-Proliferation Act of 1978, to deny an export license application or to revoke an existing export license for nuclear exports to Taiwan.

(6) For purposes of the Immigration and Nationality Act, Taiwan may be treated in the manner specified in the first sentence of section 202(b) of that Act.

(7) The capacity of Taiwan to sue and be sued in courts in the United States, in accordance with the laws of the United States, shall not be abrogated, infringed, modified, denied, or otherwise affected in any way by the absence of diplomatic relations or recognition.

(8) No requirement, whether expressed or implied, under the laws of the United States with respect to maintenance of diplomatic relations or recognition shall be applicable with respect to Taiwan.

(c) For all purposes, including actions in any court in the United States, the Congress approves the continuation in force of all treaties and other international agreements, including multilateral conventions, entered into by the United States and the governing authorities on Taiwan recognized by the United States as the Republic of China prior to January 1, 1979, and in force between them on December 31, 1978, unless and until terminated in accordance with law.

(d) Nothing in this Act may be construed as a basis for supporting the exclusion or expulsion of Taiwan from continued membership in any international financial institution or any other international organization.

Overseas Private Investment Corporation

SEC. 5. (a) During the three-year period beginning on the date of enactment of this Act, the $1,000 per capita income restriction in clause (2) of the second undesignated paragraph of section 231 of the Foreign Assistance Act of 1961 shall not restrict the activities of the Overseas Private Investment Corporation in determining whether to provide any insurance, reinsurance, loans, or guaranties with respect to investment projects on Taiwan.
(b) Except as provided in subsection (a) of this section, in issuing insurance, reinsurance, loans, or guaranties with respect to investment projects on Taiwan, the Overseas Private Insurance Corporation shall apply the same criteria as those applicable in other parts of the world.

The American Institute in Taiwan

SEC. 6. (a) Programs, transactions, and other relations conducted or carried out by the President or any agency of the United States Government with respect to Taiwan shall, in the manner and to the extent directed by the President, be conducted and carried out by or through--
(1) The American Institute in Taiwan, a nonprofit corporation incorporated under the laws of the District of Columbia, or
(2) such comparable successor nongovernmental entity as the President may designate (hereafter in this Act referred to as the "Institute").
(b) Whenever the President or any agency of the United States Government is authorized or required by or pursuant to the laws of the United States to enter into, perform, enforce, or have in force an agreement or transaction relative to Taiwan, such agreement or transaction shall be entered into, performed, and enforced, in the manner and to the extent directed by the President, by or through the Institute.
(c) To the extent that any law, rule, regulation, or ordinance of the District of Columbia, or of any State or political subdivision thereof in which the Institute is incorporated or doing business, impedes or otherwise interferes with the performance of the functions of the Institute pursuant to this Act, such law, rule, regulation, or ordinance shall be deemed to be preempted by this Act.

Services by the Institute to United States Citizens on Taiwan

SEC. 7. (a) The Institute may authorize any of its employees on Taiwan--

(1) to administer to or take from any person an oath, affirmation, affidavit, or deposition, and to perform any notarial act which any notary public is required or authorized by law to perform within the United States;

(2) to act as provisional conservator of the personal estates of deceased United States citizens; and

(3) to assist and protect the interests of United States persons by performing other acts such as are authorized to be performed outside the United States for consular purposes by such laws of the United States as the President may specify.

(b) Acts performed by authorized employees of the Institute under this section shall be valid, and of like force and effect within the United States, as if performed by any other person authorized under the laws of the United States to perform such acts.

Tax Exempt Status of the Institute

SEC. 8. (a) The Institute, its property, and its income are exempt from all taxation now or hereafter imposed by the United States (except to the extent that section 11(a)(3) of this Act requires the imposition of taxes imposed under chapter 21 of the Internal Revenue Code of 1954, relating to the Federal Insurance Contributions Act) or by any State or local taxing authority of the United States.

(b) For purposes of the Internal Revenue Code of 1954, the Institute shall be treated as an organization described in sections 170(b)(1)(A), 170(c), 2055(a), 2106(a)(2)(A), 2522(a), and 2522(b).

Furnishing Property and Services to and Obtaining
Services from the Institute

SEC. 9. (a) Any agency of the United States Government is authorized to sell, loan, or lease property (including interest therein) to, and to perform administrative and technical support functions and services for the operations of, the Institute upon such terms and conditions as the President may direct. Reimbursements to agencies under this subsection shall be credited to the current applicable appropriation of the agency concerned.

(b) Any agency of the United States Government is authorized to acquire and accept services from the Institute upon such terms and conditions as the President may direct. Whenever the President determines it to be in furtherance of the purposes of this Act, the procurement of services by such agencies from the Institute may be effected without regard to such laws of the United States normally applicable to the acquisition of services by such agencies as the President may specify by Executive order.

(c) Any agency of the United States Government making funds available to the Institute in accordance with this Act shall make arrangements with the Institute for the Comptroller General

of the United States to have access to the books and records
of the Institute and the opportunity to audit the operations
of the Institute.

Taiwan Instrumentality

SEC. 10. (a) Whenever the President or any agency of the
United States Government is authorized or required by or pursuant
to the laws of the United States to render or provide to or
to receive or accept from Taiwan, any performance, communication,
assurance, undertaking, or other action, such action shall,
in the manner and to the extent directed by the President, be
rendered or provided to, or received or accepted from, an
instrumentality established by Taiwan which the President
determines has the necessary authority under the laws applied
by the people on Taiwan to provide assurances and take other
actions on behalf of Taiwan in accordance with this Act.

(b) The President is requested to extend to the
instrumentality established by Taiwan the same number of offices
and complement of personnel as were previously operated in the
United States by the governing authorities on Taiwan recognized
as the Republic of China prior to January 1, 1979.

(c) Upon the granting by Taiwan of comparable privileges
and immunities with respect to the Institute and its appropriate
personnel, the President is authorized to extend with respect
to the Taiwan instrumentality and its appropriate personnel,
such privileges and immunities (subject to appropriate conditions
and obligations) as may be necessary for the effective performance
of their functions.

Separation of Government Personnel for Employment with the Institute

SEC. 11. (a)(1) Under such terms and conditions as the
President may direct, any agency of the United States Government
may separate from Government service for a specified period
any officer or employee of that agency who accepts employment
with the Institute.

(2) An officer or employee separated by an agency under
paragraph (1) of this subsection for employment with the Institute
shall be entitled upon termination of such employment to
reemployment or reinstatement with such agency (or a successor
agency) in an appropriate position with the attendant rights,
privileges, and benefits which the officer or employee would
have had or acquired had he or she not been so separated, subject
to such time period and other conditions as the President may
prescribe.

(3) An officer or employee entitled to reemployment or
reinstatement rights under paragraph (2) of this subsection
shall, while continuously employed by the Institute with no
break in continuity of service, continue to participate in any
benefit program in which such officer or employee was participating
prior to employment by the Institute, including programs for
compensation for job-related death, injury, or illness; programs

for health and life insurance; programs for annual, sick, and
other statutory leave; and programs for retirement under any
system established by the laws of the United States; except
that employment with the Institute shall be the basis for
participation in such programs only to the extent that employee
deductions and employer contributions, as required, in payment
for such participation for the period of employment with the
Institute, are currently deposited in the program's or system's
fund or depository. Death or retirement of any such officer
or employee during approved service with the Institute and prior
to reemployment or reinstatement shall be considered a death
in or retirement from Government service for purposes of any
employee or survivor benefits acquired by reason of service
with an agency of the United States Government.

(4) Any officer or employee of an agency of the United
States Government who entered into service with the Institute
on approved leave of absence without pay prior to the enactment
of this Act shall receive the benefits of this section for the
period of such service.

(b) Any agency of the United States Government employing
alien personnel on Taiwan may transfer such personnel, with
accrued allowances, benefits, and rights, to the Institute without
a break in service for purposes of retirement and other benefits,
including continued participation in any system established
by the laws of the United States for the retirement of employees
in which the alien was participating prior to the transfer to
the Institute, except that employment with the Institute shall
be creditable for retirement purposes only to the extent that
employee deductions and employer contributions, as required,
in payment for such participation for the period of employment
with the Institute, are currently deposited in the system's
fund or depository.

(c) Employees of the Institute shall not be employees of
the United States and, in representing the Institute, shall
be exempt from section 207 of title 18, United States Code.

(d)(1) For purposes of sections 911 and 913 of the Internal
Revenue Code of 1954, amounts paid by the Institute to its
employees shall not be treated as earned income. Amounts received
by employees of the Institute shall not be included in gross
income, and shall be exempt from taxation, to the extent that
they are equivalent to amounts received by civilian officers
and employees of the Government of the United States as allowances
and benefits which are exempt from taxation under section 912
of such Code.

(2) Except to the extent required by subsection (a)(3)
of this section, service performed in the employ of the Institute
shall not constitute employment for purposes of chapter 21 of
such Code and title II of the Social Security Act.

Reporting Requirements

SEC. 12. (a) The Secretary of State shall transmit to the
Congress the text of any agreement to which the Institute is
a party. However, any such agreement the immediate public

disclosure of which would, in the opinion of the President, be prejudicial to the national security of the United States shall not be so transmitted to the Congress but shall be transmitted to the Committee on Foreign Relations of the Senate and the Committee on Foreign Affairs of the House of Representatives under an appropriate injunction of secrecy to be removed only upon due notice from the President.

(b) For purposes of subsection (a), the term "agreement" includes—

(1) any agreement entered into between the Institute and the governing authorities on Taiwan or the instrumentality established by Taiwan; and

(2) any agreement entered into between the Institute and an agency of the United States Government.

(c) Agreements and transactions made or to be made by or through the Institute shall be subject to the same congressional notification, review, and approval requirements and procedures as if such agreements and transactions were made by or through the agency of the United States Government on behalf of which the Institute is acting.

(d) During the two-year period beginning on the effective date of this Act, the Secretary of State shall transmit to the Speaker of the House of Representatives and the Committee on Foreign Relations of the Senate, every six months, a report describing and reviewing economic relations between the United States and Taiwan, noting any interference with normal commercial relations.

Rules and Regulations

SEC. 13. The President is authorized to prescribe such rules and regulations as he may deem appropriate to carry out the purposes of this Act. During the three-year period beginning on the effective date of this Act, such rules and regulations shall be transmitted promptly to the Speaker of the House of Representatives and to the Committee on Foreign Relations of the Senate. Such action shall not, however, relieve the Institute of the responsibilities placed upon it by this Act.

Congressional Oversight

SEC. 14. (a) The Committee on Foreign Affairs of the House of Representatives, the Committee on Foreign Relations of the Senate, and other appropriate committees of the Congress shall monitor—

(1) the implementation of the provisions of this Act;

(2) the operation and procedures of the Institute;

(3) the legal and technical aspects of the continuing relationship between the United States and Taiwan; and

(4) the implementation of the policies of the United States concerning security and cooperation in East Asia.

(b) Such committees shall report, as appropriate, to their respective Houses on the results of their monitoring.

Definitions

SEC. 15. For purposes of this Act—
(1) the term "laws of the United States" includes any statute, rule, regulation, ordinance, order, or judicial rule of decision of the United States or any political subdivision thereof; and
(2) the term "Taiwan" includes, as the context may require, the islands of Taiwan and the Pescadores, the people on those islands, corporations and other entities and associations created or organized under the laws applied on those islands, and the governing authorities on Taiwan recognized by the United States as the Republic of China prior to January 1, 1979, and any successor governing authorities (including political subdivisions, agencies, and instrumentalities thereof).

Authorization of Appropriations

SEC. 16. In addition to funds otherwise available to carry out the provisions of this Act, there are authorized to be appropriated to the Secretary of State for the fiscal year 1980 such funds as may be necessary to carry out such provisions. Such funds are authorized to remain available until expended.

Severability of Provisions

SEC. 17. If any provisions of this Act or the application thereof to any person or circumstance is held invalid, the remainder of the Act and the application of such provision to any other person or circumstance shall not be affected thereby.

Effective Date

SEC. 18. This Act shall be effective as of January 1, 1979.

H. LETTER FROM PRESIDENT REAGAN TO VICE CHAIRMAN DENG XIAOPING, April 5, 1982

Dear Mr. Vice Chairman:

The establishment of diplomatic relations between the United States and China was an historic event which improved the prospects for peace and served the interests of both our peoples. Yet we now find ourselves at a difficult juncture in those relations.

I am writing to you because it is important for the leadership of both our countries to resume the broad advance to which you have contributed so much. This is particularly important today, as we face a growing threat from the Soviet Union and its satellite nations throughout the world. Though our interest and thus our policies are not identical, in Afghanistan and Iran, in Southeast Asia, in my own hemisphere, and in the field of nuclear weaponry, your nation and mine face clear and present dangers, and these should impel us toward finding a firm basis for cooperation.

We have come far together in a very short time. I strongly support the continuation of this progress. We must work together to expand the benefits to both our countries. My Administration has taken a number of initiatives to further this process, and we intend to do more.

Clearly, the Taiwan issue had been a most difficult problem between our governments. Nonetheless, vision and statesmanship have enabled us in the past to reduce our differences over this issue while we have built a framework of long-term friendship and cooperation.

The United States firmly adheres to the positions agreed upon in the Joint Communique on the establishment of diplomatic relations between the United States and China. There is only one China. We will not permit the unofficial relations between the American people and the people of Taiwan to weaken our commitment to this principle.

I fully understand and respect the position of your government with regard to the question of arms sales to Taiwan. As you know, our position on this matter was stated in the process of normalization: The United States has an abiding interest in the peaceful resolution of the Taiwan question.

We fully recognize the significance of the nine-point proposal of September 30, 1981 and the policy set forth by your government as early as January 1, 1979. The decisions and the principles conveyed on my instructions to your government on January 11, 1982 reflect our appreciation of the new situation created by these developments.

In this spirit, we wish to continue our efforts to resolve our differences and to create a cooperative and enduring bilateral and strategic relationship. China and America are two great nations destined to grow stronger through cooperation, not weaker through division.

In the spirit of deepening the understanding between our two countries, I would like to call your attention to the fact that Vice President Bush will be travelling to East Asia toward the end of April. The Vice President knows and admires you. He is also fully aware of my thinking about the importance of developing stronger relations between our two countries. If it would be helpful, I would be delighted to have the Vice President pay a visit to Beijing, as part of his Asian trip, so that these matters can be discussed directly and personally with you and other key leaders of the People's Republic of China.

                Sincerely,

                Ronald Reagan

I. LETTER FROM PRESIDENT REAGAN TO PREMIER ZHAO ZIYANG, April 5, 1982

Dear Mr. Premier:

The present state of relations between our two countries deeply concerns me. We believe significant deterioration in those relations would serve the interest of neither the United States of America nor the People's Republic of China.

As the late Premier Zhou Enlai said in welcoming President Nixon to China in 1972, "The Chinese People are a great people, and the American People are a great people." We are two strong, sovereign nations sharing many common interests. We both want to build a structure for long-term friendship. We both face a common threat of expanding Soviet power and hegemonism. History has placed upon us a joint responsibility to deal with this danger.

The differences between us are rooted in the long-standing friendship between the American people and the Chinese people who live on Taiwan. We will welcome and support any peaceful resolution of the Taiwan question. In this connection, we appreciate the policies which your government has followed to provide a peaceful settlement.

As I told Vice Premier Huang in Washington, we welcome your nine-point initiative.

As I also told the Vice Premier, we expect that in the context of progress toward a peaceful solution, there would naturally be a decrease in the need for arms by Taiwan. Our positions over the past two months have reflected this view. We are prepared, indeed welcome, further exchanges of view in the months to come. I hope you share my conviction that the United States and China should work together to strengthen the prospects for a more peaceful international order. While our interests, and thus our policies, will not always be identical, they are complementary and thus should form a firm basis for cooperation.

In my letter to Vice Chairman Deng, I have suggested that a visit to Beijing by Vice President Bush at the end of April could be a useful step in deepening the understanding between our two countries. The Vice President will be travelling in Asia at that time, and could visit Beijing if you feel it would be useful.

Sincerely,

Ronald Reagan

J. LETTER FROM PRESIDENT REAGAN TO CHAIRMAN HU YAOBANG, May 3, 1982

Dear Mr. Chairman:

The visit of Vice President Bush to China affords a welcome opportunity to convey my regards to you.

As sovereign nations, our two countries share a common responsibility to promote world peace. We face a grave challenge from the Soviet Union which directly threatens our peoples and complicates the resolution of problems throughout the globe. It is vital that our relations advance and our cooperation be strengthened.

Vice President Bush is visiting China as my personal emissary. He is prepared to discuss a wide range of issues of mutual concern. My sincere hope is that we can achieve, through his discussions, enhanced mutual understanding, at the highest levels of our governments.

Among the issues the Vice President will address is the question of United States arms sales to Taiwan. This remains an area of residual disagreement, as our governments acknowledged at the time of U.S.-China normalization. I believe, so long as we exercise the statesmanship and vision which have characterized our approach to differences over the past decade, we will be able to make progress toward the removal of this issue as a point of bilateral contention.

In the meantime, as stated in my recent letters to Vice Chairman Deng and Premier Zhao, the United States will continue to adhere firmly to the positions agreed upon in the Joint Communique on the Establishment of Diplomatic Relations between the United States and the People's Republic of China. Our policy will continue to be based on the principle that there is but one China. We will not permit the unofficial relations between the American people and the Chinese people on Taiwan to weaken our commitment to this principle.

On this basis, and with good faith on both sides, we are confident that a means can be found to resolve current differences and deepen our bilateral and strategic cooperation. It is my hope that you and I will have an opportunity to meet soon. Please accept my best wishes in your efforts to build a secure and modernizing China.

Sincerely,

Ronald Reagan

K. U.S.-PRC JOINT COMMUNIQUE, August 17, 1982

1. In the Joint Communique on the Establishment of Diplomatic Relations on January 1, 1979, issued by the Government of the United States of America and the Government of the People's Republic of China, the United States of America recognized the Government of the People's Republic of China as the sole legal

government of China, and it acknowledged the Chinese position that there is but one China and Taiwan is part of China. Within that context, the two sides agreed that the people of the United States would continue to maintain cultural, commercial, and other unofficial relations with the people of Taiwan. On this basis, relations between the United States and China were normalized.

2. The question of United States arms sales to Taiwan was not settled in the course of negotiations between the two countries on establishing diplomatic relations. The two sides held differing positions, and the Chinese side stated that it would raise the issue again following normalization. Recognizing that this issue would seriously hamper the development of United States-China relations, they have held further discussions on it, during and since the meetings between President Ronald Reagan and Premier Zhao Ziyang and between Secretary of State Alexander M. Haig, Jr., and Vice Premier and Foreign Minister Huang Hua in October, 1981.

3. Respect for each other's sovereignty and territorial integrity and non-interference in each other's internal affairs constitute the fundamental principles guiding United States-China relations. These principles were confirmed in the Shanghai Communique of February 28, 1972 and reaffirmed in the Joint Communique on the Establishment of Diplomatic Relations which came into effect on January 1, 1979. Both sides emphatically state that these principles continue to govern all aspects of their relations.

4. The Chinese government reiterates that the question of Taiwan is China's internal affair. The Message to Compatriots in Taiwan issued by China on January 1, 1979 promulgated a fundamental policy of striving for peaceful reunification of the Motherland. The Nine-Point Proposal put forward by China on September 30, 1981 represented a further major effort under this fundamental policy to strive for a peaceful solution to the Taiwan question.

5. The United States Government attaches great importance to its relations with China, and reiterates that it has no intention of infringing on Chinese sovereignty and territorial integrity, or interfering in China's internal affairs, or pursuing a policy of "two Chinas" or "one China, one Taiwan." The United States Government understands and appreciates the Chinese policy of striving for a peaceful resolution of the Taiwan question as indicated in China's Message to Compatriots in Taiwan issued on January 1, 1979 and the Nine-Point Proposal put forward by China on September 30, 1981. The new situation which has emerged with regard to the Taiwan question also provides favorable conditions for the settlement of United States-China differences over the question of United States arms sales to Taiwan.

6. Having in mind the foregoing statements of both sides, the United States Government states that it does not seek to carry out a long-term policy of arms sales to Taiwan, that its arms sales to Taiwan will not exceed, either in qualitative or in quantitative terms, the level of those supplied in recent years since the establishment of diplomatic relations between

the United States and China, and that it intends to reduce
gradually its sales of arms to Taiwan, leading over a period
of time to a final resolution. In so stating, the United States
acknowledges China's consistent position regarding the thorough
settlement of this issue.

7. In order to bring about, over a period of time, a final
settlement of the question of United States arms sales to Taiwan,
which is an issue rooted in history, the two governments will
make every effort to adopt measures and create conditions conducive
to the thorough settlement of this issue.

8. The development of United States-China relations is
not only in the interest of the two peoples but also conducive
to peace and stability in the world. The two sides are determined,
on the principle of equality and mutual benefit, to strengthen
their ties in the economic, cultural, educational, scientific,
technological and other fields and make strong, joint efforts
for the continued development of relations between the governments
and peoples of the United States and China.

9. In order to bring about the healthy development of
United States-China relations, maintain world peace and oppose
aggression and expansion, the two governments reaffirm the
principles agreed on by the two sides in the Shanghai Communique
and the Joint Communique on the Establishment of Diplomatic
Relations. The two sides will maintain contact and hold
appropriate consultations on bilateral and international issues
of common interest.

L. **U.S. PRESIDENTIAL STATEMENT ON AUGUST 17 COMMUNIQUE, August 17, 1982**

The U.S.-China Joint Communique issued today embodies a
mutually satisfactory means of dealing with the historical question
of U.S. arms sales to Taiwan. This document preserves principles
on both sides, and will promote the further development of friendly
relations between the governments and peoples of the United
States and China. It will also contribute to the further reduction
of tensions and to lasting peace in the Asia/Pacific region.

Building a strong and lasting relationship with China has
been an important foreign goal of four consecutive American
administrations. Such a relationship is vital to our long-term
national security interests and contributes to stability in
East Asia. It is in the national interest of the United States
that this important strategic relationship be advanced. This
communique will make that possible, consistent with our obligations
to the people of Taiwan.

In working toward this successful outcome we have paid
particular attention to the needs and interests of the people
of Taiwan. My long-standing personal friendship and deep concern
for their well-being is steadfast and unchanged. I am committed
to maintaining the full range of contacts between the people
of the United States and the people of Taiwan--cultural, commercial
and people-to-people contacts--which are compatible with our
unofficial relationship. Such contacts will continue to grow

and prosper, and will be conducted with the dignity and honor befitting old friends.

Regarding future U.S. arms sales to Taiwan, our policy, set forth clearly in the communique, is fully consistent with the Taiwan Relations Act. Arms sales will continue in accordance with the Act and with the full expectation that the approach of the Chinese government to the resolution of the Taiwan issue will continue to be peaceful. We attach great significance to the Chinese statement in the communique regarding China's "fundamental" policy; and it is clear from our statements that our future actions will be conducted with this peaceful policy fully in mind. The position of the United States Government has always been clear and consistent in this regard. The Taiwan question is a matter for the Chinese people, on both sides of the Taiwan Strait, to resolve. We will not interfere in this matter or prejudice the free choice of, or put pressure on, the people of Taiwan in this matter. At the same time, we have an abiding interest and concern that any resolution be peaceful. I shall never waver from this fundamental position.

I am proud, as an American, at the great progress that has been made by the people on Taiwan, over the past three decades, and of the American contribution to that process. I have full faith in the continuation of that process. My Administration, acting through appropriate channels, will continue strongly to foster that development and to contribute to a strong and healthy investment climate, thereby enhancing the well-being of the people of Taiwan.

M. PRC STATEMENT ON AUGUST 17 COMMUNIQUE, August 17, 1982

1. Following discussions, the government of the People's Republic of China and the government of the United States of America have reached agreement on the question of United States sale of arms to Taiwan. The two sides have released the Joint Communique simultaneously today.

The United States sale of arms to Taiwan is an issue which affects China's sovereignty. Back in 1978 when the two countries held negotiations on the establishment of diplomatic relations, the Chinese Government stated in explicit terms its opposition to the United States arms sales to Taiwan. As this issue could not be settled at that time, the Chinese side suggested that the two sides continue discussions on the issue following the establishment of diplomatic relations. It is evident that failure to settle this issue is bound to impair seriously the relations between the two countries.

With a view to safeguarding China's sovereignty and removing the obstacle to the development of relations between the two countries, Premier Zhao Ziyang held discussions with President Ronald Reagan on this issue during the Cancun meeting in Mexico in October 1981. Subsequently, Vice-Premier and Foreign Minister Huang Hua continued the discussions with Secretary of State Alexander M. Haig, Jr., in Washington. As from December 1981, the two sides started concrete discussions through diplomatic channels in Beijing. During this period, U.S. Vice-President George Bush, entrusted by President Reagan, paid a visit to China in May 1982 when he held discussions with the Chinese leaders on the same subject. The Joint Communique released by the two sides today is the outcome of repeated negotiations between China and the United States over the past ten months. It has laid down the principles and steps by which the question of U.S. arms sales to Taiwan should be settled.

2. The Joint Communique reaffirms the principles of respect for each other's sovereignty and territorial integrity and non-interference in each other's internal affairs as embodied in the Shanghai Communique and the Joint Communique on the establishment of diplomatic relations between China and the United States. Both sides also emphatically state that these principles continue to govern all aspects of their relations. That is to say, the question of U.S. arms sales to Taiwan must be settled on these principles. Needless to say, only by strictly observing these principles in dealing with the existing or new issues between the two countries, will it be possible for their relations to develop healthily.

3. In compliance with the above principles governing the relations between the two countries, the U.S. arms sales to Taiwan should have been terminated altogether long ago. But considering that this is an issue left over by history, the Chinese Government, while upholding the principles, has agreed to settle it step by step. The U.S. side has committed that, as the first step, its arms sales to Taiwan will not exceed, either in qualitative or in quantitative terms, the level of those supplied in recent years since the establishment of diplomatic relations between the two countries, and that they will be gradually reduced, leading to a final resolution of this issue over a period of time. The final resolution referred to here certainly implies that the U.S. arms sales to Taiwan must be completely terminated over a period of time. And only a thorough settlement of this issue can remove the obstacles in the way of developing relations between the two countries.

4. In the Joint Communique, the Chinese Government reiterates in clear-cut terms its position that "the question of Taiwan is China's internal affair." The U.S. side also indicates that it has no intention of infringing on Chinese sovereignty and territorial integrity, or interfering in China's internal affairs, or pursuing a policy of "two Chinas" or "one China, one Taiwan." The Chinese side refers in the Joint Communique to its fundamental policy of striving for peaceful reunification of the motherland for the purpose of further demonstrating the sincere desire of the Chinese Government and people to strive for a peaceful solution to the Taiwan question. On this issue, which is purely China's internal affair, no misinterpretation or foreign interference is permissible.

5. It must be pointed out that the present Joint Communique is based on the principles embodied in the Joint Communique on the establishment of diplomatic relations between China and the United States and the basic norms guiding international

relations and has nothing to do with the "Taiwan Relations Act" formulated unilaterally by the United States. The "Taiwan Relations Act" seriously contravenes the principles embodied in the Joint Communique on the establishment of diplomatic relations between the two countries, and the Chinese Government has consistently been opposed to it. All interpretations designed to link the present Joint Communique to the "Taiwan Relations Act" are in violation of the spirit and substance of this Communique and are thus unacceptable.

6. The agreement reached between the governments of China and the United States on the question of U.S. arms sales to Taiwan only marks a beginning of the settlement of this issue. What is important is that the relevant provisions of the Joint Communique are implemented in earnest, so that the question of U.S. arms sales to Taiwan can be resolved thoroughly at an early date. This is indispensable to the maintenance and development of Sino-U.S. relations.

N. ROC STATEMENT ON AUGUST 17 COMMUNIQUE, August 17, 1982

With regard to the Joint Communique issued on August 17, 1982 by the government of the United States of America and the Chinese communist regime, the government of the Republic of China hereby reiterates its solemn position that it will consider null and void any agreement, involving the rights and interests of the government and people of the Republic of China, reached between the United States government and the Chinese communist regime.

The government of the Republic of China makes further declarations as follows:

The supply of adequate defensive weapons to the Republic of China is an established arms sales policy of the United States of America, formulated by and executed within the stipulations of the Taiwan Relations Act. Now the United States government has mistaken the fallacious "peaceful intention" of the Chinese communists as sincere and meaningful and consequently acceded to the latter's demand to put ceilings on both the quality and quantity of the arms to be sold to the Republic of China. It is in contravention of the letter and spirit of the Taiwan Relations Act, for which we must express our profound regret.

The Chinese communists would always justify the means they choose to employ in attaining their aims. The alternating employment of peace talk and military action is their traditional, inveterate trick. The Chinese communists are exerting all efforts in waging an international united front campaign, with a view to further isolating the Republic of China. They are seeking all possible means to interrupt and discontinue U.S. arms sales to the Republic of China, trying to pave the way for their military invasion of this country. It is a serious mistake that the United States government, failing to comprehend the real nature of the trick and fraud of the Chinese communists, unwittingly issued the above-said document jointly with them.

During the process of discussions on the so-called Joint Communique, the U.S. side has kept the government of the Republic of China informed of its developments, and at the same time the government of the Republic of China has presented to the United States its consistent position of firmly opposing the issuance of such a document. On July 14, 1982, the U.S. side, through appropriate channels, made the following points known to the Republic of China that the U.S. side:

1. has not agreed to set a date for ending arms sales to the Republic of China,
2. has not agreed to hold prior consultations with the Chinese communists on arms sales to the Republic of China,
3. will not play any mediation role between Taipei and Peiping,
4. has not agreed to revise the Taiwan Relations Act,
5. has not altered its position regarding sovereignty over Taiwan,
6. will not exert pressure on the Republic of China to enter into negotiations with the Chinese communists.

We earnestly hope that the United States government will not be deceived by but will see through the Chinese communists' plot in attempting to annex our base of national recovery and to divide the free world. We also hope that the United States, upholding her founding spirit of freedom and justice, will fully and positively implement the Taiwan Relations Act to continue providing us with defensive arms so as to maintain the stability and prosperity of the Republic of China and to safeguard the peace and security of the Asian-Pacific region.

Selected Bibliography

Atlantic Council of the United States. *China's Policy for the Next Decade*. Washington: Atlantic Council, 1983.

Baker, Howard H. *The United States and China: A Report to the United States Senate by the Senate Majority Leader*. Washington: GPO, 1982.

Barnett, A. Doak. *The FX Decision*. Washington: Brookings Institution, 1981.

_____. *U.S. Arms Sales: The China-Taiwan Tangle*. Washington: Brookings Institution, 1982.

Bonds, Ray. *The Chinese War Machine*. London: Salamander Books Ltd., 1979.

Bunge, Frederica M. and Rinn-Sup Shinn. *China: A Country Study*. Washington: American University, 1981.

Camilleri, Joseph. *Chinese Foreign Policy: The Maoist Era and Its Aftermath*. Seattle: University of Washington, 1980.

Carpenter, William M. *Long-Term Strategic Forecast for the Republic of China*. Arlington, VA: SRI International, 1980.

Chaffee, Frederick H. *Area Handbook for the Republic of China*. Washington: American University, 1969.

Clough, Ralph N. *Island China*. Cambridge, MA: Harvard University, 1978.

Copper, John F. and George P. Chen. *Taiwan's Elections: Democratization and Political Development in the Republic of China*. Baltimore: University of Maryland School of Law, 1984.

Downen, Robert L. *The Taiwan Pawn in the China Game*. Washington: Georgetown University, 1979.

Ellison, Herbert J. *The Sino-Soviet Conflict: A Global Perspective*. Seattle: University of Washington, 1982.

Fairbank, John K. *The United States and China*. Cambridge, MA: Harvard University, 1979.

Furuya, Keiji. *Chiang Kai-shek: His Life and Times*. New York: St. John's University, 1981.

Garrett, Banning N. *Soviet Perceptions of China and Sino-American Military Ties*. Arlington, VA: Harold Rosebaum Associates, 1981.

Garver, John W. *China's Decision for Rapprochement with the United States, 1968-1971*. Boulder, CO: Westview, 1982.

Gelber, Harry G. *Technology, Defense, and External Relations in China, 1975-1978*. Boulder, CO: Westview, 1979.

Gilbert, Stephen P. *Northeast Asia in U.S. Foreign Policy*. Beverely Hills, CA: Sage Publications, 1979.

Godwin, Paul H. B. *The Chinese Defense Establishment: Continuity and Change in the 1980s*. Boulder, CO: Westview, 1983.

Goldwater, Barry M. *China and the Abrogation of Treaties*. Washington: Heritage Foundation, 1978.

Gottlieb, Thomas M. *Chinese Foreign Policy Factionalism and the Origins of the Strategic Triangle*. Santa Monica, CA: Rand Corporation, 1977.

Gregor, A. James and Maria Hsia Chang. *The Republic of China and U.S. Policy*. Washington: Ethics and Public Policy Center, 1983.

_____, and Andrew B. Zimmerman. *Ideology and Development: Sun Yat-sen and the Economic History of Taiwan*. Berkeley, CA: University of California, 1981.

Han, Lih-wu. *Taiwan Today*. Taipei: Cheng Chung Book Co., 1982.

Heaton, William R., Jr. *A United Front against Hegemonism: Chinese Foreign Policy into the 1980s*. Washington: National Defense University, 1980.

Hinton, Harold C. *Communist China in World Politics*. Boston: Houghton Mifflin Co., 1966.

_____. *Peking-Washington*. Beverly Hills, CA: Sage Publications, 1976.

_____. *The China Sea*. New York: National Strategy Information Center, 1980.

_____. *The Sino-Soviet Confrontation*. New York: National Strategy Information Center, 1976.

Hsiung, James C. *The Taiwan Experience: 1950-1980*. New York: American Association for Chinese Studies, 1981.

Jacobsen, Carl G. *Sino-Soviet Relations Since Mao*. New York: Praeger, 1981.

Jencks, Harlan W. *From Muskets to Missiles: Politics and Professionalism in the Chinese Army, 1945-1981*. Boulder, CO: Westview, 1982.

Johnson, Stuart E. *The Military Equation in Northeast Asia*. Washington: Brookings Institution, 1979.

Kenny, Henry J. *The American Role in Vietnam and East Asia*. New York: Praeger, 1984.

Kintner, William R. *A Matter of Two Chinas*. Philadephia: Foreign Policy Research Institute, 1979.

Kissinger, Henry A. *White House Years*. Boston: Little, Brown and Co., 1979.

Kuo, Shirley W. Y., Gustav Ranis, and John C. H. Fei. *The Taiwan Success Story*. Boulder, CO: Westview, 1981.

Lasater, Martin L. *Taiwan: Facing Mounting Threats*. Washington: Heritage Foundation, 1984.

_____. *The Security of Taiwan*. Washington: Georgetown University, 1982.

Lieberthal, Kenneth. *Sino-Soviet Conflict in the 1970s*. Santa Monica, CA: Rand Corporation, 1978.

_____. *The Strategic Triangle*. Colgne: Federal Institute for East European and International Studies, 1979.

Pollack, Jonathan D. *The Sino-Soviet Rivalry and Chinese Security Debate*. Santa Monica, CA: Rand Corporation, 1983.

Pye, Lucian W. *Chinese Commercial Negotiating Style*. Santa Monica, CA: Rand Corporation, 1982.

Rees, David. *Soviet Border Problems: China and Japan*. London: Institute for the Study of Conflict, 1982.

Republic of China: A Reference Book. Taipei: United Pacific International, Inc., 1983.

Robinson, Mary Ann. *The American Military and the Far East*. Colorado Springs, CO: USAF Academy Library, 1980.

Rothenberg, Morris. *Whither China: The View from the Kremlin*. Miami, FL: University of Miami, 1977.

Shaw, Yu-ming. *The Prospects for ROC-US Relations under the Reagan Administration*. Taipei: Asia and World Institute, 1983.

Shen, James. *The U.S. and Free China*. Washington: Acropolis Books, 1983.

Snyder, Edwin K., A. James Gregor, and Maria Hsia Chang. *The Taiwan Relations Act and the Defense of the ROC*. Berkeley, CA: University of California, 1980.

Solomon, Richard H. *The China Factor: Sino-American Relations and the Global Scene*. Englewood Cliffs, NJ: Prentice-Hall, 1981.

Stuart, Douglas T. and William T. Tow. *China, the Soviet Union, and the West*. Boulder, CO: Westview, 1982.

Sullivan, David S. *Redressing the Strategic Nuclear Imbalance in Northeast Asia*. Arlington, VA: SRI International, 1982.

Sun, Yat-sen. *San Min Chu I*. Taipei: China Publishing Company, n.d.

Sutter, Robert G. *Future Sino-Soviet Relations and Their Implications for the United States*. Washington: Library of Congress, Congress Research Service, 1982.

_____. *The China Quandary*. Boulder, CO: Westview, 1983.

Swanson, Bruce. *Eighth Voyage of the Dragon*. Annapolis, MD: Naval Institute Press, 1982.

The Military Balance: 1983-1984. London: International Institute of Strategic Studies, 1983.

The Twelfth National Congress of the CPC. Beijing: Foreign Languages Press, 1982.

U.S. Congress, House of Representatives. *The United States and China: Communication from the Speaker Transmitting a Report*. Washington: GPO, 1983.

_____, Committee on Foreign Affairs. *China-Taiwan*. Washington: GPO, 1982.

_____, Subcommittee on Asian and Pacific Affairs. *Implementation of the Taiwan Relations Act*. Washington: GPO, 1980.

_____. *The New Era in East Asia*. Washington: GPO, 1981.

_____. *The United States and the People's Republic of China*. Washington: GPO, 1980.

_____. *United States-China Relations Eleven Years after the Shanghai Communique*. Washington: GPO, 1983.

_____, Subcommittees on Asian and Pacific Affairs and on Europe and the Middle East. *The Soviet Role in Asia*. Washington: GPO, 1983.

_____, Senate, Committee on Foreign Relations. *East-West Relations: Focus on the Pacific*. Washington: GPO, 1982.

_____. *Implementation of the Taiwan Relations Act, the First Year: A Staff Report*. Washington: GPO, 1980.

_____. *Taiwan*. Washington: GPO, 1979.

_____. *The Future of Taiwan*. Washington: GPO, 1984.

_____. *U.S. Policy toward China and Taiwan*. Washington: GPO, 1982.

_____, Subcommittee on East Asian and Pacific Affairs. *Oversight of Taiwan Relations Act*. Washington: GPO, 1980.

_____, and Library of Congress, Congressional Research Service. *The Implications of U.S.-China Military Cooperation: A Workshop*. Washington: GPO, 1981.

_____, Committee on the Judiciary, Subcommittee on Separation of Powers. *Taiwan Communique and Separation of Powers*. Washington: GPO, 1983.

U.S. Department of Defense. *Soviet Military Power*. Washington: GPO, 1983.

Whiting, Allen S. *The Chinese Calculus of Deterrence: India and Indochina*. Ann Arbor, MI: University of Michigan, 1975.

Wich, Richard. *Sino-Soviet Crisis Politics*. Cambridge, MA: Harvard University, 1980.

Wolff, Lester L. and David L. Simon. *Legislative History of the Taiwan Relations Act*. New York: American Association for Chinese Studies, 1982.

Zagoria, Donald S. *The Sino-Soviet Conflict: 1956-1961*. Princeton, NJ: Princeton University, 1962.